5259

The
Sailing Cruiser

W.M. Nixon

The
Sailing Cruiser

Illustrated by Peter A.G. Milne

DODD, MEAD & COMPANY · NEW YORK

Copyright © W. M. Nixon 1977
All rights reserved
No part of this book may be reproduced in any form
without permission in writing from the publisher
First published in the United States of America 1978
Printed in Great Britain

1   2   3   4   5   6   7   8   9   10

Library of Congress Cataloging in Publication Data

Nixon, W. M.
    The sailing cruiser.

    Includes index.
    1. Yachts and yachting. 2. Sailboats. I. Title.
VM331.N59   623.82'2   77–28372
ISBN 0-396-07573-8

Contents

Photographs are by the author, or supplied by builders, except as follows:

Helen Anderson, page 14; Stephen Bath, 230; Beken of Cowes, 101; Butch Dalrymple-Smith, 51, 107; Trevor Davies, 186; Ford Jenkins, 132; Peter Johnson, 19, 63; Tom Lawlor, 17; Anthony Linton, 145; Brian Manby, 111, 173 (all); Oppenheim, 9; Frank Stimpson, 120; *Yachting World*, 84, 137, 139, 140, 146.

1 Series built sailing boats

Of all the changes in the last half-century which have affected the sport of cruising in sailing boats, the introduction of plastics in boatbuilding is the most significant. You and I may love wooden boats, but we sail those made of glass reinforced plastics, which you can shorten to glass fibre in England or fiberglass in America.

The usefulness of the material for boats manifests itself in many ways. It lends itself to series production and to the manufacture of the complex curves needed in yacht building.

The commercial benefits of series production have led to the establishment of boat building plants which seem very much like any other factory, but even here individuality is evident. Often such plants only build hulls and other large modules, the actual finishing being done by the much smaller yards. So, far from tolling the death knell of the little boatyard beside a hidden creek at the end of a leafy lane beloved by traditional sailing folk, GRP has actually helped to perpetuate it.

The ancient Egyptians made fibres of glass in 1500 B.C. by rapidly drawing and cooling molten sand, at a time when boatbuilding in wood had scarcely started in Europe. The first plastics of the modern era appeared in about 1860, and by 1940 it was possible to combine plastics and fibres of glass to produce GRP, roughly as we know it today.

The first boats of GRP were landing craft and lifeboats, but among pleasure craft, dinghies and runabouts first appeared to be followed by more sizeable craft such as a 45-ft motor yacht *Perpetua* (a somewhat optimistic name), built by Halmatic, Portsmouth, England, in 1954. Halmatic followed this by building sailing yachts to the design of the

American John Alden for the U.S. market. As is usual with a new material, there were many mistakes made in the early days. For instance a first experience of glass fibre for some cruising men came through timber boats being sheathed with it. This is not a good practice and only served to divert attention from sounder glass fibre boats.

1959, which was in any case a booming year in general economic terms, saw many new plastic yachts in Europe. Small cruisers were begun with modest production runs in GRP, such as the first Kingfisher 20 built by Westfield Engineering, designed by R. A. G. Neirop.

The Kingfisher 20 has continued in production, one new lease of life being the fitting of a Hasler Chinese lugsail to the basic design. This modest craft has contributed more than her fair share to the acceptance of GRP construction in Britain. With one of the most highly developed yachting histories of any sailing nation, Britain came reluctantly to GRP, whereas France with burgeoning new enthusiasm saw the possibilities of the material and by the late '50s was already acquiring her formidable reputation for small plastic cruisers, the best known of that day being the Golif built by Jouet.

British yachtsmen, with their numbers increasing by something like 20 per cent every year by the late '50s, couldn't resist for ever, and in addition to the Kingfisher 20, 1959 was notable for the debut of the Pionier, while the following year another step along the road to acceptance of GRP was made with the Elizabethan 29.

They make a fascinating pair, for the 30-ft Pionier, from the board of the Dutch designer E. G. Van de Stadt, who was establishing himself as a world leader in both innovative design and design for GRP, seemed designed to be as utterly plastic a boat as is humanly possible, while the Elizabethan 29 from the board of Kim Holman was very much a wooden boat that happened to be built in plastic.

Subsequently, the development of GRP yacht design has tended to be between the two ideas, for while the design of the coachroof of the Pionier may be structurally impeccable, those great big curves on the corner of the coachroof take up space on which it is impossible to stand, greatly reducing the effective working deck area. At the time some experts insisted that the smallest permissible curve in a GRP construction was of six inches radius, which seems small enough but in reality is very big indeed, and in the interests of both looks and space on deck, designers and builders have since evolved construction with much more compact cabin-tops.

Below decks both boats are inevitably restricted by a narrow beam, but within their limits they are comfortable and there are something like a hundred Elizabethan 29s and two hundred Pioniers continuing to give their owners good sailing.

For the yachting public at large, the early impact of these two designs

One of the first GRP cruisers to be built in Europe, the Pionier represented a very complete commitment to the newly introduced material.

came chiefly from each winning the Queen's Cup at Cowes, the Pionier in 1960 and the Elizabethan 29 in 1963. The instant publicity of a major racing win was of considerable commercial significance, and the builders involved – Southern Ocean Shipyard with the Pionier and Peter Webster Ltd – soon had many orders.

By the early 1960s a remarkable array of designs in GRP was appearing. Some of them were eminently forgettable, but new names began to appear which have since become major features of the contemporary scene. In 1960, for instance, Eddie Tyler of Kent decided he wanted a 48-ft yacht in GRP to van de Stadt's design. He set up a workshop and in 1961 *Glass Slipper* was sailing, and the Tyler Boat Company was in being; it has since developed like the pioneering firm of Halmatic Ltd as specialized moulders of GRP hulls to numerous different designs.

In 1962 Halmatic Ltd moulded on an almost experimental basis some 36-ft hulls for the long established firm of Camper and Nicholsons Ltd. The boats were finished with wooden decks and coachroof, and became the Nicholson 36, winning many races. Adlard Coles's *Cohoe IV* of this class was beaten by only six minutes from being overall winner of the very breezy 1963 Fastnet Race.

Good as they were, they made splendid cruisers as well – the

Elizabethan 29. *One of the earliest series built GRP cruiser.*
LOA 29 ft, LWL 20 ft, beam 7 ft 6 in, draft 4 ft 2 in, displacement 6,384
lb, sail area 308 sq. ft.

Nicholson 36s represented only a half commitment to GRP. But Campers did not stop there, and under the direction of Peter Nicholson – himself a formidable offshore racing and cruising man – the Nicholson 32 was coming along, a GRP yacht built with the cruising man in mind.

Nicholson 32

The resulting boat merits study, for she did more than any other single design in England to establish glass fibre. There were other notable designs of the time, such as Southern Ocean's offshore racing Excalibur 36, but the importance of the Nich 32 is that she was accepted by cruising men, traditionally the most conservative section of yachtsmen, and having accepted her, they have stuck to her, for the boat is now into its Mark X version with numbers built approaching the 500 mark.

Her design is particularly interesting as she has the cod's head–mackerel tail lines of Nicholson's yachts of the time, being full forward and comparatively fine aft. The waterline is pretty well symmetrical, and this has resulted in a boat docile on the helm, and with a powerful and roomy hull shape to boot.

If anything, the hull is too powerful, and will stand up to some really heavy going, the boat's only weakness being those rather large windows in the doghouse. In the first boats, the windows were set in rubber, and so stiff was the hull design that in rough water it was known for the windows to be broken in. Subsequently the windows were properly bolted in place, but even that has proved insufficient *in extremis*, and the latest version of the design has seen an increase in hull freeboard with a lowering of the coachroof and a less vulnerable window.

That may be an improvement, but addicts of the design – and I admit to being one of them – preferred almost everything else the way it was on the original boat, for the newer boats have a 'marina layout' down below without some of the excellent seagoing characteristics of the original accommodation. The very first plan is shown here, and for a boat of the size it is hard to fault for serious cruising. The pilot berth – which has been done away with in the 'improved' version – is mighty comfortable at sea, and is one of the main features of an eminently seaworthy layout in the saloon area, the galley in particular being extremely practical.

It has to be admitted that the most recent examples of the boat in which the chart table is athwartships – albeit facing aft – is a rather better arrangement in this department than the fore-and-aft chart-table of the original. Fore-and-aft chart-tables are a nuisance, as you're either falling into or out of them, and so are the charts and all your drawing instruments; moreover, unless you can arrange some sort of a navigator's seat, either hinged outwards or supported on a pillar from

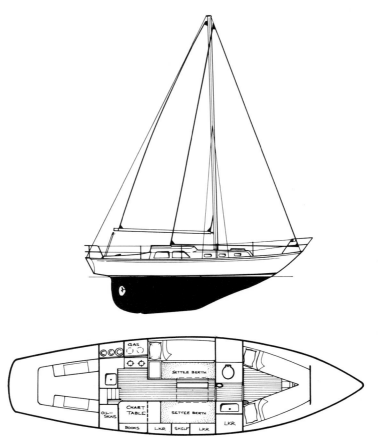

Nicholson 32. *Although she first appeared in 1963, the Nicholson 32 is still being built in modified form. She was particularly important in the acceptance of GRP as a boat building material.*
LOA 32 ft, LWL 24 ft, beam 9 ft 3 in, draft 5 ft 6 in, displacement 13,440 lb, sail area 463 sq. ft.

the cabin sole, working unsupported at such a table is at least a pain in the neck, and probably in sundry other regions as well.

Despite this, for a boat of its size the Nich 32's basic original layout offered much for the serious seagoing cruising man, the accommodation being further augmented with an ample toilet-washroom immediately forward of the mast, and a proper two-berth cabin in the fo'c'sle. This was theoretically to provide a dimension of privacy when the boat was in port, but in fact thanks to the power of the hull shape I've known some people – admittedly with strong stomachs – to continue sleeping in a Nich 32's forecabin through all conditions at sea.

Some GRP cruising yachts have been around for twenty-five years, and the oldest of them will give some indication of the staying power of the material. One of the first classes to go into production was the Block Island 40, built by the American Boat Building Company of Rhode Island to a design of the late Bill Tripp. Being a product of the latter half of the 1950s, the boats of the type made famous by Carleton Mitchell's *Finisterre*, hefty, broad-beamed yachts with centreboards.

In the early days they were a force to be reckoned with on the American offshore racing scene. Nowadays, they have been a little outdated for racing, but they've established themselves as one of the classic designs of all times, and continue to give fine service as excellent fast

The handsome Block Island 40 Phalarope *was built in 1959, and is a good example of the lasting qualities of sound GRP construction.*

cruisers. One of them, *Phalarope*, built in 1959, has had as varied a cruising career as you could wish, and in all she seems to put paid to most of the practical objections to GRP, while her photo shows her to be a handsome craft which can hold her own in any company.

After spending her first few years cruising extensively on America's Eastern seaboard, *Phalarope*'s owner, Dr. Richard Warren, sailed her

Classic cruising yacht evolved from the transom-sterned workboats of the English Channel. In this case it is the Halcyon 27, John and Helen Anderson's Kyon *seen in the Galapagos during a round the world cruise which they successfully completed in September 1976. Although retaining most of the characteristics of the standard Halcyon 27. Kyon's coachroof had been given extra strengthening, and the cabin windows had been reduced to the more seamanlike portholes.*

across the Atlantic in 1966, and based her in Ireland, commuting across from time to time to cruise in Europe. Eventually he sold a half share in her to Professor J. B. Kinmonth, who in time became the sole owner, and from her new home port of Chichester Harbour *Phalarope* has continued a cruising career of high quality – apart from her cruises on Ireland's West Coast, she has covered a lot of ground in Brittany and Spain, and the only really untoward event in her cruising came in 1974 while heading for Norway – a jet plane zoomed out of the sky and crashed into the sea nearby, to be followed a little later by the pilot floating down under a parachute!

Professor Kinmonth owned wooden yachts before *Phalarope*, but is now a complete enthusiast for GRP construction. Of course, for cruising purposes he has a particularly good example of the breed, because having appeared in the early days of GRP, *Phalarope* is substantially over-built, though comparable in weight with the average timber yacht of her time. Parts of her are mighty thick, so much so that when Camper and Nicholsons slipped her once for routine maintenance, they described her as 'bullet-proof'.

Maintenance has been minimal, the topsides still being unpainted in 1975; the professor thinks he will have to do it sometime, but fortunately (see Chapter 10) every year sees the products for doing this improving in quality. The boat is generally laid up afloat, which has proved entirely satisfactory in every respect except that the only bits of varnished wood – the cockpit coamings and the toe rail – are more trouble to maintain than the rest of her put together. She has been particularly trouble free, the only job of any significance being a new bronze rudder stock in 1968 – galvanic action had attacked the original, but a sacrificial zinc anode has prevented any recurrence of the trouble. With alloy masts and terylene sails, *Phalarope* must have seemed the very soul of modernity when she first took to the water, but now she is totally normal.

Different types

It would be absurd to claim that all GRP cruisers match up to the very high standard she sets. Subsequent to the time of her construction, there was much experimentation with the strength-weight parameters of GRP construction, and boats appeared which positively squeak their way across the seas, those that are still afloat. Inevitably, too, the production techniques which could be copies from the automobile industry led in the larger plants to the building of boats by operatives who had no concept of the finished product, and there is always a hazard in drawing any analogy with the motor industry, for if your car breaks down you have a fair chance of walking away from it, whereas the breakdown of a boat may involve considerable swimming.

On the plus side, the continuing dynamic interaction between the industry and its enthusiastic market has led to remarkable advances in basic designs, and boats generally sail much better these days – even the heftiest cruisers – than they did twenty years ago, while anything which is rubbish generally doesn't last long in an industry where most of the personnel are in it for the love of boats rather than any idea of making millions.

When buying a boat the question is how much can be afforded, but right away I would knock about 20 per cent off your top limit to allow for extra expense and the fact that running costs nowadays are generally between 10 per cent and 25 per cent per year of the boat's value. Of course, with today's special economic conditions, there is a school of thought which reckons that yachts of all kinds are a hedge against inflation; perhaps this is greatest in the case with the more expensive ones.

Disregarding the financial aspects for the moment, we find an almost infinite number of other factors involved in making your choice. It used to be said that a cruising man should have a foot of waterline length for every year of his age; with today's improved designs, I should think that a foot of overall length would give the same relative performance for what still not a bad basic rule at all.

Performance is another element in the equation; if your main interest is in the act of sailing itself, then your preference will be for moderate displacement craft with lots of sail, reflecting the offshore racing influence to a considerable extent. Against this, of course, there is considerable satisfaction to be derived from getting the best possible performance from a hefty cruising yacht, a really solid heavy displacement craft, and if you have lots of time available to cruise long distances, and prefer to sail in comfort with a small crew, then a heavy displacement yacht will look after you very well indeed, and her performance will not be unduly affected if you wish to carry lots of creature comforts.

Your time may be limited but you want to visit a number of ports and have a reasonable certainty of keeping to a general schedule – in this case a powerful engine will be an integral part of the selection, and dyed-in-the-wool sailing fanatics will describe your boat as a motor-sailer. If she's a good example of the type, she will sail very well indeed, but with a good engine this extra dimension of time-keeping certainty is for many owners a primary requisite.

Fin and skeg

Then of course there's the hoary old chestnut about the basic underwater shape – should it be fin-and-skeg or closed profile? There is something rather attractive about building a new boat with the traditional long-keel shape underwater, it is a statement that the boat will be an out-and-out cruiser with no racing pretensions. The longer your holidays, the longer your keel! Yet most of the criticisms of fin-and-skeg on one hand and praises of long-keel on the other are demonstrably inaccurate. For instance, there is a notion that only long-keel boats can dry out alongside a quay; actually, many of them are distinctly unsafe doing this, as they tend to pivot around the toe of their keel. The fin'n'skeggers, because their keel has to be located accurately about the centre of lateral resistance (provided they have a minimum of straight edge along the bottom of the keel), will dry out very comfortably indeed.

. . . but the sun doesn't always shine, and the winds aren't always gentle, so part of cruising is coping with brisker conditions as they arise. Aboard the 47 ft sloop Tritsch-Tratsch II *during a cruise to the Scilly Isles, on passage from Dartmouth to the Hamble, running fast with a small genoa boomed out. With a wind which eventually gusted to 45 knots, and very favourable tides, a passage of 100 miles was made in ten hours.*

As to allegedly poor steering characteristics of fin-and-skeg boats, they are admittedly livelier, but this is because they tend to be faster. In many conditions the rudder, being right at the aft end of the waterline, actually provides much more positive control than a rudder on the aft end of the keel, and nearer amidships.

Another stone flung at fin'n'skeg is that warps and what not get fouled between the keel and skeg, and round the exposed propeller with its shaft supported by a P bracket. Certainly this is possible, but in six years of cruising a variety of fin-and-skeg yachts, I've only seen it happen once, and it was soon cleared. Against this, provided the propeller is located in the right relationship to the skeg-hung rudder, the manœuvrability under power of such boats is remarkable, a real advantage in today's crowded harbours.

One criticism of today's profile which cannot be refuted is that in the last analysis, being an appendage, a skeg-hung rudder cannot be as structurally strong as the closed-profile shape. Undoubtedly this is the case, and there are known cases of yachts running aground, or even of unsoundly built yachts in heavy weather at sea, where the rudder and skeg has been torn off. There is no denying it, and if you don't mind adversely affecting your yacht's sailing performance in order to ensure that you can safely pile her ashore, then fin'n'skeg ain't for you.

Over the cruising and offshore sailing population as a whole, people will inevitably tend towards the moderate boat – moderate displacement, and moderate profile, probably fin-and-skeg but with the keel and rudder blended at least a little into the hull for greater strength. Such a yacht will give the best possible performance over a wide range of conditions; while she'll always sail well she'll never be so lively as to exhaust her crew, and with her moderate displacement she'll carry enough creature comforts to make staying at sea enjoyable instead of a matter of mere existence. Inevitably the development of such yachts owes a great deal to the fast-moving world of offshore racing design and it's one of the reassuring features of world I.O.R. racing in the mid-1970s that among the top performers are those from the board of the Argentinian designer German Frers, yachts of refined good looks and almost incredible normality. To conservative cruising men, their only drawback seems to be an almost excessive spread of sail, but to cope with such sail new techniques with new equipment are always being refined and developed, and such yachts, the purest expression of sailing the high seas, can provide their own special high-powered kind of cruising. Whether or not they are for you is a matter of taste, but hereafter I hope we have a sufficiently wide-ranging selection of cruising yachts to interest everyone, always remembering that with today's increasingly sophisticated marine industry, trial sails are always available and if you want a more prolonged assessment, a charter cruise can always reveal if the boat which has taken your fancy bears up to prolonged acquaintance.

Sonata 7
Just how small you can go in sailing cruisers is a moot point, often a matter of balancing between physical and financial fitness. For serious cruising it has to be remembered that the very smallest craft are much

The David Thomas-designed Sonata *carries a 3/4 rig, being a performance-oriented cruiser.*

more at the mercy of the weather – in strong winds, a little boat is simply being blown helplessly away when a larger craft is still sailing along, and therefore with the smallest craft good sailing performance is of first priority.

One of the best known performance craft of small size is the little Hunter, designed by Oliver Lee, one of which took part in the 1972 OSTAR, *Willing Griffin*. Hunters are now found all round the coast and with experience gained in their building, Hunter Boats have developed the 'seagoing performer' concept further with the slightly larger Sonata designed by David Thomas. She provides excellent club racing as a one-design, competes offshore as a Mini Tonner at the smallest rating allowed under the IOR, cruises fast and surprisingly comfortably, and yet is easily handled by the family for pottering around. The cockpit is big enough to hold a family or a racing crew (the designer himself sails his own *Piccolo* crewed just by his family) and yet is not excessively large to induce nervousness in rough weather.

The deck layout offers ease of working, and the three-quarters rig is easily handled with a light or inexperienced crew. Not least of the

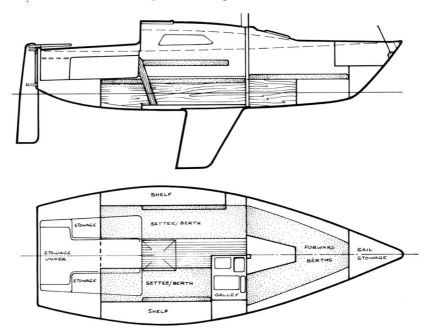

Sonata 7. *The Sonata 7 sets an effective three-quarter rig above her high performance yet roomy hull, and is proving popular for club racing and family cruising.*
LOA 21 ft, LWL 18 ft, beam 8 ft 2 in, draft 4 ft 6 in, displacement 2,453 lb, sail area 245 sq. ft.

interesting features about her is that a dinghy style spinnaker chute is offered as part of the racing package, a device which makes setting the spinnaker very much easier, and several cruising owners who like the pleasure of good sailing have included this item. It is a familiar fitting to those dinghy sailors who have just taken the plunge into cruising.

Galion 22

When I first appeared at the home port with a Galion 22, one of the would-be wits in the yacht club advised me that I had become the proud skipper of 'the best of the Mickey Mouse cruisers'. A back-handed compliment if ever there was one, but of devastating accuracy for, despite her small size, this ingenious design by Ian Hannay, a Scottish airline pilot, really can cruise, as she sails sublimely and yet provides enough comfort for living aboard – we'd a highly enjoyable four weeks family cruise with her.

With the Galion 22, you move into a size where performance can be coupled with good accommodation. By using a hull with fairly slack sections and a narrow cabin sole located well down in the boat, together with a dashing coachroof which exploits the potential of GRP to the full, the designer manages a headroom of 5 ft 9 ins (1·75 m) for much of the 'saloon', with slightly more at the aft end where the hatchway is capped by a slight blister to enable easy access without the leak producing factor of a sliding hatch.

Such headroom is remarkable, but has its drawbacks, because generally speaking a golden rule of accommodation is that there should be full standing headroom, or else you should sit down – anything in between is worse than useless, and a positive menace to anyone with back trouble. Be that as it may, for many people the Galion 22 really does have full headroom, the height in the cabin gives an attractively airy feel down below, and the accommodation is set out to make the best possible use of space.

The Galion 22 Ringhaddy *tramping along with light genoa set. She has a useful 5/6 rig, and for her size is remarkably comfortable.*

A Galion being towed behind a car of average size, thereby greatly increasing the selection of cruising areas available in a limited time.

The two 'settee quarter berths' aft are extremely comfortable at sea, the double berth in the fo'c'sle works very well in port, and we frequently had four sleeping aboard in comfort. Of course, with the toilet located amidships opposite the galley, a certain tolerance and routine is required of a morning, but by comparison with most other 22-footers she has real comfort.

On deck, the cockpit is another exercise in the full use of GRP – it is roomier than the cockpits of many ten tonners of two decades ago, and yet is perfectly seaworthy, being properly self-draining with a good bridge-deck between it and the cabin. The cabin-top admittedly restricts movement on deck, but as all halyards are led aft to the cockpit, and the mainsail is roller reefed by means of a reel from which a wire is likewise led aft, much of the deck work can be done from the cockpit, and indeed I had one cunning crew-member who was busy contriving notions of lengthening the main halyard and reefing cable so that he could do the job without getting out of his bunk. . . .

The rig itself is 5/6 sloop, for at the time the design appeared – 1966 – the designer reckoned that the masthead rig then becoming common was not at such an advanced stage as the 5/6 rig as employed on dinghies and inshore keelboats, and to augment his little boat's already sparkling performance he gave her a rig which is meant to be flexed dinghy fashion. It's a little disconcerting, and we may have overdone the flexing at times, for our deck-stepped mast caused a partial collapse of its supports which we had to reinforce with a steel strengthener, but there's no doubt that through a wide variety of conditions her sophisticated rig and easily driven hull gave her a performance which frequently outstripped much larger cruising yachts.

On the foredeck the pulpit is set inboard from the forestay to enable the deck-sweeping genoa to set without interference from the guardrails – certainly the genoa set very nicely, but in every other respect that pulpit was a confounded nuisance and if we still had the boat, I think we'd have changed it by now. Auxiliary power was a Watermota Shrimp, the little $3\frac{1}{2}$ h.p. model running on incredibly small quantities of paraffin. It pushed the little boat on at $5\frac{1}{2}$ knots with no trouble.

The Quarter Tonners

Moving a fraction further up the size scale, we find a complete selection of small production cruiser/racers which have been developed from boats designed to take part in Quarter Ton racing, that is rating at $18 \cdot 0$ ft under the International Offshore Rule, and a varied bunch they are indeed from 23 ft to 27 ft in LOA.

For a while during the early 1970s there was a rash of almost freakish Quarter Tonners, boats of ultra-light displacement which led observers to think that little further useful development of mini-cruiser/racers would come from this source. Ultra light displacement has only a very limited usefulness, even in racing boats, for it is only of marked advantage while sailing in a blow off the wind; in such circumstances there is no doubt that the ULD boat planes away good-oh to a well deserved win. The win is well-deserved because in any other conditions the ULDB is at a distinct disadvantage.

In any other sailing conditions, the ULDB is a curse, a temperamental bitch which won't perform at all unless you have exactly the right amount of sail set in precisely the required configuration; even far offshore a relatively steady wind can vary through 10 knots in as many minutes, so it's obvious that the ULDB's improvement in performance if you keep changing sail in such conditions is going to be completely offset by the interference with trim during sail-changing operations, and the reversion in jig time to the original wind conditions in any case.

On top of all this, your ULDB bounces about all over the place, and with her almost nonexistent bilge even a cupful of water below is going to find its way everywhere, with consequent miserable conditions in the accommodation. Clearly a cruising man can have no interest whatever in such a craft, but fortunately for the continuing development of the craft available to him, very few racing men have been able to make much of them either, and over the years at all size levels it is the moderate displacement boats which have proved to have the best overall performance, boats which have a high tolerance of wind strength variation, and can equally tolerate sound basic accommodation in order to maintain their crews at peak performance.

Galion 22. *In many ways an advanced design for her time, the Galion 22 exploited fully the potential of GRP construction.*
LOA 22 ft, LWL 18 ft, beam 7 ft 3 in, draft 3 ft 3 in, displacement 3,584 lb, sail area 220 sq. ft.

Ecume de Mer

At the Quarter Ton size, this has produced boats which combine good performance with seaworthiness and workable accommodation, real sailing cruisers, in other words. Undoubtedly the world's most successful example of this has been the Ecume de Mer, which first appeared in 1969 to a design by Group Finot of Paris. Since then Jean-Marie Finot's individual and attractive design has become very well known, as the builders Chantiers Mallard have produced over 700 of these able and roomy cruiser/racers.

The design is imaginative in many ways, none more so than in the accommodation which manages five full size berths in a layout which functions well both in port and at sea, while on deck the seemingly

Ecume de Mer. *One of the most numerous production yachts in Europe.*
LOA 26 ft 3 in, LWL 19 ft 4 in, beam 8 ft 8 in, draft 4 ft 1 in and 5 ft,
displacement 4,180 lb, sail area 366 sq. ft.

severe coachroof design quickly becomes totally acceptable when you
find out how very easy it is to work the sails with that lovely roomy deck.

Anyone contemplating a boat around this size is almost embarrassed
by the selection available. If your tastes run to something rather more
individual, there is the David Thomas design Quarto, which is also
produced in a 'cruiser' version with a raised coachroof known as
Quartet. With a less roomy hull, she doesn't offer as much room down
below as the Ecume – indeed practically none of the other Quarter
Tonner variants do – but her seagoing ability was proved beyond
question during the 1974 Round Britain Race when in sometimes
abominable conditions one of the very best performances was put up by

two young Swiss sailors with a Quarto appropriately called *Petite Suisse*; these two – Beat Guttinger and Albert Schiess – had never sailed on anything other than the Swiss lakes, but they proved their mettle and that of their little craft beyond all doubt, and such a test demonstrated to cruising men generally the real sea-keeping ability of the Quarter Tonners.

Ruffian 23
One of the most attractive of the other Quarter Tonners is the Ruffian 23. This Billy Brown design has a certain elegance which makes it seem completely stylish some years after it first appeared. The boats are absolute charmers to sail, and fulfil all functions so well that classes have been started in many places, for instance Hong Kong. The cruising capacity of the design was demonstrated particularly well during 1974 by Ian Baird, a Scottish Ruffian 23 owner; having completed his boat to his own designs with a special forecabin with three bunks, he cruised for three weeks on the West Coast of Scotland in very mixed weather crewed by his wife and three children, and the family's large black labrador dog.

Eygthene 24
Another individual and interesting Quarter Tonner development is the

Ecume de Mer

A Ruffian 23 in squally weather.

Ron Holland-designed Eygthene 24, which has been on the American scene since 1973 as the Kiwi 24. Evolved from *Eygthene* which won the World Championship at Weymouth in 1973, these attractive boats are particularly noted for their very roomy decks, a welcome feature in such small craft, and brought about by flared topsides. Part of the original design concept was that moderately heavy displacement would enable the boat's cruising function in production form to include carrying creature comforts without spoiling performance, and this requirement has been shown to be well fulfilled.

The H Boat
Here is an example of a sailing cruiser which provides performance, in contrast for instance with the Centaur (page 36). It is the H Boat. Each is a valid design concept admirably fulfilling two different sets of requirement. In the Centaur the emphasis is on accommodation, and it is a bonus that for her type her sailing performance is particularly good; with the H Boat, we have a truly sparkling sailing performance, yet it is a pleasant surprise to find comfortable accommodation, albeit limited by the sitting headroom.

Designed by Hans Groop of Finland, she is essentially of Scandinavian concept, having her ancestry in one direction with the elegant Skerries cruisers of which the best-known example was probably the 30 Square Metre, while a more robust ancestor is the Folkboat. As a result the H Boat exudes elegance and style, and within a few years of her introduction numbers are steadily increasing past the two thousand mark, with the emphasis naturally in the Scandinavian countries, but with other nations also being attracted by her undoubted appeal and sparkling performance.

'Sparkling performance' is almost an understatement, as in certain conditions she can outsail the Soling, the Olympic three-man keelboat, and yet by a skilful estimate of just how much such a sailing boat can manage to carry in the way of cruising comfort, Hans Groop has been unable to produce a yacht which can be cruised and lived aboard extensively. 'Lived aboard' is of course a relative term – in reality she best lends herself to the camping-cruising, living-in-the-cockpit style of sailing which the Scandinavians have developed to a fine art, and to which their mainly sheltered waters are so well suited. But an added

H Boat. *Designed by Hans Groop of Finland, the H Boat provides regatta racing and camping-cruising in the classic Baltic style.*
LOA 27 ft 2 in, LWL 20 ft 8 in, beam 7 ft 2 in, draft 4 ft 3 in, sail area 262 sq. ft.

advantage is that with a proper self-draining cockpit, complete with a seamanlike step into the accommodation, she can withstand rough water in safety, although giving her crew a hectic and wet ride.

Even in such conditions, she is a distinct improvement on her somewhat aged relative, the International Dragon, as her increased freeboard and better hull-shape forward makes for a comparatively drier sail, but it would be fatuous to suggest that compared with chunkier cruiser types she is anything other than wet, for the faster a boat is, the wetter she must be, and speed is of the essence with the H Boat.

Thus her best all-round use is to be found on fairly smooth water, of which the Baltic has an abundance, but if we are really honest with ourselves, a surprising number of cruising people spend a great deal of time sailing on virtually smooth water, and so the boat's usefulness may be more extensive than at first seems the case. Indeed when you think of some of the cruises that have been done in times past with yachts of the wet old Metre type, such as Iain Rutherford's notable ventures out to St. Kilda and across to Norway in the Six Metre *Suilven*, then the possibilities with the H Boat are almost endless, provided you have a crew who can withstand a fast but tough sail. In smooth water because of her extremely good sailing manners, she can give good sailing at almost any level of physical involvement. The thing to remember is that she is first and foremost a sailing boat, she is least effective when sitting still just being a floating caravan, but as no one in their right mind would buy an H Boat if looking for a floating caravan, her limited room below is unlikely to upset anyone.

One concession to accommodation comfort is the deck-stepped mast, which greatly improves one's moveability in the critical galley area, without having an unduly adverse effect on rig tuning, and anyway as H Boats nowadays get their best racing against their One Design sisters, all with deck-stepped masts, from a racing point of view it's irrelevant and it makes cruising comfort sense. The rig itself is just right, a flexible three-quarter configuration which gets the best possible performance from the boat, and if properly handled makes a much more useful knockabout cruising rig for this type of boat than would a masthead rig, which would unduly overpower the slim hull.

Having so much of the day sailer in her makeup, inevitably the cockpit is proportionately large, a comfortable place in which to get the best performance from a yacht which responds willingly to enthusiastic treatment. Cockpit layout varies among the half-dozen or so builders of the boat, in some the mainsheet is on a track right across the cockpit at coaming level; this makes mainsheet handling marginally easier for the helmsman, but it is a drawback in that it divides the cockpit overly much, and for more general use an athwartships track at seat level might take up less room and make movement within the cockpit easier, indeed with a really effective kicking strap arrangement it might be possible to have the mainsheet led to a fixed eye on the cockpit sole, the most convenient of all arrangements.

In terms of volume, she should really be compared with other cruisers of less than 25 ft, and therefore she lends herself readily to auxiliary power by outboard, with a 4½ h.p. engine of this type giving her a speed of 5 knots, perfectly adequate as she will start to sail very effectively in the faintest of zephyrs. In order to maintain this performance it is essential that she isn't overloaded with personal and cruising gear, but overloading is unlikely as the kind of cruising undertaken will be in line with her somewhat spartan accommodation.

Trapper 500

The Canadian design team of Cuthbertson and Cassian, otherwise known as Big George and Little George, have achieved world-wide renown with a distinctive range of yachts which have their own discernible style of firm good looks based generally on a sweeping line and shortish overhangs, yachts which have sailed well enough to win races yet can also be guaranteed to provide real cruising comfort. These yachts come in all sizes, a notable example being the striking C & C 61 sloop, of which something like half a dozen raced at boat-for-boat level in the Southern Ocean Racing Conference around Florida during the early 1970s. Even by the standards of that remarkable regatta, 'One Design Racing' in such large yachts – for with their short overhangs their 61 ft of overall length is an even bigger boat than you'd expect – is pretty startling, but the C & C reputation doesn't rest solely on such a spectacular display, in fact in Europe they are probably much more renowned for their sensible smaller cruisers, of which the Trapper 500 is one of the best known.

She appeared originally in 1970 as the C & C 27, but is now built as the Trapper 500 by Trapper Yachts of Poole, who have had a notable success with her in many European countries, a deserved success, as she is a remarkably successful compromise between accommodation require-ments and performance needs. When afloat, she is deceptive in appearance, as her high freeboard and short ends suggest an emphasis on roomy accommodation, but her hull profile underwater reveals the shark's fin keel, scimitar rudder configuration which C & C have made their trademark, a performance shape, in other words, which gives good sailing as well, and in fact like many of the best sailing cruisers, the Trapper 500 looks her best when under way in a good breeze, as this shows her potential and also reveals other attractive features, such as the comfortably wide side decks which, when the yacht is heeled, serve also to reduce the apparent size of the coach roof which tends to look rather

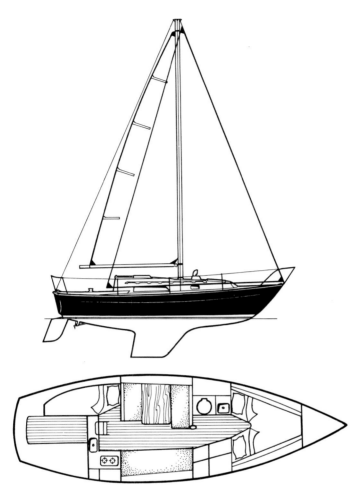

Trapper 500
*LOA 27 ft 4 in, LWL 22 ft 2 in, beam 9 ft 2 in, draft 4 ft 3 in,
displacement 5,190 lb, sail area 348 sq. ft.*

dominant in the profile drawings.

The accommodation really is amazing when it is remembered that she
has exactly the same overall length as the H Boat. With the Trapper, we
have two bunks in a separate if admittedly minimal forecabin; moving
aft, there's a toilet-washroom which can be closed off from the rest of the
accommodation; in the main saloon, a double berth to port becomes a
dinette, there's a single settee berth along the starboard side, while down
aft the galley is cleverly arranged to utilize the space available under the
bridge-deck, although the sheer pressure of space from the proliferation

Trapper 500 in a breeze.

of bunks has meant that the galley is somewhat less convenient than a real cooking enthusiast might like. To port, a full size quarter berth provides a berth which will be particularly useful at sea as it is in the position of least motion, and yet is fairly easy of access. Above it, a chart-table folds down from the aft bulkhead, and the navigator working at it sits in a twisted position on the head of the quarter berth facing aft; it's better than it sounds, but as the dinette-double berth will not tend to be used for sleeping when at sea, while the quarter berth is important sea-time sleeping room, it might be preferable to accept that the saloon table in this instance is also the best chart-table and arrange the instrumentation around it accordingly.

With so much accommodation, the cockpit inevitably has been pushed right aft, but with the short stern overhang there is plenty of aft buoyancy and so the yacht can carry her crew in the cockpit without having an unduly adverse effect on trim. One drawback of having the cockpit so far aft is that the tiller fills almost the entire length of it with the helmsman sitting at the bridge-deck while the rudder stock is at the aft bulkhead. This does not in fact take up as much room as might be thought, but it can be an inconvenient arrangement nevertheless, and any owner with a yen for gadgetry would be fully justified in fitting wheel steering, absurd as it might seem in a yacht less than 30 ft LOA.

In earlier versions the mainsheet was led from the boom by a claw roller which was an irritating few inches from the boom end; this has since been modified to have the mainsheet led to the boom end, and although the slight angling from the vertical of the mainsheet as a result can be a danger, it is preferable to having that exposed boom end jutting completely unprotected into the middle of the cockpit, a cause of some nasty accidents.

Unlike the H Boat, the Trapper 500 is of a type admirably suited to the masthead sloop rig, and her nicely proportioned rig looks very much of a piece with the rest of the boat, producing an excellent all-round performance. Indeed, it is as an all-rounder that this attractive yacht scores so well – a good family cruiser, she can give an excellent showing in local racing of all sorts, and yet can confidently face all weathers at sea. Within her compact length – a very desirable feature if marina charges loom large in your cruising costs – she provides the accommodation of many a larger yacht without adversely affecting her performance within her size range, and not surprisingly the *marque* is noted as one which holds its value very well.

Contessa 28

Although Douglas Peterson of California is deservedly renowned for his offshore racers, a number of yachts with more avowed cruising emphasis have appeared from his drawing board. So builder Jeremy Rogers, who had co-operated successfully with him on racing boats, turned to him for the Contessa 28 performance cruiser.

With marina charges, other running costs, and boatbuilding expenses seeming to escalate ever faster, 28 ft is a size which will attract increasing attention, as it is just about the smallest you can go while retaining a really zippy performance and yet provide full headroom and comfort below. It is easy to decry full headroom as a vital cruising requirement, but for family use it undoubtedly is, and anyone who has spent a lengthy period aboard a cruising yacht will be able to confirm that without proper headroom, the accommodation is often little better than a camped-in extension of the cockpit, but with real headroom the cabin becomes a separate entity which enormously improves the general atmosphere aboard. So although the coachroof of the Contessa 28 may be a little obtrusive for those who like their yachts very sleek, it certainly is not excessively so, and the advantages far outweigh any slight marring of appearance.

In any case the boat is designed as a unit, and the slight chunkiness of

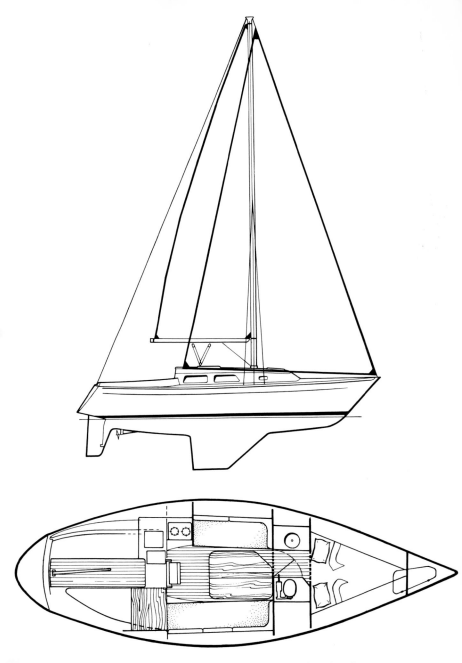

Contessa 28 *is probably the smallest size in which standing headroom can be included in a yacht with really outstanding sailing characteristics. LOA 27 ft 8 in, LWL 22 ft, beam 9 ft 5 in, draft 4 ft 10 in, displacement 6,970 lb, sail area 356 sq. ft.*

the coachroof is matched by an attractive chunkiness in the hull, but this is not a heftiness which will in any way impair performance. There are certain cruising concessions evident in her shape – for instance the keel is less deep than would be the case were she an out-and-out racer, and it is unlikely that any Peterson racer would have a skeg, however small, in front of the rudder. One very welcome feature from a cruising point of view is the sump provided for bilge water within the top of the keel, which would be lacking in the total fin keel configuration found in the racing world.

The accommodation has been kept straightforward – there is a double bunk occupying the forecabin, with the headroom carried determinedly forward a full size toilet-washroom can be provided right across the ship, and in the saloon floor space is maintained by having simple settee berths each side, the starboard one becoming a double, while an ingenious aft facing chart-table fits away over the quarter berth. The galley is rightly thought of as the heart of the yacht, with icebox and full-size cooker with oven, while the freshwater tank holds 20 gallons. The total layout is designed to provide two separate sleeping cabins when in port, and it succeeds in this, but of course one of the delights of the Contessa 28 is that she could be easily handled by a crew of three or even two, so there is no need to feel that every bunk has to be filled.

The auxiliary is a Petter AC2WM 'Mini-Twin' 12 h.p. diesel, driving through a 2 : 1 reduction gear, so if anything there is power in reserve, a comforting thing to have if you happen to be in a tight corner with just a light family crew aboard, or indeed with almost any crew. . . . Nevertheless, it is as a sailing boat that she achieves total fulfilment, for she sets a good spread of cloth in an unextreme rig. The mainsheet is carried from the top of the coachroof which certainly provides extra room in the cockpit, though my own personal preference is not to have an exposed mainboom end jutting over the cockpit in such an uncompromising way, but it is located well above the cockpit sole to provide fairly safe headroom and those of us who are particularly sensitive to the potential dangers, possibly exaggerated, of this arrangement can always pad the hostile end which sometimes seems determined to brain us.

The overall effect of the Contessa 28 is most pleasing, just what you would expect from the already proven combination between one of America's leading designers and one of Europe's leading builders. With great skill they have produced a boat with enough comfort below to please mother, while father, dear father knows that if he isn't winning club and local distance races with her, then it is entirely his own fault!

Westerly Centaur

The Centaur is undoubtedly a front runner in the 'lots-of-boat-for-your-money stakes', and deservedly so, for she successfully fills her function as a comfortable family cruiser with a more than adequate sailing performance. As she is designed by Laurent Giles and at 26 ft overall length is much the same size, she's sometimes thought of as the contemporary equivalent of the same designer's highly successful Vertue 5 tonners. But the Centaur is of much more moderate displacement, and moreover has a bilge keel configuration, so clearly she will give best results if used for short hops with shoal water a feature of the selected cruising ground.

Be that as it may, a number of Centaurs have successfully cruised long distances, and the boat is deservedly one of the most popular smaller cruising yachts in Europe. Three layouts are offered, the full ends of the hull enabling accommodation to be provided throughout the 26-ft length. Layout A with the dinette tends to be selected by the majority of owners, because for most cruising men the majority of time is spent in port, and such a layout, which enables people to move up and down the boat without disturbing anyone sitting at the table, is best for living aboard with the boat upright.

Anyone contemplating longer passage making might go for layout B, as it enables three people to sleep below in a seaway (assuming that when the boat is really hurrying along the fo'c'sle bunks are untenable through the more violent motion forward). Beginners might well think that layout A actually provides for four people to sleep in the saloon area through the dinette converting to a double bunk, but experience indicates that overly wide bunks are a nuisance in a seaway, and therefore for sleeping on passage a double bunk is not a proposition at all unless the boat is continually on her ear and the sole occupant of the bunk is well jammed against one side or other.

Knowing how gear accumulates on any cruising yacht, layout C with its big cockpit locker has its attractions, provided that the locker hatch cover is completely watertight when shut, otherwise even with the boat's noted dryness a lot of water is going to find its way below. Unfortunately, with this layout the only two seagoing berths are along the port side; were she on starboard tack, as a 26-footer, she would find her performance quite markedly hindered by the weight of two people lying in effect along the lee rail.

Despite this, bearing in mind that all accommodations are a compromise, the choices offered to the prospective Centaur buyer by Westerly Marine cover most requirements, and for a 26-footer to be able to provide all tnis with at least 6 ft headroom in all cabins is quite something. This is achieved by the rather large coachroof, but by a happy knack of design this is not so prominent as might appear from the lines drawings. One's only reservations about it would be from the safety factor – in order to maintain deck room, the sides of this are very flat and almost vertical, presenting a seemingly vulnerable target for any breaking cross-sea. Fortunately, as the Centaur is both light and small, she would tend to bounce along in such conditions rather like a ping-pong ball.

On deck, the cockpit is large and comfortable, but seamanlike as it is properly self-draining with the seats virtually at deck level. A choice is

Westerly Centaur.
LOA 26 ft, LWL 21 ft 4 in, beam 8 ft 5 in, draft 3 ft, displacement 6,700 lb, sail area 384 sq. ft.

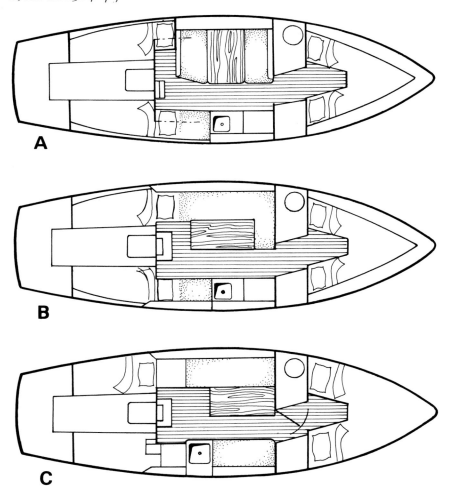

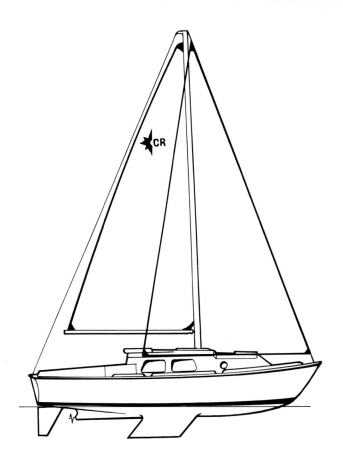

offered with the rig: you can have either the standard masthead sloop or a ketch with short bowsprit. While this latter rig is not without its charm, for most people the simplicity of the sloop will make it the obvious choice. A useful selection of headsails is available, while the mainsail is roller reefing with the sheet led handily from the end of the boom to the aft end of the cockpit. Some might describe this as an old-fashioned arrangement, bemused as we are by offshore racing mainsheets in the middle of the boat, but for a family cruiser it is much the best, as it keeps blocks, slides and ropes well clear of all the kids in the cockpit, not to mention Aunt Nellie and her pet poodle.

As to sailing performance, the Centaur is no slouch, and is noted as one of the ablest bilge keelers. Part of the notion behind bilge keels is that the yacht's angle of heel when going to windward enables the lee bilge keel to be presented to the water at the most efficient angle, and therefore in theory at least much less depth is required in order to provide sufficient lateral resistance for windward work than is the case with an ordinary keel. Unfortunately, while all this is going on, the windward bilge keel is doing nothing other than cause drag, and the twin keel combination must also adversely affect manœuvrability. Nevertheless, a properly designed configuration can provide a remarkably good performance, and of course the advantages of shoal draft coupled with the fact that you can dry out wherever you please with the boat remaining upright, makes this one of the best compromise arrangements for shoal water cruising, while in coastal cruising it just about doubles the area available to you, as you now have all that fascinating territory between low water and high water, an area which the conventional single keel boat tends to shy away from.

Laurent Giles and Partners spent some time tank-testing the bilge keel arrangement of the Centaur in order to provide maximum performance together with a configuration which enables the boat to be dried out with confidence. The result has proved eminently satisfactory, but a fin keel version called Pembroke has also been introduced.

Twister

The wooden prototype Twister appeared in 1963, the builders, J. W. and A. Upham Ltd of Brixham, having commissioned from designer Kim Holman a 6-ton cruiser with good racing potential. All their best hopes were fulfilled, as the first boat *Twister of Mersea* designed to the then RORC rating rule notched up some outstanding wins in her first season.

Production was then started with Tyler's of Kent moulding for Upham's a slightly improved hull shape – they lengthened her slightly and beefed her up generally – and the resultant craft, basically a wooden boat which happens to be built in glass fibre, like Holman's pioneering Elizabethan 29, continues to be one of the most popular small cruisers on the English market. It is something of a collectors' item among connoisseurs; they hold their value exceptionally well. Over the years, they have been modified in various ways; originally they were just GRP hulls with wooden decks and coachroof, but now an entirely GRP version is available and popular, though aficionados still go for the glass and wood mixture.

One word which perfectly describes the Twister is compact – by comparison with later designs, with rudders and keels as separated appendages, the Twister seems a tough little bulldog of a boat, and it could reasonably be argued that she is the ultimate expression of her type, for just a year after the *marque* went into production, fin-and-skeg yachts became the norm.

Having quite hefty displacement, at least by today's standards, the Twister's deepish hull provides full headroom without recourse to a high coachroof, and particularly in the glass fibre version the compact cabin top with its well-angled sides is one with which you could face breaking cross-seas with equanimity. With the deep hull form, depth is

Twister. *An older design of small cruising yacht, with her moderately heavy displacement.*
LOA 28 ft 3 in, LWL 21 ft 6 in, beam 8 ft 1 in, draft 5 ft, displacement 9,520 lb.

carried well forward, which allows a proper fore-cabin, a real asset to harmony aboard while cruising, while what could be called the seagoing accommodation in the saloon is simple but most effective.

Being rather narrow, there is no room for pilot berths, but there are two good settee berths and a quarter berth, although the latter is a bit restricted by having a folding chart table over it. For serious cruising, the boat's substantial displacement means that a myriad of lockers can be fitted without any great fear of the sailing trim being spoilt if they are filled up with books and all the items of personal gear that make cruising a pleasure instead of mere existence.

On deck, her seamanlike character is further underlined by a real offshore cockpit, the accommodation's dryness being preserved by a bridge-deck which also contributes to the boat's strength. Being low, the coachroof becomes part of the deck area, and a good working surface is available for anyone changing sail and so forth. The rig is a completely straightforward masthead sloop, and though the mast may seem a little far forward to modern eyes, for cruising men a largish mainsail is probably a positive asset.

On most points of sailing there will be little to choose between her handling and fin-and-skeg boats; perhaps on a broad reach with spinnaker set the Twister, through having her rudder that much nearer the centre of lateral resistance, will be a little wild. Against this, the reassurance of the ultimate strength of her design is very cheering on filthy nights at sea, and any of today's younger offshore sailors who think that the only boat in which to get anywhere offshore is one which skates over the water would be quite surprised by the way Twister can shift in a seaway, and in real comfort too.

Nantucket Clipper

One of the most interesting threads in the fabric of today's marine industry is the character boat business. Within character boats, there are two main sorts – detail-perfect reproductions of a known type of times past, and basically orthodox modern boats to which character features have been added to make them that little bit different from other cruising yachts.

In the reproduction category, every year some fascinating new facsimiles appear, a certain bizarre effect being achieved when as often as not they are built in modern materials such as GRP or ferro-cement; thus at the moment we have glass fibre being used to build traditional types as varied as Colin Archer ketches in Sweden, Itchen Ferry cutters in England, and catboats in America. Many such craft sail very well indeed, but this is a secondary consideration, because they are ideal for a cruising man whose great pleasure is in leisurely and slow exploration of one small piece of coastline, for the endless charm of being aboard a character boat offsets any troublesome urge to have to make long fast voyages in order to achieve enjoyment.

Perhaps the orthodox boat with character features gets the best of both worlds, as you get modern performance coupled with the existential satisfaction of old-time design. Far from being useless ornaments, many of the old features have real advantages, and one of the most successful illustrations of this is the Nantucket Clipper, which despite its name, exotic to European ears, was designed by Alan Buchanan who lives in the Channel Isles, and is built in GRP in Norfolk, England by Offshore Yachts International.

Nantucket Clipper's dominant character feature is her attractive clipper bow, which has real advantages for a cruising yacht. When hauling the anchor, the stem is kept clear of flailing flukes, and it lends

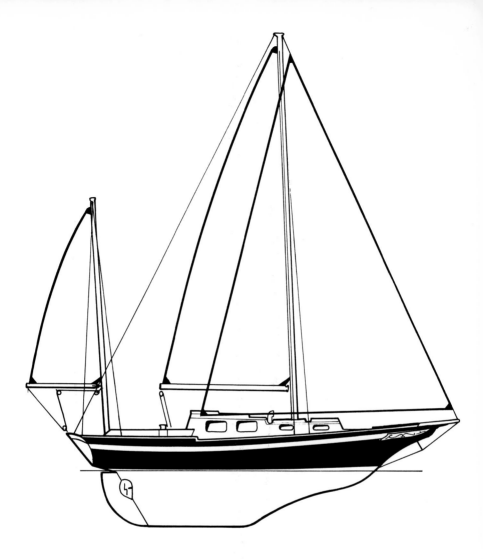

itself particularly well to a special fairlead whereby the anchor is stowed in the fairlead simply by hauling in the chain. Looking at the plans of the Clipper's accommodation, the striking feature seems to be the full hull shape – the bow looks positively bluff. But in fact this is only the case at deck level – the boat has an average waterline entry forward, well able to slice through choppy water, but the clipper bow results in a marked flaring of the topsides forward which provides a great deal more deckroom than would otherwise be the case.

Apart from the great convenience of the extra room for those working forward, the main effect of this is to make the boat seem much bigger than she really is. In fact, her real waterline length is only 21 ft (6·40 m)

Nantucket Clipper.
LOA 29 ft 10¼ in, LWL 21 ft, beam 9 ft 1½ in, draft 4 ft 3 in, displacement 8,290 lb, sail area 368 sq. ft.

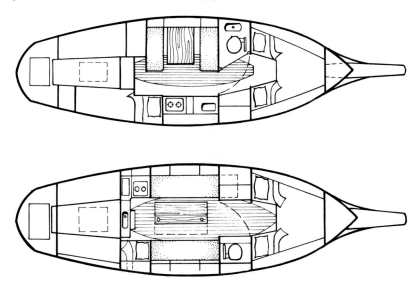

while the beam is 9 ft 1½ ins (2·78 m), and yet most people have the image of her as being much larger.

Two accommodation layouts are offered, each of which has features in its favour. For serious seagoing, the 'old-fashioned' plan with the two settee berths in the saloon together with a quarter berth offers an opportunity for more than one person to get some real sleep while on passage. With the dinette layout, the quarter berth is the only real possibility for sleeping at sea unless you are prepared to lower the table, but as this will be fulfilling two functions, as it also has to act as the chart-table, such action can only be undertaken with navigators more co-operative than I have experienced. The accommodation is pleasantly finished, there is handy access to the 10 h.p. diesel engine, and the effect is of sensible no-nonsense layout with both alternatives.

Originally, the Nantucket Clipper was designed with a separate fin and skeg profile, but now – very sensibly – she has been given a closed profile underwater, for in reality her fin was virtually a long keel with just the rudder looking a trifle silly unattached, offering little real improvement in handling characteristics. In the revised profile, she now has extra room in the keel for water and fuel tanks, and good handling ability under power has been retained by locating the propeller in the aperture in the more than adequately sized rudder. By their very nature, character boats such as this tend to lead their owners to potter round characterful little ports, places which are often cluttered with warps and other underwater hazards, where a fin and skeg boat might get herself rightly fouled up; with the compact profile of the Nantucket Clipper, you can go into any messy old place without having continually to look to your latter end. . . .

While the preference was for the simple sloop rig as opposed to the ketch for the Westerly Centaur, with the Nantucket Clipper first choice would be the yawl rig every time. Actually, owing to ingenious design the mizzen is stepped on top of the rudder post, which presumably would make the boat a kawl or a yetch, but whatever you'd call her, she has a useful-sized mizzen which does not fill up the cockpit, and the two-masted rig can function in this instance very effectively under a variety of sail combinations, the only disadvantage from a family cruising point of view being the bacon-slicer main sheet on the aft edge of the bridge-deck.

Any hardened modernist who would dismiss her as ornamental is making a bad mistake; her traditional embellishments all serve a useful purpose resulting in an individual little yacht whose seagoing ability has already been widely demonstrated, one of the most notable achievements of the design being in 1973 by Graham Donovan who with *Callipygous* won the Cruising Association's Hanson Cup for a cruise from Suffolk on England's East Coast down Channel to Brittany, then across the Bay of Biscay to north-west Spain, then on to the Azores before turning for home, coming back via the Scillies and Devon. Some of this was done single-handed, at other times his wife was with him and occasionally they'd a third hand; apart from visiting no less than 41 ports and achorages, the distance logged was 4,700 miles in 105 days. If the Nantucket Clipper is just an ornamental boat, then all cruising men should have ornamental boats!

Nicholson 31
Deliberately introduced for the cruising man, into a world of fin keels and spade rudders is the long keel old-fashioned transom Nicholson 31. The rig is an absolutely straightforward masthead sloop, which means standard spar sections and fittings are used. The large coachroof does mean that deck space is in somewhat short supply, but in this – slightly under – 31 ft overall length it gives an L-shaped galley with oven, pilot berth, quarter berth and a double cabin forward. Yet there are additionally saloon settees either side of a cabin table. The only thing to suffer from this will be speed, due to the high displacement against available sail area.

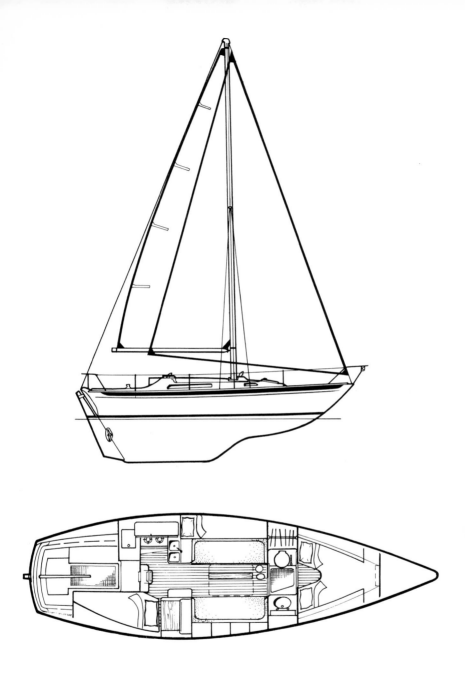

Nicholson 31. *Although introduced in 1976, the Nicholson 31 incorporates many features of older cruising yachts.*
LOA 30 ft 7 in, LWL 24 ft 2 in, beam 10 ft 3½ in, draft 5 ft displacement 8,000 lb, sail area 624 sq. ft.

Arpege.
LOA 30 ft 4 in, LWL 22 ft, beam 9 ft, 11 in, draft 5 ft, displacement 7,840 lb, sail area 430 sq. ft.

Arpege and her Half Ton younger cousins

In the early 1960s a young French engineer called Michel Dufour wanted to get himself a small cruiser, but he was so unimpressed by the glass fibre boats then available in the size range in which he was interested that he went ahead and designed and built the boat himself. The result was the 20-ft *Sylphe*, a delightful little cruiser, and before Dufour knew where he was, he was into the marine industry, with a 30-ft cruiser design coming along by 1965.

Arpege

The outcome of this – called Arpege – took France in particular and the world in general by storm in 1966. Subsequently Dufour produced other designs, both large and small, at his factory at La Rochelle.

When the Arpege first appeared she combined a number of features which have since become accepted as normal. Particularly notable is the detail of the different parts of the accommodation, each section being made up from beautifully constructed mouldings which not only fulfilled their specific function in making the boat very comfortable, but also were an integral part of the Arpege's structure, thus rationalizing the building process. It was not a totally new concept by any means – part of the attraction of the work of the great designers of the golden age of yachting, people like Herreshoff, and Nicholson, Watson, and Fife, was the way in which plush Edwardian furnishings disguised what were in fact vital members of the yacht's structure. But Dufour and other engineering-orientated yacht designers took it all a stage further such that the actual visible interior furniture was an integral part of the total strength concept of the boat.

Working from this, he was able to produce modules such as the complex galley moulding, which functions very well indeed as a galley, whether in port or at sea, and at the same time is part of the basic strengthening which is particularly important in the way of the main hatch. The same high level of moulded interior furnishing is found, for instance, in the washroom structures, and elsewhere the detailed approach is found in something as exotic as a special moulded wine locker with individual sockets for the bottles.

By using the mouldings of galleys, bunks, washrooms, navigation areas and wine lockers as part of the basic structure, Dufour arrived at a boat which was both stronger and lighter than other glassfibre boats of the time, which still were basically wooden boats built in GRP.

His real ingenuity is further revealed by the accommodation of the Arpege still being unrivalled among 30-footers. Some of his own later designs, of course, have unfortunately been influenced by an undesirable trend brought about by market insistence on boats which function well when used in a marina – strewth! Thus we have seen Dufour designs with no pilot berths at all, when for serious seagoing the pilot berths of the Arpege were among her best features.

I remember being quite astonished when sailing offshore in an Arpege for the first time to discover that six people could be aboard without the boat at any time seeming crowded. If you were cruising, the watch below could be put completely out of the way in the pilot berths, which at first looked narrow but at 1 ft 9 ins at their widest are actually the ideal width as you don't bounce about in them. If racing keenly, naturally the three below would use the three berths along the weather side, which still seemed to leave the boat practically empty, and the watch on deck had the complete use of the excellent galley and the huge chart-table, the only bother here being that the bloke in the starboard quarter berth had to be sure that he was right down the bunk, otherwise the navigator – preoccupied as a member of the breed always is – tended to sit on his head. The general feeling of roominess was further aided by the fo'c'sle being completely free for sail stowage.

The racing successes have been notable, as the Arpege for a long time was one of the leading performers in the Half Ton Cup for yachts rating at first 18·0 ft under the old RORC rule, and later 21·7 ft (6·6 m) under the IOR. Naturally she is no longer so dominant, but a properly tuned Arpege can now rate as little as 20·5 under the IOR, and if she isn't right up with the top Half Tonners, at the lower rating she is still very much a force to be reckoned with. As for her continuing capacity for serious cruising – it is really remarkable.

Of all the level rating classes, more boats have probably been built from Half Tonner origins than any other, because this size – between 28 and 31 ft overall – seems to be the smallest which can offer a boat which is also a reasonable proposition as a fast family cruiser. Admittedly, some of the better Quarter Tonners do this too, but Half Tonners offer a little more beef, and can fairly easily reach that critical $5\frac{1}{2}$ to 6 knot speed level which seems to be necessary in order to make passages of a reasonable length while cruising with limited time.

Thus while the Arpege is the biggest seller in this range, there is an astonishing variety of well-known cruiser/racers which have the same Half Ton size. At much the same time as Arpege first appeared, for instance, the She 31 came upon the scene; she too is still in production, a classic little gem of a boat from Sparkman and Stephens, though with her small accommodation about as different as possible from Arpege. Then there have been boats as diverse as the Hustler 30 and the Spinner, the Elizabethan 9 Metre and the S & S 30, and most successful of all from the racing point of view, the Norlin-designed Scampi from Sweden which is arguably the highest scoring production racing boat yet seen in offshore racing. The list could go on – Nicholson 30, T 31, Ballad, Bes, Ruffian 30, North Star, Comet.

Golden Shamrock

Ron Holland's Golden Shamrock Half Tonner is a cruiser-racer with the emphasis very much on racing, but she *can* be cruised and for someone whose greatest joy lies in pure sailing she has much to offer. The prototype wooden-built *Golden Shamrock* sailed from her builders in Cork to La Rochelle for the 1974 World Half Ton Championship; despite being dismasted in the first race, she was re-rigged and made a good enough showing to encourage South Coast Boatyard to go ahead with a production version. Part of their enthusiasm was engendered by knowing that the boat also could cruise, because after the 1974 Worlds in the filthy weather of September '74, the prototype had been cruised back to Ireland via Brittany, the Channel Isles, Cornwall and the Scillies by that formidable sailor, former Olympic helmsman Harry Cudmore. Subsequently Cudmore's name became even more closely linked with the class – he cruised one of the GRP production boats, *Golden Leprechaun*, to the Solent in 1975 and cleaned up among the Half Tonners racing in Cowes Week; then in 1976 he appeared campaigning the highly tuned *Silver Shamrock*, made an even more successful repeat performance at Cowes, and went on to win the Half Ton Worlds at Trieste in September. And if you think that has little enough to do with cruising, bear in mind that our Harry has cruising as his first love, having been a member of the Irish Cruising Club since he was 15 in 1959, and after winning the Half Ton Worlds he promptly went off with the boat for a cruise of the

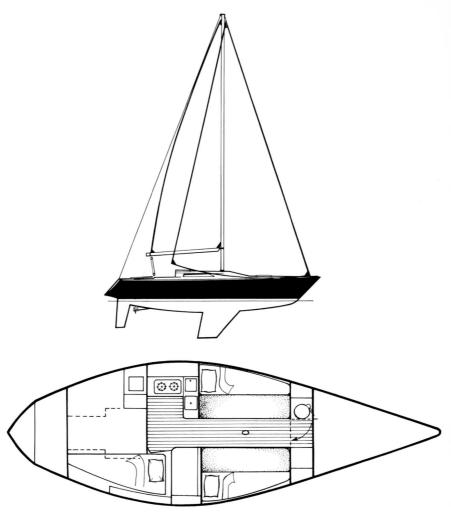

Golden Shamrock. *An offshore racing design, the Shamrock won the World Half Ton championship in 1976, but boats of this type have also notched up some notable high speed cruises.*
LOA 30 ft, LWL 24 ft 6 in, beam 10 ft 2 in, draft 5 ft 9 in, displacement 7,717 lb, sail area 538 sq. ft.

Adriatic. Other Shamrock owners have also been surprised to find that their supposed out-and-out racers also make excellent *sailing* cruisers, while Stuart Woods completed the 1976 Singlehanded Transatlantic race in his *Golden Harp*, when just to finish was an achievement, and found that she performed well with her Hasler Vane Gear, so perhaps yet again those of us who think that only an out-and-out cruiser makes for good cruising will have to think anew in light of the new developments from offshore racing.

Be that as it may, the Golden Shamrock is a classic of the type, with her large sail area above a comparatively smallish and easily driven narrow-ended hull. A spade rudder only slightly balanced gives a pleasantly firm feel to the helm, while the keel, tiny by comparison even with recent standards, is as effective as possible with the selection of the most useful possible section. With their greater relative speed, today's yachts do not need the huge lateral area of times past in order to prevent leeway, though it does mean that when lying a'hull greater leeway will be made, but enthusiasts of the type will point out that because of their greater speed they are more unlikely to be caught out by bad weather in the first place. Whether or not *that* is the case, the fact of the matter is that during the 1974 Worlds *Golden Shamrock* and her leading opponents continued racing in the open waters of the Bay of Biscay in winds of Force 9 and more, and one of them, the Billy Brown-designed *Rock 'n Goose*, emerged with absolutely no hull damage from a complete roll over, so the ultimate seaworthiness of the type seems proven. However, one disadvantage of the new type of keel is that it seems most effective hydrodynamically speaking when it juts out direct from the hull,

Yes, they do cruise! View of Venice from Silver Shamrock *cruising the Adriatic after winning the World Half Ton championship in Trieste in September 1976.*

meeting the hull at virtually a right angle with no garboard curves. This may make sound sailing sense, but it makes for doubtful engineering, and with such a yacht there is a constant need to ensure that the keel loads are properly distributed internally, with no evidence of working as the seasons pass.

The accommodation is concentrated amidships, which keeps weight out of the ends to aid performance, and also means that all the bunks are habitable in a seaway. They are habitable as far as motion is concerned, but one real drawback of the shallow hull type is that there is nowhere for bilge water to go to; thus even a cupful of water below will find its way into the lee bunk through the inevitably hectic motion of a fast-moving yacht, and so precautions have to be taken to prevent such water making for misery through a system of strategically placed electric pumps and the use of waterproof bags for clothing and bedding stowage. The arrangement is the standard one of pilot-berth/settee berth each side, with a quarter-berth/navigatorium aft on the starboard side, and galley to port. The galley is particularly large, for racing crews sail on their stomachs, and there is even room for a cooker with oven, which with the other small comforts included, makes her very much of a cruiser-racer by today's standards. Unfortunately with a yacht of this size, it is difficult to have a separate seat for the navigator, and thus he is perched awkwardly sharing the quarter berth with its hopefully sleeping occupant.

On deck, the sailing emphasis is almost total, the attractive coachroof being as low as possible yet retaining headroom below. The cockpit is very much a working one, but as a comfortable helmsman is more likely to be able to give all his attention to getting the best from the boat, the helmsman's location has much to commend it for cruising, as a footrest keeps him in place and visibility is particularly good within the limits of the deck-sweeping genoa.

Inevitably the *Golden Shamrock* has an almost total racing image, but for extended cruising the builders brought out in 1977 the Club Shamrock with longer coachroof, heavier interior and bigger engine.

Optima 92

Probably the majority of today's leading firms in the international marine industry started, however long ago, from small and often quaint beginnings. For instance, even the mighty Nautor organization began in a slightly converted stable in the far north of Finland. However, the reputation of German industry is such that you cannot escape a sneaking feeling that all major German industrial enterprises have burst into life in fully-fledged modern factories. This may be the case in other fields, but in the marine industry the humble beginning is to be found as it is found elsewhere, in fact one of the largest firms building boats in

Optima 92.

Germany, Dehler Yachtbau, started in the mid-1960s when Willi Dehler began building small boats in glass fibre in his kitchen.

The charm of the story is further increased on discovering that he did not set out to build boats, he set out to build caravans. . . . At that time, Ricus van de Stadt of Holland, the leading yacht designer, was also one of Europe's top experts on glassfibre, so when Herr Dehler decided to build caravans in GRP he took himself off to Zaandam in Holland to meet the great man, and after an intensive session returned somewhat bemused with plans of a boat, having been convinced that such things were far more interesting to build than caravans. He has remained convinced ever since, for with his younger brother Heinz he has built up his firm to be one of the leading and most respected yacht building concerns in Europe, with a factory in Germany turning out five boats a day, the link with van de Stadt being strengthened, for not only are all their cruisers to his designs, but they also took over his Zaandam yard in Holland in 1973 and have expanded it with intensive production of another of his designs, the Optima 92.

She is a fascinating boat which merits close study as she shows just what can be done when there is co-operation between a talented innovative designer and a production-oriented firm which is large enough to take full advantage of the possibilities of GRP construction. At a useful size just slightly larger than a Half Tonner, but untrammelled

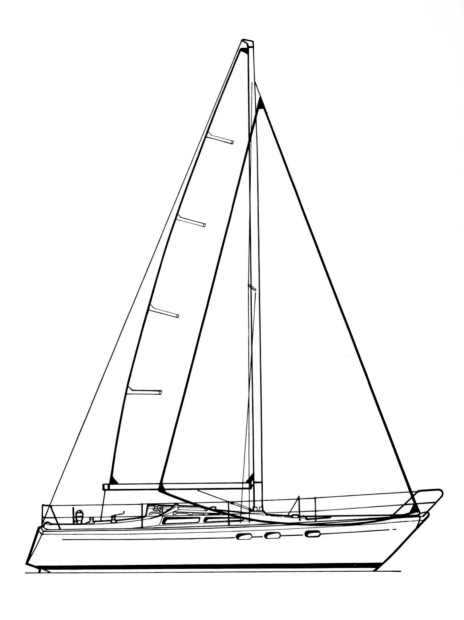

Optima 92. *This German-built fast cruiser is of particular interest as she represents some of the latest thinking by E. G. van de Stadt of Holland, a world pioneer of GRP yacht design.*
LOA 30 ft 2 in, LWL 24 ft, beam 9 ft 10 in, draft 5 ft 1 in, displacement 7,920 lb.

by any undue emphasis on rating rule requirements, the Optima is an excellent example of a modern sailing cruiser, and successfully combines a number of features which formerly seemed to require a larger size. For instance, the aft-located toilet usually seems to require a boat of at least 40 ft LOA, and in fact we discuss the possibilities of this arrangement when we come to the Swan 44, but by determined use of the roomiest part of the hull, and the skilful deployment of mouldings such as the one which enables the washbasin to hinge away against the side of the yacht, the toilet is not only in the most comfortable part of the yacht, but its compartment also includes shower facilities as part of a very workable package.

The toilet having been thus 're-located', the designer is then free to bring fresh thought to the planning of the forward end of the yacht. The forecabin, as it is not adjacent or indeed an alleyway to the toilet, has its identity more clearly defined as a separate accommodation section, and a nice touch is the provision of its own little table, which will have a host of applications, not least in helping any children aboard to think of the forecabin as their own special den, while for adults the entire cabin can become a double berth.

The saloon provides two good seagoing berths, and one of them is part of a dinette arrangement which in turn converts to a double berth, but nevertheless the total effect is pleasantly uncrowded, and much as I like a pilot berth, it has to be confessed that doing without in this case has real benefits. A substantial galley has the welcome feature of double sinks, and although the chart table is on the small side, it could be extended and in any case it is solely a table as the charts themselves stow in a special drawer above the quarter berth.

In the cockpit we find a particularly comfortable layout. Again, the wheel steering may seem a little contrived for a boat of this size, but full advantage has been taken of the potential this arrangement offers, and the possibilities of glass fibre have been fully exploited to make the cockpit both pleasant and a good working area. The mainsheet is led reassuringly from the end of the mainboom virtually vertically to a

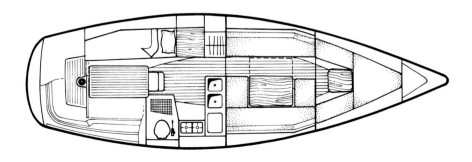

cockpit-width track on top of a semi-bulkhead moulding which includes the steering gear, easily accessible for those who have an ultimate distrust of the workings of wheel steering.

The rig of the Optima 92 is interesting, a 7/8 configuration where the main is sufficiently large really to be the *main* sail, the slight resultant decrease in genoa size being particularly welcome where light crews are carried as it is that much more easily sheeted, and at other times can be carried somewhat longer when the wind pipes up.

Thanks to a highish freeboard (which includes portlights in the topsides which always give an attractive 'big-ship' effect) the Optima is almost flush-deck, the vestigial coachroof blending smoothly into the deck. Such decks are attractive to work, but they also can have a very exposed feel about them, and with this in mind the yacht has an 'anti-roll' safety bar just forward of the mast, although one unwelcome feature of this is that it is used also to carry the navigation lights, which would be totally obscured to lee by the genoa. However, safety is generally high on the priorities list, and one thing which could with benefit be copied by virtually every cruising design is the boarding ladder mounted permanently on the transom, designed in such a way that when it is lowered into place the bottom step is well under water. Apart from convenience when swimming from the boat, it can be a real life saver if someone falls overboard.

Contessa 32

At the time of the 32's appearance Jeremy Rogers had established his name with the Contessa 26, a particularly good Folkboat refinement in glass fibre designed by David Sadler.

The Contessa 32 was seen as a larger, more modern sister to the 26, and she succeeded admirably, so much so that more than 200 have been built, with an enthusiastic owner's association formed without any egging-on whatever from the builder. The boat immediately established an enviable reputation for especially attractive and positive handling characteristics, and although she is no longer in the first flight of offshore racers, she does well at a local level, and being such a delight to sail that she also is raced as a one-design class.

As for her cruising characteristics, their high quality has been demonstrated frequently, and the 1974 season resulted in the Royal Cruising Club's Claymore Cup being won by Edward Bourne's Contessa 32 *Little Eila* for a cruise from England to Northern Spain and back with a youthful crew, while a sister-ship, Hugh Morrison's *Quaila*, won the Clyde Cruising Club's John Dobie Memorial Trophy for a season which successfully combined good offshore racing with enjoyable family cruising, a mixture which reflects the way many people use their sailing cruisers, and supports the notion that attempts to

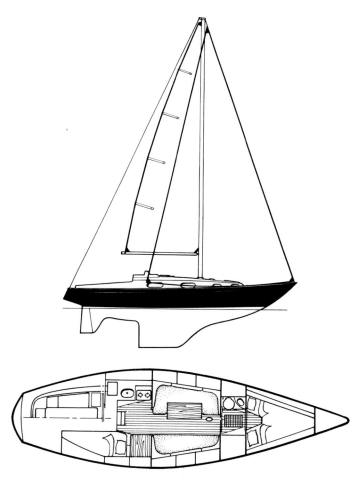

*Contessa 32 has classic good looks which withstand changes in fashion.
LOA 32 ft, LWL 24 ft, beam 9 ft 6 in, draft 5 ft 6 in, displacement
9,000 lb, sail area 562 sq. ft.*

separate local offshore racing from cruising are rather artificial.

Without in any way meaning it as denigration, the most striking feature of the Contessa 32 is her smallness, something which is emphasized by her beautiful proportions, such that beside a hefty cruiser like the Nicholson 32, she seems almost a delicate flower. In terms of volume, she is much smaller than the Arpege, for instance, but as she has that extra couple of feet of length, her motion is that much easier, she is very gentle with her crew, and there is no need to crowd up her accommodation, for she would give of her best with a crew of only three or four, and in fact many are comfortably sailed by husband and wife. Not that she won't stand hard driving – with a crowd of roughs aboard, she'll thump along with the best of them – but true to her non-extreme character her real *forte* is ably sailing the sea with no fuss and bother, crewed by two or three friends.

Bearing this in mind, it is in keeping with her character that the layout is simple but effective. You could fit a pilot berth on the port side, a number already have, but the standard boat has a pleasant dinette arrangement which in port can become a double berth, and there is the almost standard two-berth forecabin with a washroom which uses the full width of the ship.

On deck, the coachroof looks just right – it is low, the sides are angled such that breaking cross-seas will not hit it with a dreadful bang, while the cockpit is large enough to be comfortable without being so big that you get thrown about in it and worry betimes about it being dangerous if it fills with water. As for her underwater shape, it is the very essence of reasonableness, and very few long-keel boats dry out as comfortably as the Contessa 32.

Gladiateur

One of the more successful medium-sized cruisers from European builders has been the 32 ft Centurion, built by Henri Wauquiez in northern France to designs by Holman and Pye of England. Looking somewhat like a rather chunkier and shorter Hustler 35, this popular boat had intriguing design origins, as she was based on plans for a Half Ton offshore racer which won a design competition in Australia in 1966. Since then Half Tonners have tended to be smaller, settling around the 30 ft mark, but meanwhile the Centurion reappeared from this French builder who required an unextreme looking good all round cruiser-racer with emphasis on accommodation comfort; he got it with the Centurion, and it clearly filled a real market demand as the boat had topped the five hundred sales mark when production was phased out in 1977.

It was a case of getting out while on top, as there was still a considerable demand for Centurions, but shrewdly it was reckoned that this could be more strongly sustained by a completely new design to the same basic requirements, so the Gladiateur is rather fascinating as she is to 1977 what the Centurion was a decade earlier. Thus where the Centurion, while very much under the needs of cruising comfort demands, showed strongly in her appearance the influence of yachts designed for the then offshore racing rule (RORC) the Gladiateur, like a saloon car which has been breathed on by a sports car builder, shows the influence on appearance of the International Offshore Rule. But although like her earlier sister she could give a perfectly adequate

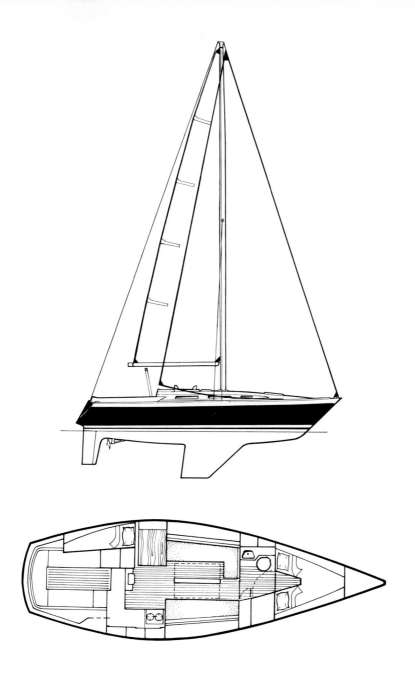

Gladiateur.
LOA 32 ft 8 in, LWL 27 ft 7 in, beam 11 ft 1 in, draft 6 ft, displacement 10,000 lb.

offshore racing performance, it is as a fast cruiser that she will really come into her own.

The Centurion is renowned for her accommodation comfort, and if anything the new boat is even more so, her huge beam allowing the provision of a very commodious saloon, indeed it seems almost too roomy and for determined seagoing the addition of a pilot berth certainly wouldn't go amiss, but apparently there is very little market demand for such a thing, which is a sad reflection on the market rather than a telling point against pilot berths. The entire accommodation is dominated by the 'living/working' space around the galley and navigation areas, and it makes for a very pleasant sense of room in the saloon, but unfortunately results in the toilet/washroom being forced rather far forward, while the forecabin is something of a regression to the cubbyhole foc's'le of yore. But as the emphasis is on cruising comfort for an uncrowded crew rather than sleeping space for a large racing crew, this arrangement is what the Centurion/Gladiateur owner will want, and he will like other features such as the substantial no-nonsense auxiliary – a Volvo Penta MD IIC – and the inclusion of a bilge sump in the top of the keel, for one of the faults in today's bilge-less offshore racers is that a mere cupful of water below can dampen everything as it has nowhere to go.

On deck the appearance is 'late 70s modern', the coachroof blending into the deck, and high freeboard alleviated visually by a broad stripe along the top of the topsides. A comfortable but not excessively large cockpit continues the no-nonsense tradition of the Centurion in having tiller steering, while forward the rig more determinedly reflects contemporary practice with a substantial spread of sail set on a tall mast supported by shrouds fastened to chainplates which are well inboard, a marked change from the original design of the Centurion which carried the shrouds in the old style from the gunwhale.

One of the attractions of the Gladiateur is that she is very complete. The well-finished interior automatically includes such features as a large oilskin locker, indeed every square inch of usable space in the usable part of the boat amidships is put to good use, and so she fulfils another item in the designers' brief in that she is ideal for a busy owner who wants to get sailing as soon as possible with a minimum of preliminary fuss. In buying this boat, such a person will know that he has a craft which will not look out of place in a fleet of the latest offshore racers, and yet he also has a boat which will provide him with fast and comfortable cruising. Not surprisingly, when the first Gladiateur was finished just in time for exhibition at the 1977 Paris Boat Show, more than twenty-five were sold immediately.

2 Larger cruising designs

Contention 33

The Contention 33 shows the influence of the Holland-Peterson (Ton Cup) revolution, not surprisingly as she is a Doug Peterson design, with a notable history of development. From the S.O.S. stable, she is seen by the Managing Director Alan Bourdon as the lineal descendant in the firm's range of their first craft, the Pioneer 9, which in turn was replaced by the successful Pioneer 10 which he himself campaigned to a Class IV win in the 1971 Fastnet. For the Contention 33, he called in that noted Poole racing skipper George Stead (of whom more anon) who outlined his proposals to Peterson, and then developed the boat which resulted into one of the most successful all-round off-the-peg offshore racers in the world.

From the beginning the project included a cruiser-racer version with a longer coachroof and greater home comforts below finished in the successful and practical way for which S.O.S. are renowned, but when the boat was announced in September 1975, such was the demand for the racing version that a year had elapsed before the cruiser-racer appeared. She is still very much a racer, but the accommodation has been modified for a pleasanter life when stopped, whereas the racing version, with bunks piled amidships and just a vestigial galley purely for working in a seaway, had no thought of stopping in its layout at all.

So one of the quarter berths has been removed to provide more cockpit lockers, and a pilot berth has gone to make way for more saloon lockers and a friendlier ambience around the cabin table. In the galley, space is now available for a proper stove with oven, the toilet/washroom forward is more luxuriously appointed, and the fo'c'sle really is a cabin,

Contention 33. *Developed from the successful Three Quarter Tonner of the same name, this is the cruiser-racer version.*
LOA 32 ft 10 in, LWL 28 ft 6 in, beam 10 ft 6 in, draft 6 ft, displacement 10,000 lb, sail area 641 sq. ft.

admittedly just for harbour use, but formerly it was solely a huge sail bin. Throughout the cruiser-racer version, too, the use of wood veneer has provided a pleasant and restful atmosphere which was lacking in the harshly functional atmosphere of the racer.

Contention 33, shorter coachroof version.

No one would argue other than that to describe this craft as a 'cruiser' is a relative matter – she is simply a cruiser by comparison with the extreme austerities of her out-and-out racing sisters. But anyone who wishes to dismiss her utterly as a cruiser would do well to remember the cruising achievements which have already been notched up both by the Contention 33 and her arch-rival, the Ron Holland-designed Nicholson 33, of much the same type, and which seems to take it in turns with the Contention to emerge the champion from various local Three Quarter Ton series. The far-ranging sailing of Alan Milton's *Pepsi* is just one example; *Golden Delicious*, the prototype of the Nich 33, sailed to Norway through some fierce weather to take part and place second in the 1975 Three Quarter Ton Worlds; she then crossed the North Sea again to do the Fastnet Race of that year, in which she was overall winner in a record fleet; subsequently she has continued to cover more distance cruising than racing. And whatever you think of the present, it is worth remembering that when the Three Quarter Ton size first appeared, the S & S 34 and the Hustler 35 were generally thought of as racers, yet now we would class them as good fast cruisers.

Peterson 33

By way of contrast among these GRP boats is another design by Doug Peterson, but in wood for amateur building. It may be that in terms of building cost related to size she could turn out to be the cheapest boat in the book. Such good value has been the central feature of the design concept from the start; Peterson was asked by some impecunious Californian friends (poverty is a relative business) if he could design them a cruising sloop which they could build for themselves as economically as possible. Somehow he found the time, with all his international racing design commitments, not only to do the job, but also to give it very considerable thought, as any study of the design will reveal.

With glass fibre costs going through the roof since the various oil crises, he reckoned that a correctly-judged wooden method would give the cheapest hull, but instead of going for some form of hard-chine construction using marine plywood, he chose edge-glued strip planking which produces a much more attractive and normal-looking hull. A strip-planked hull may take marginally more time (even that is doubtful) but it requires less skill, patience being the top priority. If you look at the photograph of the hull of my Half Tonner on p. 120 after it had been removed from the building plug on the left, it will be noted that the plug itself looks not unlike a boat, and yet we had to build this before we could even begin to think of building the hull proper. Building an edge-glued hull is really only a tidying up the plug-building process, with the great encouragement that you are building the actual boat itself almost from the word go, the only scrapping being of the builder's frames which are removed when the shell is finished prior to the fitting of the frames proper, indeed a cautious builder might leave the building forms in until the frames had been fitted.

The actual skin is constructed of strip planks, preferably good mahogany as it is texturally consistent, usually about 1in x 1in, but it makes sense to have the hull thickness greater than that designed in order to have something in hand when planing down the exterior to get a good finish. With each strip plank, some shaping will be required before gluing, but it is surprisingly little, skill at it comes quickly, and the whole essence is to take it slowly at first. Properly done, the result is most attractive and has a much more expensive look about it than it really costs.

In this way the hull of the Peterson 33 is constructed, and other features have been included to keep her cheap and easily built. For example, a transom stern not only gives you as much boat as possible for the money, but it is also the easiest way to finish a boat and greatly facilitates rudder installation. The simplest deck is just a flush one, but in a boat of this size and type such an arrangement would lack headroom.

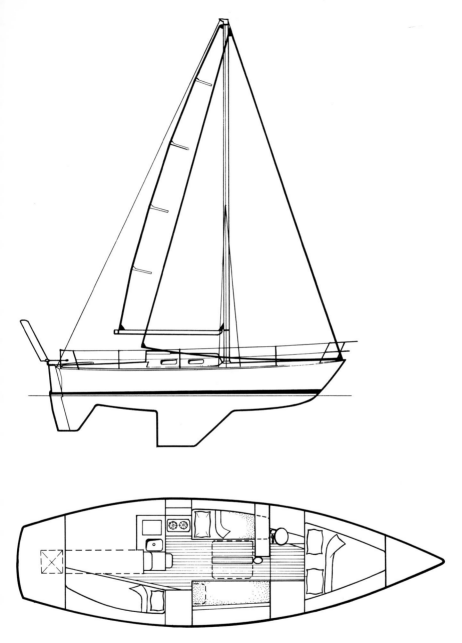

Peterson 33. *An easily constructed craft built in edge-glued strip planking.*
LOA 32 ft 10 in, LWL 28 ft 6 in, beam 9 ft 11 in, draft 5 ft 10 in, displacement 11,600 lb, sail area 497 sq. ft.

However, the designer has stopped the coachroof aft of the mast partners in order to ease building problems which can be annoyingly difficult when a mast goes through a coachroof.

This particular arrangement has been aided by the designer's notions about cruising boats. He doesn't think they should be as beamy as today's high-powered offshore racers, arguing that more comfort is provided at sea where there is a good length to beam ratio with the accommodation kept in the steadiest part of the yacht amidships. Admittedly if marina charges loom large in your running costs, enthusiasm for sailing length just for occasional comfort's sake has to be kept severely under control, but if such charges do not particularly affect you, it is nice to know that one of the world's top designers thinks that length is a good idea in a cruising boat, with an easily driven hull of modest beam the goal to aim for.

Thus the accommodation ends up largely amidships in a very simple and straightforward layout, the foc's'le having only stowage and sleeping uses, in one case a Peterson 33 owner already has it earmarked solely to stow his bicycles! From a cruising point of view, the large skeg at the rudder makes steering almost unbelievably steady, and even when suddenly heeled in gusty weather, thanks to this and her slim canoe shape the boat shows no tendency to broach at all. Indeed, for confined manoeuvring she is too slow in turning. A better boat has resulted over-all by making the skeg somewhat smaller.

In many ways the Peterson 33 represents a number of wheels coming full circle, more remarkably so as they do so in the hands of a leading American designer. He finds that after all, wood may still be the cheapest building material – wood enthusiasts have never doubted it. He reckons that when all is said and done, even for an amateur builder the construction of a round bilge hull is as easy as the supposedly simpler hard-chine method – old boat-building hands have often claimed this, to the disbelief of their listeners. And finally he concludes that for cruising comfort, a properly-designed slim and easily driven hull is best; European yacht design commentators used to insist that this was the case back in the 1950s when fast fat boats like *Finisterre* made slim boats seem inadequate.

Tradewind 33

This 33 ft ocean cruising yacht makes for an intriguing comparison with the Contention 33, for though both are virtually the same overall length, and both are designed to sail offshore, there are few pairs of boats in this book which offer greater contrast. And yet John Rock, who designed the Tradewind 33, and George Stead, who was the mastermind behind the Contention 33, started together in the boatbuilding business back in the 1960s; they called themselves Rockstead Marine, and built van de

Despite her heavy displacement the Tradewind 33 leaves relatively little wake astern, while her transom is a particularly elegant feature.

Stadt designed 26 ft Invictas down in Poole.

Since that time George Stead has acquired a deserved reputation as a phenomenally successful offshore racing man, both in sailing boats and building them, while John Rock, as a result of making a transatlantic passage with Russell Anstey, taking one of the attractive Rustler 31s out to the West Indies for charter work, found his own great love in ocean cruising. He has since sailed extensively in deep water in a number of boats, notably in a Bowman 36 sloop which he finished himself to a very high standard, and while doing this he has talked with other ocean cruising folk and has gradually built up a dossier of requirements for the ideal ocean cruising yacht, from which the Tradewind 33 is the result. She is a successful result, too, as she has already attracted many buyers from all over the world, a number of them proven cruising experts. Perhaps one of the factors in her appeal is that, the hulls having been moulded by Seaglass Ltd, the professional builders (for many owners are finishing their own boats) are F. C. Mitchell of Poole, which really is

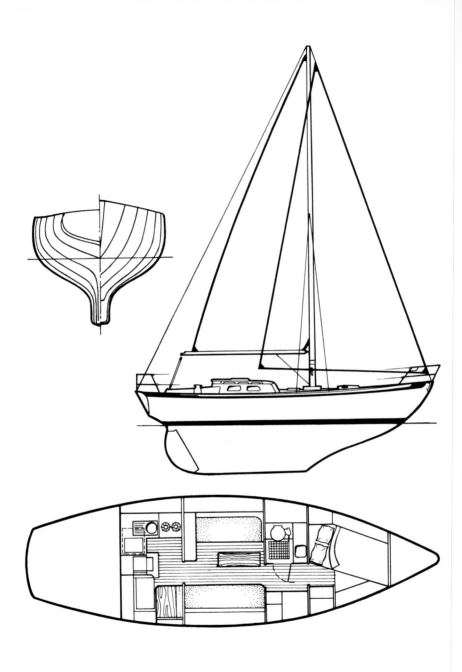

Tradewind 33. *For many people the Tradewind 33 will be the ultimate dreamship, as she is designed to carry a crew of two on long voyages. LOA 33 ft, LWL 25 ft 10 in, beam 10 ft 6 in, draft 5 ft 6 in, displacement 19,443 lb, sail area 544 sq. ft.*

a yachtsman's dream of a boatyard as it is situated right on the water-front at the end of a leafy lane!

The main attraction of the Tradewind 33 is that within her clearly defined ocean cruising limits, she comes very near to being most people's dreamship. The requirements assessed here are ultimate safety at sea in the severest knockdown conditions, ease of handling by one or two people, room and comfort below with sufficient displacement to allow long distance cruising stores and comforts to be carried without unduly impairing performance, and characterful good looks.

If anything the Tradewind 33 is built overstrength and her size of 33 ft was selected as being the smallest possible which still could have a flush deck, so this extra desirable feature has been incorporated, adding both to strength and ease of sail handling. The coachroof is small, but knowing the incredible strains which can be put on any coachroof during a knockdown, some owners might prefer to make it even lower, as there is some headroom to spare, and this can be done as the deck moulding just has a gap where the house is fitted, and it can be tailored to personal taste.

The long keel makes sense under this heading as well, as it adds strength, and though a Tradewind 33 owner might not expect to visit all that many ports, those he visits will be far distant. If they are cluttered with underwater obstructions and fouling, the protection afforded by the closed profile is doubly reassuring. The designer has also been at pains to ensure that the toe of the keel is well forward, so drying out alongside can be undertaken confident in the knowledge that the boat won't go down on her nose.

However, the long keel will not affect ultimate manœuvrability as the boat's heavy displacement will ensure that she carries her way, and though she may tack slowly, she will tack positively. She has the best kind of heavy displacement hull as she is designed to go sweetly *through* the water rather than fussily over it, so in fact for such a hefty boat (19,433 lb) she leaves surprisingly little wake.

A number of different engines have been used; many owners have gone for a 42 h.p. Mercedes diesel, but John Rock's own preference is for a 15 h.p. Bukh, as he reckons this is the largest engine which he can manage to hand-start in the event of electrical failure. You pays your money and you takes your choice. The sail-plan is modest, as the designer's own preference is for unhurried progress, though with a bit of a breeze she can certainly move along in style. However, some extra length in the mast would not go amiss for more general cruising, although I think the temptation to add a bowsprit should be resisted.

In the question of appearance, the Tradewind 33 is one of those extra special yachts which looks even better afloat, and even better again when sailing, than she does in her plans. Seen in the flesh, her every line speaks of strength and seagoing ability, and she has details such as a particularly handsome sawn-off counter with an elegant tumblehome which will look especially well when lying stern to quay in some of the world's more exotic harbours. She is definitely a yacht on which dreams are made, and there are few vessels afloat which come so near to being the dreamship of so many experienced cruising people. (See jacket.)

Jouet 33

As we move gradually up the size scale, we arrive among yachts where large areas of space inevitably go unused. It can be argued that one of the advantages of a larger yacht is that empty space becomes a positive and worth-while feature of her layout, and those of us with misanthropic tendencies would find cruising insufferable unless we had some distance between us and the rest of the crew – our friends, would you believe – for at least part of the time. One way in which distance and space utilization have both been achieved is through the centre cockpit layout, and while it can be done in smaller boats than the Jouet 33, such craft tend to err on the bulky side, and so this is one of the smallest hulls where good sailing characteristics are successfully combined with a central cockpit layout, though 'central cockpit' is almost a misnomer, as the cockpit is only slightly further forward than would be the case with an orthodox layout, the aft cabin being of minimal size.

Jouet 33 is designed by Yves Mareschal, who shows his faith in the design by cruising every summer in the prototype; the boats are built by Arcoa-Jouet under the Yachting France umbrella at Arcachon, that unusual harbour which is the only gap in the unbroken line of beach in the upper Bay of Biscay which extends the whole way from the Spanish border to the mouth of the Gironde.

Depending on what you want from a boat, the accommodation of Jouet 33 is either very ingenious or it is a rabbit warren, for in her relatively small but high performance hull she provides berths for seven, plus an eighth small one, in no less than three cabins. This layout is particularly suited to family cruising with small children; the parents bundle them into the aft cabin in order to have a party in the saloon. When the children get older they bundle the parents into the aft cabin and have a party themselves. . . .

The saloon itself provides an elegant circular dinette which, if need be, can become a double bunk; there is a quarter berth separate from the navigator's throne, a really good galley, a slightly crowded loo and a good fo'c'sle.

Besides all this there is an aft cabin which is self-sufficient – it even has its own toilet. It does make the best possible use of the space available to it, but obviously it can only go so far. Straight away, its usefulness in heavy

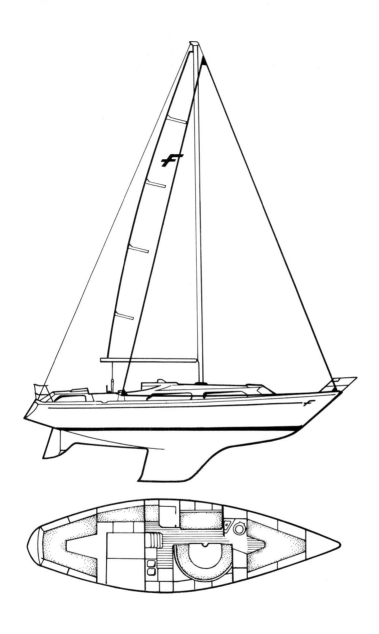

Jouet 33. *An attractive cruising yacht which shows real Gallic ingenuity
in providing the maximum possible number of bunks and cabins.
LOA 32 ft 9 in, LWL 25 ft, beam 10 ft 4 in, draft 5 ft 7 in, displacement
10,000 lb, sail area 460 sq. ft.*

weather at sea is restricted by the hatch facing forward, the boat being too small to have the redeeming feature of an alternative access via a corridor under the side deck, though I suppose if you were really desperate in a grim northern climate, you could do away with the quarter berth.

Another hazard for anyone attempting to make home sweet home in that aft cabin is that the temptation to use it as a sail locker – however temporarily – must be wellnigh overwhelming, even though there is a large sail locker along the starboard side of the cockpit. Warps and fenders could too easily go in there, too.

Clearly a certain amount of crew discipline is going to be necessary to get the best of the layout, but with up to eight people sailing aboard a 33 footer, discipline and forbearance are both going to be needed. (The Jouet 33 was previously called the Fandango 33.)

Hustler 35

Before going into discussion of the design of the Hustler 35, special interest must be admitted. I spent one of my happiest seasons afloat in a Hustler 35, Ronnie Wayte's *Setanta of Skerries*. The first of the class had appeared the year before, 1970, and seemed to offer an ideal mixture of performance and comfort for the combination of racing and cruising he had in mind. As he was a very busy man, I ended up virtually having the use of the boat on many occasions, and 1971 was the year of years. We cruised *Setanta* to many places, we took part in Cowes Week, and then raced her in the Fastnet, getting second in the class. It was the sort of season you dream about, an ideal marrying of racing and cruising, and on reflection, perhaps there is no need to say much about the Hustler 35 plans, our memories of the 1971 say all that's necessary. The fond memories were revived in the spring of 1975 when Leslie Landamore, who builds the Hustler range, loaned us his *Pala II* for a fortnight's leisurely family cruising in the Thames Estuary. Some people would argue that ideally for such shoal waters one should have a handy shallow draft craft, but despite her 6 ft draft, the Hustler 35 found her way into all sorts of remote places, while in more open water, despite our being just an ordinary family crew, she behaved like a perfect lady at all times, indeed in behaviour and appearance she was such a lady that at times we felt a bit wrong in taking her into the mucky creeks which are an integral part of East Coast cruising; but even in such muddy situations she still won top marks for style, and of course comfort.

The Hustler 35's hull is one of the most beautiful afloat, and has a certain charm nowadays in that it seems slightly dated beside such aggressively racing boats as the Contention 33. The effect is a little spoilt by the high coachroof, which also is something of a safety drawback because when you are standing on deck beside the mast your feet are

Hustler 35. *Originally developed as a Three Quarter tonner, she makes a fine cruiser.*
LOA 35 ft, LWL 25 ft 9 in, beam 10 ft 7 in, draft 6 ft, displacement 12,120 lb, sail area 560 sq. ft.

almost at the level of the upper guard rail, but such a coachroof is necessary in order to provide the excellent accommodation which is a feature of the boat, and the coachroof itself is skilfully designed to obtrude as little as possible.

When the design first appeared in 1970 she was one of the most striking boats of that year, and though nowadays more freeboard would be expected – which would enable the coachroof to be that little bit lower – nevertheless of itself that hull shape has a timeless elegance which draws favourable comment. I remember once in an anchorage Down West we'd picked up a mooring, having been wrongly informed that the boat to which it belonged was away for a couple of days. To our embarrassment this boat reappeared after a couple of hours, and we set about moving *Setanta* off the mooring, but the skipper of the other boat told us to stay where we were, remarking that the Hustler 35 looked far better there than his boat did. Praise indeed, knowing the fond eye with which most owners look upon their own craft.

However, while the outward appearance may be beautiful, the most remarkable thing about the Hustler 35 is her accommodation, which is ingenious without being too clever, and makes a fascinating comparison with the ocean-going layout of the Tradewind 33. In the Tradewind 33, a small crew, and her function, leads to an open layout with lots of what might be thought of as waste space, because if you are going to spend long periods at sea you need a certain amount of room around you. With the Hustler 35, engaged in local passage racing or cruising, you will tend to have a larger crew aboard who will be moving the boat along, and you need accommodation which will contain a large number of bodies in as small a space as possible in as much short term comfort as possible, and this she does admirably.

This is not to say that the Hustler 35 could not go ocean cruising, she certainly could, and equally so could the Tradewind 33 be used for shorter ventures, but the two boats give much better value when used for their real function, and in the case of the Hustler 35 this is a busy summer season of local cruising, local distance racing, and an annual cruise in the holidays. For this she is admirable, providing a sparkling performance and good manners with it.

The firm of Holman and Pye have a deservedly good reputation for their interior layouts, and the Hustler 35's merits special study. Note how in the saloon the feet of all the berths disappear into cubbyholes under chart-tables or lockers. Thus there is no need for the saloon to be any longer than is necessary, and if it looks somewhat confined in the standard layout as shown, aboard *Setanta* we had in fact two pilot berths, and she still provided complete comfort for six racing fanatics in the Fastnet of 1971, so much so that we did the whole race, picking up our second place in class, with scarcely any rude remarks being made, and that shows *exceptional* harmony!

For general cruising use, however, a better layout might be the one fitted in *Pala II*, where the pilot berth is a real seagoing narrow one along the starboard side – very comfortable too – while the extra room thus provided enables the settee berth to port to be L-shaped, making the saloon that much more cosy for nights in port.

With the height of the coachroof carried uncompromisingly forward, both the toilet – big enough to be a washroom – and the forecabin are very roomy. Moving aft, the galley is excellent, and in the navigatorium one particularly good feature is the 'bundling board' between the navigator's seat and the quarter berth. All too often the navigators seem to find themselves sitting on the head of whoever is in that berth. In all, the accommodation is excellent, and everything you would expect in a 35-footer, but because it has been so skilfully compressed, the boat still has a very roomy and comfortable cockpit and that long and stylish counter.

The profile is classic fin-and-skeg, which makes her a delight to sail, and yet because the fin keel is placed so precisely amidships, with a horizontal lower edge, she dries out a treat. The engine, a capable Volvo Penta MD2, drives through the usual P-bracket, folding prop arrangement, which makes her very manœuvrable when going ahead, but somehow I have always found the boats a bit temperamental going astern, but perhaps I was not giving them enough power, sometimes when you are trying to reverse you should take your courage in both hands and drive her to it.

Nicholson 35

At first glance the Nicholson 35 may seem to be a slightly larger Nicholson 32 with a somewhat modernized underwater profile, but there are some quite significant variations. Chief of these is the general shape of the hull. With the Nicholson 35, we find the 'cod's head and mackerel tail' has gone and a much more normal hull shape. In some localities, you will find the boat being used for distance racing, but really her performance is not designed to be so sparkling as to make this a rewarding exercise. However, with her substantial displacement – 16,000 pounds – she is an eminently comfortable yacht which can keep at sea for long periods without tiring her crew, and yet her performance is good enough to be covering the ground at a healthy rate all the time, even if not aspiring to out-and-out racing ability.

Everything about her speaks of a sensible no-nonsense boat which will inspire complete confidence in her crew. For instance, while retroussé transoms are very dashing and increase sailing length, the benefit they give to performance is only very slight, and in today's crowded harbours their pointed end is vulnerable. Equally, tumblehome in the topsides is something which some stylists introduce, but after a season or two of busy use, that elegant bulge in the topsides can become a sorry mess of scuffs and scrapes. So it is completely in character that the Nicholson 35 has a standard transom and no bulging topsides. Also from the purely seagoing point of view, her coachroof is a model of its kind, unobtrusive with well angled sides that will deflect any

On deck, the Nicholson 35's coachroof is a model of its kind. While providing full headroom where needed in the accommodation, it is still low in profile, and with well-angled sides would deflect a cross-sea while the small windows contribute to the overall strength.

crashing cross-sea, and the cockpit, while large, certainly is not so big that having it fill with a breaking crest will cause trouble.

Thus, while she is not so completely orientated to long distance work as the Tradewind 33, it is not surprising that a number of Nicholson 35s have successfully completed transoceanic passages; equally, while she will not have quite the turn of speed of the Hustler 35, she will give a good showing when asked to do a short and detailed cruise with five or even six aboard; this is a design which offers a different emphasis, and judging by sales, fulfils very well many experienced sailors' notions of what a 35-ft cruising yacht should be like.

The accommodation, without being overcrowded, manages to get

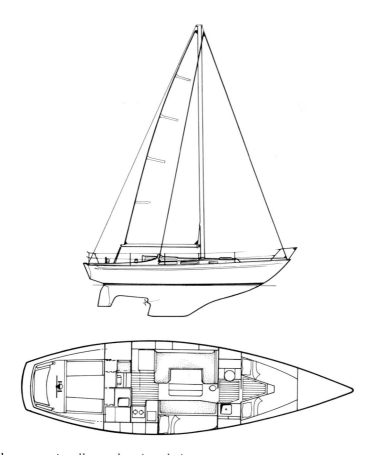

Nicholson 35. *An all round cruiser design.*
LOA 35 ft 3 in, LWL 26 ft 9 in, beam 10 ft 5 in, draft 5 ft 6 in,
displacement 15,700 lb, sail area 737 sq. ft.

everything in. The aft-facing chart-table may seem unusual at first, but having spent the last couple of seasons on a boat with an aft-facing chart-table, I can only say that after a couple of minutes it does not make the slightest difference. It enables the instruments and so forth to be located in under the bridge deck and makes a great deal of room available which would otherwise be taken up in the middle of the ship.

One particularly welcome feature in this area is the seat in the companionway which could be most useful at sea, provided people do not make a habit of perching in it while there is a lot of traffic through the hatch. Exposure can quickly begin to sap the stamina of even the fittest crew member during heavy weather, but in this seat he can be sheltered and dry, and yet readily on hand if called by the helmsman.

The galley is really substantial, the working surface immediately forward of the cooker being a desirable feature which cannot be included in smaller boats simply because of lack of space. Lack of space is no problem in this case, the toilet compartment which uses the full width of the hull can easily combine a shower system if required. Indeed, I will always remember an acquaintance, somewhat addicted to older wooden boats often with minimal toilet arrangements who went off for his first venture in 'one of these tupperware boats', which happened to be a 600-mile delivery cruise in a brand new and very fully equipped Nicholson 35. The last two days of the trip were in abominable weather, but when they reached the home port he came ashore soon after they had picked up the moorings looking quite immaculate and clean shaven. 'Oh well,' he explained, 'we were coming along in that sou'easter, filthy driving rain and no visibility, but then we picked up the lightship just down the coast so I went below and had a shave and a hot

An aft-facing chart table in the Nicholson 35 permits a more roomy arrangement of the galley-navigatorium area.

shower, and she was so comfortable you couldn't even tell what the weather was like outside. . . .'

That was well-earned praise, and just the kind of comfort the boat was designed to provide. Comfort in other ways comes from her hefty displacement and moderate sail plan, which will mean that you are not rushing on deck at all hours of the night to change sail, and if the wind does happen to be light, well, by the standards of twenty years ago she is a motor-sailer, with a 48 h.p. Perkins diesel as standard. This drives through a hydraulic unit to a fixed propeller – none of that folding prop nonsense – on the aft side of the keel, which also means that a strut is avoided.

In the profile, the rudder is hung separately on a skeg, as the builders reckon that the improved manœuvrability which results from this rather than the enclosed profile which they have retained in the 32 is necessary in today's marinas, and as the boat is obviously based on worth-while market research, such must be the case. However, personally my only quibble about the design is in the profile, in that I would like to see the toe of the keel a little further forward in order to ensure completely secure drying out, with no possibility of the boat going down on her nose. Far from having an adverse effect on sailing performance, such a thing would improve it, as the leading edge of the keel which does most of the work when sailing to windward. Doubtless more than half of the Nich 35's overall weight is well aft of this pivot point, but it is not a thing one would want to test unduly in a strange harbour.

In 1977 the builders introduced the Mark V version of the Nich 35 which had a number of alterations. They reduced the size of the skeg to improve handling, altering the engine to an orthodox direct drive with the propeller immediately forward of the rudder. There was a new arrangement for accommodation to appeal more to the average buyer, but as the original layout was more 'interesting' in many ways, it is being shown here.

Olympic Adventure

This characterful 47-ft ketch is another illustration of the increasing internationalism of today's marine industry, as she was designed by Edward Brewer, the noted American designer, and writer about yacht design, and is build by Olympic Yachts S.A. at their plant at Piraeus in Greece.

The adventure was developed in response to a real market demand; visitors to the Olympic plant, where they built both offshore racers, lifeboats, and fast patrol boats, often included cruising enthusiasts who talked of a dreamship which, while she would sail well, would not in any way be a cruiser-racer as she would have her emphasis on comfort, seaworthiness and ease of handling by a small crew. Over the years Ted

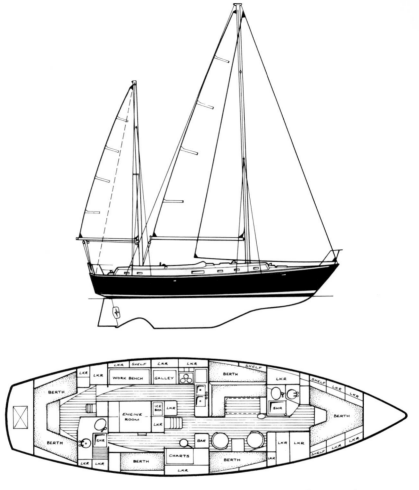

Olympic Adventure 47. *Designed by Ted Brewer, the Adventure is a characterful yacht for serious but comfortable cruising.*
LOA 47 ft, LWL 38 ft, beam 14 ft 3 in, draft 5 ft 10 in, displacement 30,000 lb, sail area 1,098 sq. ft.

Brewer has been developing his own distinctive designs of hefty, short-ended seagoing cruisers, and the result of the interaction between builders and designer is the Adventure, in many ways as modern as tomorrow, and yet also a true descendant of a discernible type of yacht which has been required by out-and-out cruising men since cruising began.

Because we are used to all sorts of extreme shapes these days, the moderation – moderate overhangs, moderate beam, moderate displacement, moderate sail area in particular – and from the cruising point of view her perfectly adequate draft of 5 ft 10 in opens up access to all those magic anchorages within the one fathom line.

Like the Nicholson 35, she has a good hull for bashing about in some less than civilized places, as she has no tumblehome in the topsides, and the nonretrossé transom is much less vulnerable to harbour damage than the sweeping sterns beloved of naval architects today. Underwater, she has a long keel both to facilitate drying out and to provide lateral area lost through shallow draft. One concession to fin-and-skeg configuration is the bite out of the keel profile to make the rudder semi-skeg. This looks so little as to seem insignificant, but apparently it does make for improvement in handling characteristics. Although the toe of the rudder skeg is an inch or so higher than the foot of the keel proper, perhaps a larger differential might be desirable to protect the rudder installation when drying out. One feature which could with benefit be introduced in other yachts with aperture-located propellers is the way most of the Adventure's aperture is taken from the skeg, leaving the rudder with an almost intact leading edge. When manœuvring under power, great control is obtained from deflecting the propeller's initial thrust with the rudder; where a chunk has been taken out of the rudder to provide an aperture, deflection is negligible and there is virtually no manœuvrability until the boat has gathered way: with the Adventure, steps have clearly been taken to retain this asset.

As the original brief specified only total accommodation for seven people, the entire layout has a refreshing roominess and absence of clutter which will greatly help living aboard for long periods, which is what owners of the Adventure are envisaged as doing. In a yacht of this size, the raised cockpit immediately aft of centre makes a lot of sense, as it can be made large enough for comfort without spoiling the look of the ship, it provides first-class visibility for the helmsman, something which is all-too-often lacking in larger yachts, and it leaves virtually all of the roomy 38-ft waterline hull free for cabin space.

Somewhere that a change might be worked is the aft cabin, where the angle of the bunks from the centreline might make them a little uncomfortable when the yacht is heeled. One gets so used to desk-type chart-tables across the ship that fore-and-aft tables of the type shown may be irritating, even if they do provide more work surface in a specified space; and when you've an L-shaped settee in the saloon, it always seems more pleasant to have the shorter athwartships leg of it across the forward end, so that the owner – who , God knows, will have worked hard enough to pay for such a magnificent ship – can ensconce himself nicely in the corner. Then he is able to see his friends without straining his neck as they come below when those evenings of pure gold are being created aboard a yacht in port.

Mirage 37

When the Mirage 37 first appeared in 1975 she surprised many people, as her builders, Thames Marine, had been chiefly noted as the producers of the Snapdragon range, cruising sloops between 20 and 30 ft which had specialized in what could be called the 'family economy' end of the market. With the Mirage 37 the builders are into a different league, and if she could still be called that very general thing, a 'family cruiser', she shows signs of some very original thinking by the design team involved.

Basically, they have taken a 37 ft moderately high performance hull, complete with fin-and-skeg configuration. They have fitted into it a centre cockpit maximum accommodation layout and have put on top a nicely proportioned ketch rig. It does not sound all that startling, but with the combination of some novel features and some older ideas used in new ways, the total package merits close study.

To begin with, the cockpit is well aft, as far aft as some long sterned boats of orthodox layout, and so in the Mirage the crew sailing the boat are not as exposed as is usually the case with central cockpits, but in any case the design incorporates a windshield which may not be to everyone's liking in a sailing boat, but certainly adds a little to the shelter.

Further potential in the design has been realized with a skilful shaping of the mouldings around the cockpit to enable features of the accommodation to be part of what would often in other cases be waste space. The problems of a forward facing hatch for the aft cabin is by-passed completely with a corridor along the starboard side of the boat under the cockpit coamings – so much room is provided with this that it also contains an extra berth, while on the port side the space is filled by part of the roomy galley and the toilet compartment for the aft double cabin.

From the safety point of view, rapid exit from the aft cabin is provided by a hatch in the afterdeck – otherwise, all access is from the main part of the accommodation, and for cruising in northern waters the dryness and warmth which will be gained from the absence of a direct companionway should be most welcome.

Using the short settee berth on the port side of the saloon, the boat *could* sleep eight; it would seldom be the case, but even with the six who can have their own bunks living aboard, ventilation is going to be of primary importance; in all, including the hatch in the aft cabin, there are three opening hatch-skylights in the boat, together with other small ventilators, all of which will be necessary in normal conditions and especially in a seaway when the remarkable layout might seem a little oppressive.

The specified power unit is a 53 h.p. Ford Tempest diesel, driving through a fixed propeller, all of which can guarantee a very effective

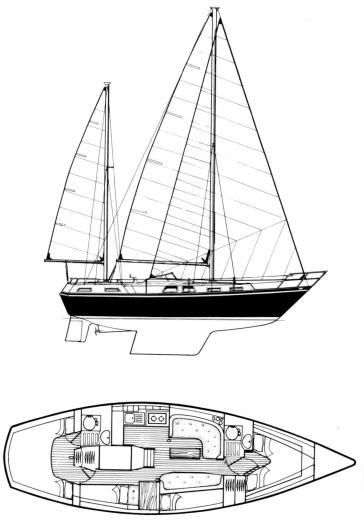

Mirage 37. Designed as the roomiest possible family sailing cruiser with full power, the Mirage 37 is especially interesting for the layout of the aft cabin and its access.
LOA 36 ft 3 in, LWL 27 ft 6 in, beam 11 ft 6 in, draft 5 ft 6 in, displacement 15,000 lb, sail area 609 sq. ft.

performance under engine. The engine itself is located in a box under the cockpit, which in fact allows total access all round, the only drawback being that you will be working at different parts of the engine from different cabins. The boat's construction uses the accepted technique of having separate moulded units for each area.

On deck, one possible area for improvement is around the afterdeck, where the raised coachroof is so far above the rest of the deckline that the guardrails on it are very low in order to retain some uniformity of appearance; anyone interested in really going to sea with the boat would be well advised to change this feature immediately, as it means that there is almost no guardrail around the aft part of the cockpit, while the afterdeck is hazardous.

One other slight carp is that the hull shape of the Mirage 37, which is otherwise a fine powerful lump of a boat, seems somewhat weak forward. No reason can be discerned as to why the boat should not have more freeboard and more powerful sections forward of the mainmast: this would improve her looks and performance and would give a roomier and drier foredeck.

The Mirage 37 incorporates a number of novel and useful design features.

3 Designs more than 40 feet

Salar 40

Time was when yachtsmen's minds were much exercised by earnest discussion about 'motor-sailers'. The concept of a sailing boat with sufficient power to have motoring as a real alternative is not new; in the last quarter of the 19th century the Napier brothers built a number of noted large yachts, virtually small ships, which successfully combined steam power with sail, the most famous being the 532-ton three-masted tops'l schooner *Sunbeam*, owned by the railway king Lord Brassey, which sailed and steamed round the world in 1876–77. Being so large, such craft coped with the difficulties of combination in ways impossible for smaller yachts, and later as motor cruisers became more popular a new breed emerged, at first using sail for steadying purposes for seagoing, and then as auxiliary propulsion until there evolved that unfortunate creature the '50–50', whose motive power was supposed to be half supplied by sails and half by engine, but which generally was reckoned only half as good as a sailing yacht, and half as good as a motor-boat.

However, with the continuing improvement in marine engines, there was no doubt that a successful combination in small craft of both sail and power could be developed which would greatly ease matters, particularly for family cruising when the joys of thrashing along under sail on a brisk day may not be shared by all on board. Thus there emerged a breed of yacht known to some as a 90–90, which is still an unfortunate reminder of the old 50–50 insult, so perhaps the description of 'fully powered sailing yacht' is more apt.

Of course, we continue to get motor cruisers with quite substantial sail areas whose owners lovingly describe as 'motor-sailers'. It is a bit of

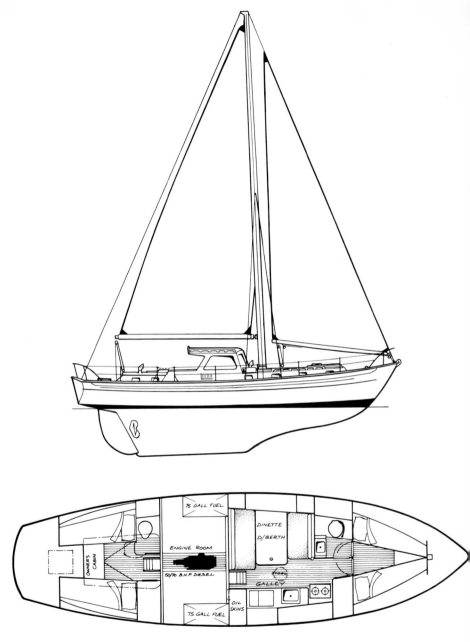

Salar 40. *A powerful all round cruiser with the unmistakable design stamp of Laurent Giles.*
LOA 40 ft, LWL 31 ft, beam 11 ft 4 in, draft 5·6 ft, displacement 23,300 lb, sail area 560 sq. ft.

a misnomer, as the sails really only are for steadying purposes – indeed no displacement motor cruiser should go to sea without steadying sails unless she has stabilizers – and their driving power is only sufficient to give a few knots on a reach in a strong wind. The true modern motor-sailer has a hull shape which is akin to a hefty sailing yacht, but in addition she has substantially more power than would normally be the case, and frequently has a wheelhouse or some sort of shelter over the cockpit; in fact, your modern motor-sailer is a sailing yacht below the water and in her rig, but she is a motor cruiser above the water and in her engine-room.

With such a combination, used for real seagoing, inevitably the sailing aspect becomes dominant, because there is nothing more uncomfortable in a seaway than a sailing hull being driven along under power; the rolling and pitching is unbelievable, and some sort of sail has to be set at least for steadying purposes. In time the crew becomes adept at getting the right combination of sail and power to get to places in the shortest time consistent with the required degree of comfort, for the motor-sailer particularly appeals to cruising men whose time is limited but who want to cover a lot of ground keeping to schedule. An able modern motor-sailer will be sailed when possible and she will do it well, but when the wind becomes light there is no compunction about starting the engine to keep moving fast. Where a nasty bash to windward is in prospect, the experienced motor-sailer skipper knows that he can make remarkable headway with just his mainsail set, sheeted almost dead amidships and the boat with her engine running.

For many people such a boat provides the ideal cruiser, and the development of the motor-sailer during the past twenty years has been one of the most welcome aspects of the yachting revolution. Indeed, it could be argued that with contemporary international offshore racing getting to levels even more hectic than Olympic sailing, we have reached the stage where any seagoing auxiliary yacht can be only a racer or a motor-sailer, the motor-sailer being the pure cruising yacht. Perhaps not, but the fact that such a point of view might be tenable shows just how successfully motor-sailers have been developed.

One design firm which has played a leading role in motor-sailer development is Laurent Giles and Partners Ltd. The firm designed sailing craft which could be effective motor-sailers if the owner wished. *Donella*, a cutter of 1958 for instance, had a diesel of only 18 h.p., but later power potential was generally more fully realized with engines around the 30 h.p. level. A layout with a central cockpit sheltered with a semi-wheelhouse over the forward end became their style. When GRP became available it was only a matter of time before a production version of the Giles motor-sailers appeared.

This was the Salar, at 39 ft in length with a beam of 11 ft 3 in she had a greater TM than either, and is every bit as roomy. Although the design first appeared in the mid-'60s, she is still being built, and everything about her appearance speaks of Jack Giles' style in producing a yacht which looks well, if a little different, which sails well, and which can keep the sea in all weathers.

Cockpit shelter on the Salar. A fixed semi-wheelhouse arrangement such as this is a real comfort in harsher climates, but it has to be acknowledged that in knockdown conditions in open water it coould become a hazard.

The first time I met a Salar when cruising, she was being sailed by the owner, his wife and family; there seemed to be children everywhere, but the yacht coped admirably in all situations, and it was a classic case of the separate aft cabin providing a haven of sanity for the adults. The second Salar I met with was being sailed by two serious cruising men who found the boat's layout gave both of them breathing space, while the actual sailing side was easily coped with by just two.

Thus the layout wins approval on two sets of requirements, and while she may look a little unusual to those of us accustomed to yachts with cockpits placed orthodoxly aft, undoubted benefits do accrue. Of course, there is no way such a cockpit could be used in all conditions without that substantial forward shelter, and one's instinctive aversion to a large deckhouse arises at first sight of it. But it is just a shelter, and in ultimate weather if it were damaged the safety of the yacht as a whole would be relatively little affected, though you would have to accept that your navigation gear and so forth, which is located under the shelter, might suffer disarray in such a disaster. Against that, in the conditions under which most of us sail, that shelter makes all the difference to comfort, and I have known dyed-in-the-wood rugged cruising types go off cruising with scepticism in a Salar and return fully converted.

One of the Salar's charms is her three separate cabins when everyone is sleeping in port, and as each cabin has its own access to one of the two toilets, the effect is that of private luxury.

Nowadays, we seem to be in the era of the great aft cabin, with a raised deck right across the stern of the boat, and there is a version of the Salar which features this, known as the Buccaneer. But while this does provide a feeling of greater airiness in the owner's stateroom aft, it rather spoils the unmistakably Jack Giles line of the boat's appearance, and aficionados would probably prefer her in the original style.

She is truly a motor-sailer with the specified engine being around the 70 h.p. mark, but her sailing ability has been proved beyond doubt. Robin Collins, whose ketch-rigged Salar *Wild Wing* has notched up transatlantic crossings and West Indies cruises, comments that the thing that really surprised him at first was her exceptional sailing performance, as her appearance had initially led him to expect a docile family cruiser.

Alternative sloop or ketch rig is available, and it really is a matter of personal choice as the yacht is big enough to carry a worth-while ketch rig, but still small enough to be manageable by a small crew when rigged as a sloop. *Wild Wing* is rigged as a ketch, but other notable cruising Salars have used the sloop rig. The only qualification that Robin Collins makes is that the club boom on the staysail is just a nuisance, cluttering the foredeck and limiting the sail plan. To get the best of the Salar's almost unexpectedly good performance on her fairly heavy hull you can carry larger headsails.

Her shape is both orthodox and unusual. The profile is standard long-keel sailing cruiser; perhaps for persistent drying out alongside one might prefer to see the toe of the keel a little further forward, there certainly seems at the moment to be a very great deal of yacht sticking out in front of it, even if the greater weight is aft. However, what is important is that a good all round sailing shape has been obtained with only 5 ft 6 in draft; even with a substantial loading of stores for long-distance cruising, she is still within the magic one fathom mark in remote anchorages.

At first glance the deck plan might be assumed to be that of a clipper bowed yacht, so full is it forward. But I do not think that Jack Giles ever used the clipper bow in any of his designs; instead he remained faithful to his own special line, but in several designs, especially the Salar, he introduced marked flare in the forward sections, resulting in a roomy and dry foredeck.

While we may have to readjust our thinking to a considerable degree in order to accept the Salar's viability as a real seagoing yacht, once we begin a critical assessment of her both as a design and in reality we find that she fulfils most requirements, albeit at times in an unorthodox way.

The Freedom 40 is a refreshing combinati[o]n of some old concepts [in] a new guise.

Freedom 40

The original concept of the Freedom 40 blew like a fresh breeze, more like a howling gale, in fact, through the world of sailing. Today's yachts, thought Garry Hoyt whose notion it all was in the first place, if anything get us away from the pleasures of sailing. Their electrics break down – *do without electrics, use oil lamps*. Their engines are such that we become slaves to the things – *do without engines*. Any man likes privacy and comfort, and if he buys a boat he surely has earned it, but many of today's boats mix in owners and crews in unprivate chaos – *give the owner the best cabin in the most comfortable part of the ship, and let the crew doss down elsewhere, it will be good for their immortal souls*. Masts, rigging and sails, especially headsails, are crucifying with cost, as well as being difficult to handle – *do without rigging, after all aircraft have done without it for years, do without headsails and let's take it from there*. Today's boats are ugly and they all look much the same – *get a hull design from L. Francis Herreshoff, an elegant sweeping New England shape of classic yet individual beauty unlike anything going afloat these days, and then put it out without disfiguring life-lines because the crew will all be in a large and safe well amidships*. Today's boats, despite everything, still sink now and again – *fill the new dreamship up with synthetic foam in any empty spaces, that will keep her up whatever you do*.

Perhaps the most surprising thing about the Freedom 40 is that she has managed to adhere so closely to the original tingling fresh concepts. Admittedly an engine has found its way aboard, and so have the inevitable electrics, but for all that she is very much a cruiser which puts the sail back in sailing. Never having sailed aboard her I do not pretend to know how the rig works. David Pelly, whose nice line in dry humour is one of the attractions of *Yachting World* magazine, observed that at first glance her plans looked to him like a wardrobe chasing a couple of Windsurfers, but judging by her photographs she looks much more handsome in the flesh, and she certainly looks interesting. As well as that, she really can make the bubbles fly astern, and in racing in the Caribbean has been known to see Swan 44s and suchlike handily tucked astern.

Of course, if she were not fast it would be because the rig was not doing its stuff, as there is really very little to stop Herreshoff's long-waterlined and strikingly handsome hull going very fast indeed. Inevitably there is a certain weakness to windward, but that is only by comparison with out-and-out racers. She is well up with other cruisers, and reaching – with a huge staysail set from the after mast – she takes off, a mode of progress maintained dead running as the two working sails can be effectively goose-winged. When the wind pipes up, extensive sea trials have evolved effective sail shortening systems which involve a minimum of effort. and though it is not immediately clear why the two-ply wrap-around sails on the masts should come down easily despite the

The novelty of the Freedom 40 has been continued in her deck layout.

inevitable friction, apparently they do, and when they are set the wishbone boom arrangements keep them nicely in shape without the usual strain of an orthodox boom and vang.

The accommodations are quite splendid, the owner getting his well-earned great cabin aft, while forward, although everything is provided, it all is achieved with a pleasantly uncluttered air. That the Freedom 40 is startlingly novel goes without saying, but perhaps her greatest attraction lies in the fact that her novel effect is obtained by returning to the highest standards of a bygone age.

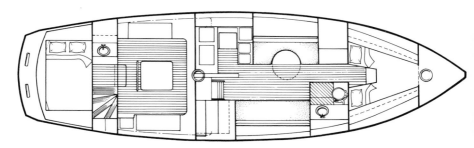

Freedom 40.
LOA 40 ft, LWL 35 ft, beam 12 ft, draft 3 ft 4 in (plate down 6 ft), sail area 780 square ft.

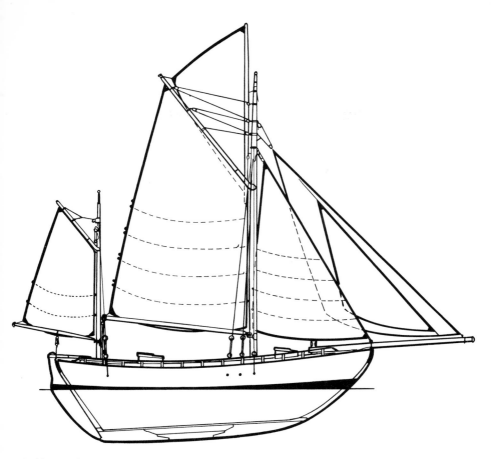

Colin Archer 40. *Perhaps the most remarkable thing about this design is the fact that though built in GRP in the 1970s, the hull lines are exactly those drawn by Colin Archer.*
LOA 39 ft 4 in, LWL 34 ft 5 in, beam 13 ft 7 in, draft 6 ft 5 in, displacement 35,000 lb.

Colin Archer 40

That remarkable designer and builder, Colin Archer of Norway, produced his first yacht in 1873, and in time his yard at Larvik became deservedly world-renowned for able and attractive yachts. He was a man of broad maritime interests, and during the 1890s he also developed his concept of the *Redningsskøjte*, which was a sailing escort, pilot, search and rescue vessel for the Norwegian coast, craft which were designed and built specifically to keep the sea for prolonged periods in all weather, their function dictating that they should be able to keep moving in even the most extreme conditions.

The vessels which resulted were heavy double-enders, having their own special look about them which makes them instantly identifiable right down to the present day. And that perhaps is the most remarkable thing of all about Colin Archer – people still continue to build yachts exactly as he designed them so many years ago, and the production of the Colin Archer 40 in glass fibre for the Colin Archer club of Stockholm started as recently as 1973.

Because extreme conditions are so seldom experienced, cruising enthusiasts have a myriad of theories to choose from in preparing for such weather, so much so that though it may sound flippant, it can reasonably be stated that the only universally-accepted golden rule is: Stay Afloat. Based on a concept of strength through intelligently-applied weight, the Colin Archer vessel in her pure form has almost totally flush deck and an almost symmetrical hull fore and aft so that as she runs before huge seas, she will part them with a minimum of fuss, while her hugely heavy nature – this little ship displaces at least 18 metric tonnes – provides her crew with security and creature comforts as aids to survival.

The Colin Archer 40 as shown here is so utterly true to type, so much her own craft, that she lends herself to some idiotic wisecracks. Cynics might say that there is something a little curious about any boat which looks as if she could go as effectively backwards as forwards, but the true enthusiast can point out that there are many differences, some of them subtle, between the shapes of the bow and stern, all of which contribute to the validity of the total concept.

This concept inevitably includes gaff rig. Some might argue that you could get away with a Bermudian or leg-of-mutton mizzen, but even that is too much of a divergence from the purity of the basic theory, while some of the Bermudian rigs occasionally fitted to these vessels are beneath contempt. So gaff rig it is, complete with loose footed sails and massive wooden spars, and heroes to handle it all.

Moody 42
In the early 1970s the distinguished firm of A. H. Moody Ltd, Bursledon, Hampshire, departed somewhat from its image as builders of large and opulent yachts by commissioning from Angus Primrose the design of the Moody 33. Built in the firm's newly-acquired factory down in Plymouth, this centre-cockpit high-powered auxiliary sailing yacht proved to be attractive for anyone looking for a lot of yacht for the money, and the concept, with a recognizably similar style to all the designs, was successfully extended to two further designs, the Moody 30 and the Moody 39. Meanwhile at their extensive yard on the River Hamble the firm continued to build their larger range, and with the

introduction in 1977 of the Moody 42, cruising people were offered a yacht which marked the design point of the newer Moody 33 *et al.*, meeting the older Moody tradition as symbolized by the famous Carbineer and others. The new boat is finished at Bursledon, but is another Primrose design which incorporates many of the features which have been so popular with the smaller craft, and the undoubted appeal of this latest design was signalled by sixteen of them being sold before the prototype made her debut at the 1977 London Boat Show.

The Moody 42 manages to provide good accommodation with good sailing performance.

She is very much a motor-sailer in the best modern manner, providing good sailing ability with a more than adequate power performance. Design purists might object to the rather vulnerable-looking deckhouse amidships, but in fact it is more robust than it looks, and is considerably lower and more seamanlike than houses on many comparable craft.

Within, it provides a really splendid 'living room', complete with galley at the forward end, and as an extra a second interior steering position can be provided at the forward end of this saloon. Such an arrangement would not be used as often as you would expect, even the most comfort-loving yachtsman finds that he inevitably seems to prefer an open steering position for the vast majority of conditions, but just

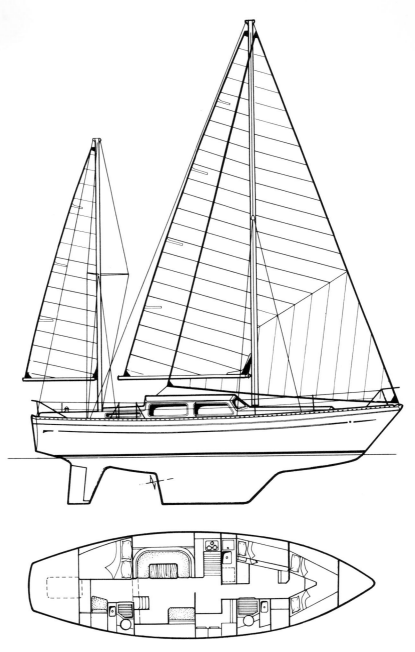

Moody 42. *An unusually successful combination of a number of features in order to meet the requirements of many cruising people.*
LOA 41 ft 9½ in, LWL 34 ft 9 in, beam 13 ft 4 in, draft 5 ft 6 in, displacement 24,200 lb, sail area 762 sq. ft.

now and again when conditions are really nasty, particularly if motoring on a cold wet day, the sheltered steering position could be a godsend.

In a motor-sailer, the engine inevitably is much more important than on a pure sailing boat, and so ease of access for maintenance is especially important. In the Moody 42, the Perkins 4.236 65 h.p. diesel is located in solitary splendour in the huge space under the main saloon. Admittedly this means that in order to get at it, the saloon is immobilized for other crew members, but engineers would insist that this is just as it should be: an awareness of the importance of the engine aboard a motor-sailer should be instilled in everyone aboard.

The rest of the accommodation is particularly well arranged. A large and comfortable aft cabin is skilfully fitted in between the saloon and the cockpit, and it is a real cabin, not just the glorified cubby-hole sometimes found in this location. Forward, the toilet-washroom to starboard could almost be called a bathroom, while the yacht is just large enough to incorporate two further separate sleeping cabins, each with a couple of bunks, in this area, and they will greatly contribute to the pleasure of sailing board, for it is very easy to have too much of the enforced bonhomie inevitable with some of today's open-plan layouts.

On deck, the steering position right aft gives a pleasant controlled feel to things, with good visibility, for although you are aware of the deckhouse amidships, it is not overly obstructive and it is just possible to see clear to the stemhead when standing at the wheel, which is the minimum visibility requirement. The journey from the companionway to the cockpit over the coachroof of the aft cabin seems a little exposed, but there is the mizzen rigging to grab and further safety could be provided by 'anti-roll' bars. Forward, the flared bow provides an exceptionally roomy foredeck.

The Moody 42 might not be the ideal boat to make prolonged passages in open water, but it must be remembered that for all its attractions, ocean cruising is very much a minority interest, and for most people cruising is a matter of coast-hopping with the occasional longer passage of two or three days' duration. For such cruising, the Moody 42 is well nigh ideal; she sails well, she motors well, she is very comfortable below and, though only a 42-footer, she provides a life style which would normally only be found on yachts ten or even twenty feet longer.

Swan 44

Pietarsaari is 200 miles south of the Arctic Circle, and is on the same latitude as southern Iceland; it is a place which is under snow for at least half of the year, while the waters of the nearby Gulf of Bothnia are usually some feet thick in ice in dead of winter. Here the Finnish firm of Nautor Ky builds yachts.

The Nautor story is an enormous triumph of Finnish craftsmanship

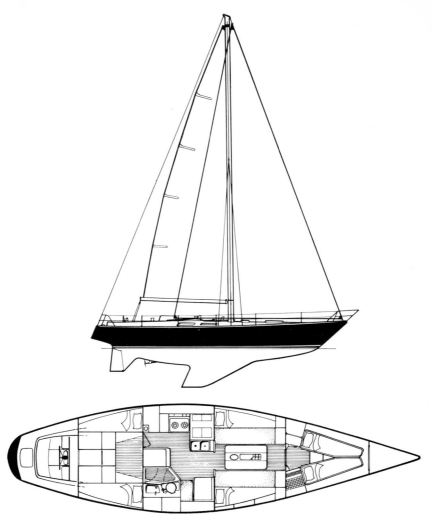

Swan 44.
LOA 44 ft, LWL 35·22 ft, beam 12·58 ft, draft 7·17 ft, displacement 23,800 lb.

and sheer quality at every stage of production. Right at the beginning they linked themselves with the talents of the design firm of Sparkman and Stephens of New York.

The first Nautor production was a GRP boat around the One Ton size; she was called the Swan 36, and the prototype was delivered to two Royal Air Force men, Dave Johnson and Mike Hurrell, in England

towards the end of the summer of 1967. The two demon aviators had
mortgaged just about everything they had to set themselves up as
Nautor Distributors, but to their dismay while the new boat looked
good and sailed sublimely, there were some faults which made the
future gloomy.

Nothing daunted, the Finns were already at work on Mark 2, and she
made her debut in the English Channel the following spring. The first
boat had been named *Casse Tete* because her low boom had clipped the
crew's heads, the new boat inevitably became *Casse Tete II*. She looked
lovely, she was superbly finished, she provided real seagoing comfort,
and she sailed like a witch, proving to be almost embarrassingly faster
than the one-off One Tonners then sailing. *Casse Tete II*, apart from
offshore successes, swept the board at Cowes Week 1968, and after the
nail-biting nerve-racking beginnings, Nautor and their agents were on
the crest of the wave.

Despite an identifiable design theme throughout, each Nautor design
has an attractive individuality; the successful philosophy has been to
introduce complete standardization in features where it does not matter,
such as in items of interior joinery work such as drawers and locker
doors, and on deck in fittings, many of which they now make themselves.
They also have their own spar plant.

With batch production introduced into separate joinery parts, an
incredibly high standard of woodwork finish can be obtained, and when
it is all assembled with that stylish Finnish craftsmanship the total effect
is breathtaking. So of course is the price when compared with production
yachts built to a more economical level, but the thing about buying a
Nautor boat is that you know exactly what you are getting, and re-sale
value is assured.

With a modern plant building to a standard which met the exacting
requirements of a shrewd and affluent international clientele, Nautor's
expansion was rapid, and the world began to beat a snow-covered track
to their door; it became fashionable to be able to talk of your expedition
into the Arctic to see your new Swan being built, and the very location
made a fascinating Baltic cruise part of your delivery trip if you wished to
sail the boat home; indeed, Pietarsaari fans would claim that if you have
not felt your way through the leads among the ice of the Gulf of Bothnia
in the early summer, then you have not taken delivery of a Swan at all.

The 44 was the outstanding production boat in the Admiral's Cup
series, and 1973 was truly exceptional in that she continued to figure at
the head of fleets for succeeding seasons. She is not a boat for genteel
ambling along; her whole design, with its flush deck and 'hole-in-the-
ground' main hatch almost amidships, involving a seemingly exposed
journey from the cockpit to get below, speaks of hard driving by fit
crews. But already some notable cruises have been notched up by yachts

of this class, and as time goes on and they become a little dated by the newest design developments in racing, cruising will become their true *forte*.

The layout does not appeal to everyone as its basic concept is rather spartan, and yet its execution is so beautifully done with luxurious woodwork and opulent upholstery that a possible criticism is that the design falls between the twin stools of out-and-out racing and comfortable cruising, not satisfying the complete needs of either.

The accommodation plan reveals the influence of offshore racing design thought in 1972; the principal 'systems workshops' for catering and navigation are kept amidships, and here too, ironically in the position of least motion, is the heads. Such an aft location for the only toilet is not a new concept – the noted cruising man A. G. MacPherson, who was in places as far distant as Iceland and Singapore when voyaging during the 1930s in his 8 ton cutter *Driac II*, made a point of having an aft toilet in a yacht only 32 ft LOA: undoubtedly the usual 'heads' in the head can be damnably uncomfortable.

Apart from safety and comfort considerations, the heads are so placed in the 44 because of the separate cabin ingeniously located aft between the main hatch and the cockpit. This too is not a totally new idea, it was standard practice in the flush deck cruising yachts of 40 ft and upwards during the Edwardian era, but in the Swan it is used in a refreshingly original way. Its separate access to the washroom provides a remarkable degree of privacy, while the location of this little stateroom is such that you could get some sleep there in almost any sea condition. Unfortunately, the curve of the waterlines means that while sleeping in the lee bunk your head would be a little lower than your feet when the boat is heeled.

If there is one real criticism of the accommodation plan, it is that so much has been packed into the boat amidships and aft, that the saloon area, with its two pilot berths and two settee berths, has been pushed so far forward as to risk being uncomfortable while sleeping there when going to windward, but as all accommodations are a compromise at best, perhaps this is a small price to pay. The alternative, which we see increasingly in the latest offshore designs where the drawbacks of over-loading forward are taken account of, would be to have four berths in that aft cabin, which from a general cruising point of view would definitely not be an improvement.

As it is, the layout of the Swan 44 gives a very reassuring air of compact strength, the plan including substantial features of athwartships strengthening particularly at deck level which could well be emulated by other designs. On deck, for those accustomed to sheltering wheelhouses and whatnot, it may all seem a little reminiscent of the tundra in winter, for apart from the mast the only things which stick up to any extent are

Adventure, and has only three inches greater beam, and yet in an accommodation typically ingenious in this designer's style one version has no less than twelve bunks, while the Adventure at the very outside would expect to sleep no more than eight, and even that would be thought of as crowding.

The philosophies of the two yachts are markedly different, for while the Bowman 57 is very much a comfortable cruising yacht, she takes her style from offshore racing, one of the first of the marque having sailed the Atlantic from her builders in Emsworth in England to her new owner in Newport in excellent time.

To provide such a performance, she gives of her best when sailed well by an able and fairly large crew, but can nevertheless continue to give a good showing when driven more modestly by a smaller complement. Certainly it would not be to everyone's taste to cruise for long periods with as many as twelve people aboard, and many cruising men would prefer to sail her with, say, seven or eight, thus leaving the saloon almost free from sleeping requirements, which may not sound much but has a surprisingly civilizing influence on life aboard.

Even with a full complement aboard, the level of privacy available is remarkable with no less than three double cabins apart from the crew's fo'c'sle; admittedly in a seaway the motion in the sleeping cabin forward could be a little violent, but she is a big yacht and so her motion in her ends is that much gentler than with smaller craft; in any case, for those with weaker digestions the double cabin immediately aft of the chart table provides minimal motion.

There is an exceptionally pleasant saloon amidships with raised sole to provide room for the engine underneath; to provide it with headroom there is a deckhouse of moderate height, an elegant structure of itself, though the rugged brigade might cavil a little at the size of the windows. One real drawback is that it restricts visibility if the aft steering position is selected, and this alone is enough to make the amidships steering position with the wheel immediately aft of the deckhouse preferable, even if it is a little more exposed to spray from forward.

Effectively, the two cockpits are one, which makes for a great deal of sheet handling space, but one disadvantage of this is that the largest sheet winches are located right above the owner's stateroom, making it a noisy place when the watch on deck are busy. But in any case that elegant aft stateroom will only really come into its own in port, as a double bunk is not much of a proposition at sea unless its width is severely restricted with what our forefathers would have called a bundling board. With so much cleverly designed sleeping accommodation throughout the length of the ship, sail stowage space is necessarily limited.

Externally, this is a yacht of style and real elegance; two forms of transom are available, either retroussé or orthodox, the former giving an overall length of 56 ft, while the latter is 58 ft. Somehow a retroussé transom never looks quite right under a mizzen, while the more traditional arrangement has the advantage of providing more room on the afterdeck, which will be welcome as the mizzen sheet will tend to cause clutter; a further advantage is the longer stern's ability to provide the mizzen with a standing backstay, something of real value in that it supports the mizzen mast when it is at its most useful, carrying a big mizzen staysail.

Two keel depths are available, of either 8 ft 4 ins or 7 ft. She is of a type which will benefit from the extra depth to give more 'zing' to windward, but for pure cruising the 1 ft 4 ins saved in the shallower version can make a surprising difference in the extra number of harbours available. Choice of keel therefore depends almost entirely on where you expect to be using the yacht.

Swan 65

With the Swan 65 we find the design idiom of the Swan offshore racer-cruiser range writ large – very large indeed. Somehow a Swan 65, being gracefully proportioned, never seems all that big at first glance, but when you study her dimensions – a beam of 16 ft 4 ins for instance – and note that even with a flush deck the large auxiliary diesel engine can be located under the saloon floor without disturbing the attractive straight-through line of the cabin sole, an awareness begins to build up of just what a massive yacht she is.

The Swan 65 has been written for ever into the history of sailing with the overall win of Ramon Carlin's *Sayula II* in the Round the World race of 1973–74. It would in any case have been an impressive win, for by comparison with most of the other entries she was a privately owned comfortably equipped cruiser-racer, while they were in a number of cases one-off specials, either virtual government entries crewed by service personnel, or heavily sponsored ventures; but *Sayula*'s triumph was made all the greater by her having withstood a capsize to at least 150 degrees while running through the notorious waters away to the south of the Indian Ocean.

There are many cases, relatively speaking, of yachts which have survived being rolled over, but *Sayula* is probably the biggest one which has done it and emerged more or less unscathed. Caught up in the breaking crest of a huge sea, this yacht of around 25 tons deadweight was flipped like a surfboard, and the outcome was a complete vindication of the design philosophy behind the construction of the Swan designs; with nothing to be swept off her clean deck, nothing carried away; miraculously her rig remained intact, though later wear and tear indicated the enormous strains to which it had been subjected; happily, safety harnesses held sufficiently to keep the watch on deck

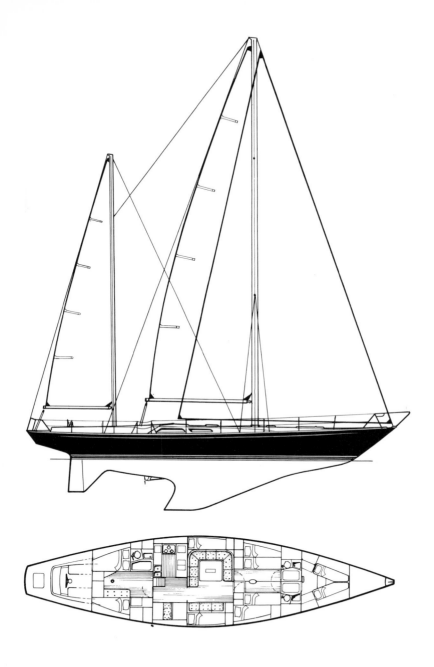

Swan 65. *For a number of years this was the largest yacht in the famous Finnish-built Nautor range.*
LOA 64 ft 10½ in, LWL 47 ft, beam 16 ft 4 in, draft 9 ft 3 in, displacement 57,400 lb.

with the ship; structurally, with her large hull strengthened both by the deck and strategically placed bulkheads, she remained sound; and so, despite somewhat wet chaos below, she was able to proceed, not only with the race but to a subsequent career of successful family cruising.

With a yacht this size, we have moved from the problem of fitting the required accommodation into the available space to the problems of having so much space that an interior designer's sensitivity is required in order to give the cabins the grace the yacht deserves. Of course, it is still necessary to provide a layout which is seaworthy, and where open space of itself is used as an interior design feature, it has to be remembered that too much open space is an accommodation hazard in a seaway, and the need for it has to be tempered with the need at least for substantial handholds, and also for items of interior furniture which contribute both to stowage and to personal support.

With the Swan 65, the result is a series of cabins which are pleasant to be in, and yet also impart an air of seaworthiness in its broadest sense. Galley and chart area are well placed amidships, the former virtually a separate 'kitchen', while the latter is conveniently placed near the main companionway.

As with the Bowman 57, the owner's stateroom aft suffers a little from noise of winches and so forth when the yacht is being actively sailed, indeed this is inevitable with any sailing cruiser with an aft cabin, but the relatively motion-free advantages of such a cabin outweigh the disadvantages, even though the rather wide bunks – both single and double – have a number of seagoing disadvantages.

The two pilot berths in the saloon will probably be the most comfortable berths in the ship in rough weather, though it would be absolutely necessary to ensure that your bunkboards are keeping you secure when in the weather bunk – fall out of one of those, and you will be going at quite some speed when you fetch up in the lee side of the saloon. The saloon itself is a friendly spot, though anyone sitting in the middle of the settee berth with everyone sitting down would probably find it quicker to walk over the table if he wants to get out in a hurry.

The two sleeping cabins ahead of the saloon are quite far forward, particularly when it is remembered that the mast shown is that of a ketch and in a sloop rig the bunks would in fact be completely forward of the mast. Still, they provide a measure of real privacy, very pleasant even with the most amiable crew, and in most conditions will provide real comfort.

Forward of this, the fo'c'sle is effectively a sail bin in which it is also possible to sleep; a yacht of this size will inevitably carry at least one paid hand, and possibly two or even three, but any owner interested in a happy ship will probably make arrangements for one of the guest cabins to be used as crew quarters.

With the likelihood of at least ten people sailing aboard regularly, the provision of three washroom/heads is not by any means excessive, and indeed if the yacht is used continuously for seagoing one might like to see one of the forward heads located a little further aft.

With the determined adherence to the flush-deck configuration, special efforts have to be made to ensure that the accommodation does

The number of crew handling sails on the Swan 65 emphasizes the considerable deck space.

not become tomb-like; the use of light woods for trim helps, as does the provision of really first class ventilation.

On deck, the helmsman has good visibility, although the fact that he is all of sixty feet aft of the stemhead may make him seem a little remote from his forward end, and the sheer size of the two masts between him and the foredeck is a further restriction. Most active helmsmen find that they prefer this aft location as it seems to give a better sense of how the yacht is moving, but it has to be accepted that it is somewhat exposed.

The sense of exposure is contributed to by the unusually long length of the counter, made so in order to accommodate the exceptionally large mizzen, which thus can have the real advantage of a standing backstay without an unsightly and vulnerable bumpkin sticking out astern of the yacht. With the size of the Swan 65, the ketch rig is inevitably preferred (though a sloop rig is available with a retroussé transom), but in order to provide a really sizeable mizzen, the sail is so close to the leech of the mainsail as to make the sail useless to windward. This is a problem with most ketches, but it is a fact that a Swan 65 in particular, when hard on the wind, will almost invariably have her mizzen stowed.

With sheets eased, of course, the mizzen begins to provide real power, and the mizzen staysail can be a really effective pulling sail in the right conditions. As well, the mizzen is big enough to provide effective power when used in conjunction with a headsail with the main stowed, a popular rig with short-handed ketches, and for such crews the Swan 65 also has a cutter rig for the fore-triangle if required.

It is a presumption to discuss a yacht such as this in one sub-section of a chapter in a book on sailing cruisers. Craft such as the Swan 65 represent the upper levels of a continuing theme of seagoing ability.

Ocean 75

Having discovered that with the Bowman 57 and the Swan 65 we had moved into a discernibly different type of yacht mainly because of their size, a study of the Ocean 75 leaves one with the inescapable feeling that we have moved on again, from very large yachts into the realm of small ships. While there have been and still are much larger yachts than this in the world, it is generally accepted that the Ocean 75 is the largest GRP sailing cruiser which could truly be described as a production yacht.

Although only 10 ft longer overall than the Swan 65, the Ocean 75 is very much bigger, being 7 ft 6 ins longer on the waterline with more than a foot extra beam, in a hull which is proportionally fuller aft and flared forward, giving acres of deck room with considerably more volume below. Indeed though the price of the Ocean 75 seems astronomical, in terms of hull volume rated against price she probably represents excellent value for money when compared with any other boat in this book.

She is of such a size that ship management requirements will almost inevitably come into consideration. There is no trouble, for instance, in visualizing a Bowman 57 or even a Swan 65 being used all the time as a private yacht, but with an Ocean 75, unless she is used continuously as a floating home, chartering considerations will loom large, and most of the Ocean 75s launched have had this as a major priority.

For her size, the displacement of around 30 tons in cruising trim is

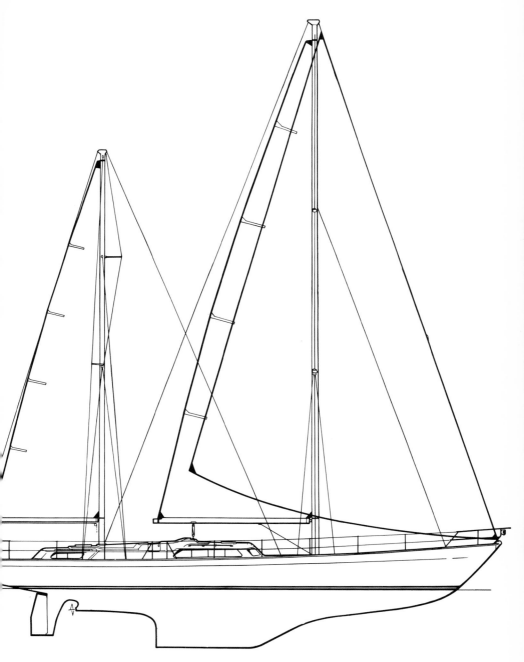

Ocean 75 sail plan and profile.

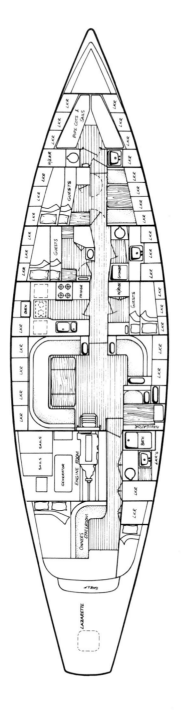

Ocean 75. *Developed from the successful Ocean 71, for several years the world's largest GRP production yacht. LOA 75 ft, LWL 60 ft, beam 17·4 ft, draft 8·5 ft, displacement 85,800 lb, sail area 2,648 sq. ft.*

The power of an Ocean 75 is evident from this photo.

fairly light, and so a relatively small crew can handle the conveniently sized rig provided things like spinnakers are left severely alone. But the Ocean 75 is a development of the noted *Stormvogel*, Cees Bruynzeel's famous world-girdling and offshore racing ketch, and it would only be fair to give her a bit of a canter now and again, when a crew of fifteen would not go amiss, particularly when you are keeping tabs on the 3,200-square-foot spinnaker.

I was lucky enough to sail aboard one of the best known Ocean 71s, *Second Life*, when Roddy Ainslie and his merry men were doing some limbering up, prior to going off in the 1973–74 Round the World race. Having been built for racing, she was somewhat stripped out down below, but this saved six tons in the displacement, and made her particularly pleasant to handle; even so, it was difficult to accept that when you turned the wheel, this small action was responsible for the mightly stemhead – which seemed miles away – swinging across the horizon.

Setting the spinnaker was a bit of a laugh as the skipper had to use the loudhailer from the cockpit to let the foredeck crew know he wanted them to go ahead with things, while moving the huge spinnaker poles about for gybing was not something to be undertaken lightly. *Second Life*, compared to anything else other than her sister ships, had a style all her own, and an attractive one at that, and despite her huge size and her acres of GRP, she was a yacht for which one could feel a real affection. Racing to the Clyde that summer, she was tearing down the east coast of the Isle of Man, broad reaching in a gale, when a steep sea from astern just caught her perfectly, she would sustain a surge of 24 knots. So elated were her crew by all this that when they brought the wind slightly more aft, they tried to set the spinnaker. It went up, but blew out with a loud and expensive bang. When Johnny MacWilliam came to make them another, he had to rent the City Hall in Cork for a day, so that he could spread it out for finishing.

The layout as shown is the basic suggestion as provided by the builders – all sorts of variants are available, but as the builders are now so experienced in finishing these craft no matter how eccentric your requirements it is probably more economical in the long run to stick with the builders instead of hopefully shopping around.

The size scale is immediately evident from the main stateroom aft. Not only is this luxurious cabin accessible from for'ard via the passageway along the outside of the engine-room, but the problem of direct access to the deck is solved by having a second aft cockpit, with a companionway to the stateroom. The cockpit serves a number of purposes, and is especially useful with a charter party aboard.

The remainder of the accommodation shown could be described as 'orthodox', certainly as far as there is an orthodoxy for the layout of 75-ft ketches. The saloon is a veritable lounge, the galley could only be described as a kitchen, and forward of that there are four sleeping cabins which provide comfort for seven or eight without any undue crowding. Lack of crowding, in fact, is a feature of this particular layout, as there are berths only for 12, but another four berths could be provided without any hardship for anyone.

On deck, the short mainboom leaves the cockpit pleasantly clear of flailing sheets and blocks and some of the more opulently appointed Ocean 75s have a wheelhouse over most of this main cockpit. Despite the motor-yacht appearance which this may seem to give, the Ocean 75 is nevertheless a yacht for sailing, and the fact that such a craft under sail can be controlled from inside a wheelhouse more comfortably than on many small ships only serves to add a special flavour to it all.

For cruising, her power is such that a cutter-rigged foretriangle is almost obligatory, even though her deck space is such that it makes her sails seem smaller than they really are. With half a dozen regular crew aboard, it would be possible to use the full-size in the foretriangle with confidence, and a number of Ocean 75 skippers do just that, but for peace of mind and some sense of control a double-head rig is a real advantage.

City Halls to spread out the sails, loudhailers to talk to the foredeck, surges of 24 knots . . . it is a different world altogether, but if you can find the resources to build an Ocean 75 in the first place, and feel you can withstand the nervous strain which will be an inevitable part of the high-powered chartering she will attract, then there is no doubt that she can provide you with the ultimate sailing cruiser.

4 Wood, tin and stone

It is hoped that this discussion of some thirty-six different sailing cruisers, mostly in GRP and to a greater or lesser extent series or even mass produced, will have outlined the basic sizes and types generally available.

All the versions of the yachts discussed are those offered by the leading, in fact generally the sole builders, but undoubtedly there are many owners who, while acknowledging the advantages of GRP, have so many individual requirements that it is only with the largest yachts that such special needs can be met by the main builders.

Finishing her yourself

Fortunately, all sorts of other avenues are open to such individualists. Many leading hull moulders are prepared to sell bare hulls for completion either by owners or other yards which they prefer. Be warned that to start on such a project requires enormous will-power, because the trouble is that the bare GRP shell of a yacht looks to the fond eye very much like a boat; in fact it is something of a snare and a delusion, as it scarcely represents 10 per cent of the finished craft.

A more realistic approach may be to buy from the builders a boat at a certain stage of completion. The wide selection of craft now available in this way is partially owed to the spread of Value Added Tax.

The completion kits movement is a healthy modern development of the previous do-it-yourself hard chine plywood boat building. When properly approached it is a worth-while way to get yourself a boat in which you can have a personal involvement without suffering from nervous exhaustion at the end of it all. You have to find premises in

Many leading hull moulders are prepared to sell bare hulls for home completion, but be warned that this is not something to be undertaken lightly, for though the moulding looks very like a boat, it represents only about 10 per cent of the finished seagoing craft. As well, during home completion like this it will dominate not only the household but the entire neighbourhood as well, with launching day seeming to fade for evermore into the future.

which to finish her off, and then having selected the design you favour, analyse the different stages of completion available in order to assess at what level you can take over. If you have a proper workshop with people to help with overhead gantries and so forth, you can start with a bare hull. Then dropping in bulkheads, modules, the engine and fittings is simply a question of time. With more limited space, and less help, it is much more sensible to leave such things to the builders, retaining for yourself the final jobs, many of which have the advantage of being within the scope of one person. Do not think for a moment that such an approach is cheating the DIY code – even with bulkheads, modules and engine fitted, and the deck on, you are still hardly three-quarters of the way there!

Such a stage, nevertheless, is still much less disheartening than the chilling discovery of just how little of a finished boat a bare shell actually comprises, but your dyed-in-the-wool individualist will still want to start with this, and better still, will want a GRP hull to an individual design. The construction of a mould being prohibitive, a number of approaches to producing one-off hulls in GRP have been developed with varying success.

The one with the longest history is foam-sandwich construction, where a rough plug is covered with fitted sheets of synthetic foam, a layer

Foam sandwich construction – fixing the synthetic foam to the mould at the beginning of the laying-up process.

of GRP is put over the outside, and then when the hull is turned a further layer of GRP on the inside produces a double-skin hull of considerable strength. There is still a nasty sanding and filling job required on the outside of the hull to bring up a gloss finish, but a number of successful craft have been produced by this method.

Enthusiasts would argue that all GRP hulls should have some sort of sandwich construction in order to provide extra strength and act as a preventative against condensation. Certainly condensation prevention and the fitting of separate mouldings inside cabins to give a better finish

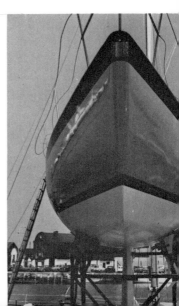

With proper finishing, a foam sandwich hull such as this one on High Tension, *the successful prototype of the High Tension 36 cruiser-racer class, can be fair and smooth.*

has resulted in frequent use of foam filling in decks, where end-grain balsa is also generally used to provide strong points for winch bases and so forth. It is another instance of the rapid development of the petro-chemical industry facilitating a boatbuilding revolution, as nowadays with most builders it is less a question of whether or not they use foam, but rather of what type.

In hulls, many builders are still content to have the straightforward GRP mould, but increasing use is being made of double skins and foam fillings at least to provide local strength. The Tyler Boat Company has evolved a method of foam sandwich which produces a hull with a satisfyingly strong feel to it. When the moulding has reached something like half thickness during the lay-up process, fore and aft 'planks' of synthetic foam are laid along the hull slightly more than their own width apart; further layers of GRP are applied, and then the gaps are filled with more 'foam planks'; more layers of GRP, and this 'Tyton' process, as it is called, results in a hull with the perfect finish resulting from a mould, and yet has the strength of a foam-sandwich hull; in fact, it is an improvement on some of the more primitive one-off hulls, as the fore and aft 'stringers' linking the two GRP layers through the sandwich are an extra strength factor; both the Hustler 35s in which I cruised in 1971 and 1975 were built by this method, and the result was a well finished and solid job, for all the world like sailing in a steel hull.

Another method of one-off construction of GRP hulls is the C-Flex method of 'glass fibre planking'. C-Flex is a glass fibre sheeting material made up of rods of GRP alternating with bundles of unsaturated glass fibre rovings, held together between two layers of lightweight open weave glass fibre cloth. The effect is of a very flexible plank, and with an open framework in the basic shape of the boat, a hull can be built by experienced personnel very quickly, with resin applied by rollers.

Wood

While there can be little doubt that at the moment GRP is the most convenient material for the construction of the majority of sailing cruisers, as we hurtle along towards the end of this frenetic 20th century, there is an increasing awareness of the finite nature of Earth's resources. Thus the petro-chemical industry, which is the basis of most of the raw materials involved in the manufacture of glass fibre, is itself based on a dwindling supply of crude oil. To a lesser extent mankind is also using up the basic materials involved in the other relatively recently developed boatbuilding methods using steel and ferro-cement. So it happens that it is enormously reassuring to know that once upon a time people built seagoing sailing craft which were based entirely on regenerating materials, and that if need be in the future we can draw upon nautical archaeology to tell us how to build timber ships fastened entirely with hardwood 'tree nails', rigged with hemp with sails made from cotton or flax, and powered across the sea by the winds which rely not upon the continuing functioning of oil refineries.

Nowadays, where wood is used it is generally with modern methods using glues which have been developed as an offshoot of the growth in petro-chemicals, all a far cry from the traditional methods. Multi-skin construction is now the norm, and the nature of wood, with its lengthwise grain, is such that the benefits of double skin planking, laid diagonally, have been recognized for some time – E. F. Knight's ex-lifeboat, *Falcon*, which he cruised to the Baltic in 1887, was built in this way.

Early experiments were hampered by the relative inefficiency of glues then available, and it was wartime urgency which speeded things up: wooden aircraft were 'hot moulded' using heated presses which facilitated the forcing of the thin skins of wood into all sorts of shapes, and speeded the curing of the glues. After the war, these presses were made to build boats.

Meanwhile, cold-moulding was possible with only modest temperatures due to the new chemically cured glues. For instance, W. A. Souter and Son of Cowes developed this to a fine art, building multi-skin yacht hulls upside down on plugs, evolving what has rightly been called 'timber engineering'. More recently they have further developed this with the use of wood and foam sandwich, and also with carbon fibre.

Garland of Howth

I was involved with the construction of a 28 ft 6 in Half Tonner to a design of Billy Brown's using what was basically the Souter method. Being obsessed with weight saving, we made this little boat with three skins of silver spruce, charming timber but really not robust enough. The wood which best lends itself to multi-skin construction is Honduras mahogany owing to its constant quality, but if you are using this be sure it *is* Honduras you are getting, as there are reputedly at least forty woods claiming to be mahogany, and many of them are utter rubbish.

It was a truly beautiful way to build a boat, and Don Conlon, who put her together in his shed down in the West of Ireland, was a master of multi-skin construction, as he knew exactly how much of the resorcinol glue to apply to ensure that the wood was sufficiently saturated to give maximum adhesion, and yet not too much so that you had a filling of glue which would be weakening. The resulting shell impressed even the most experienced boatbuilders who came to look at it, and impressed us as well, which was partially our undoing, for it looked so much like a boat that we felt it was a boat, whereas – just as it is with a bare GRP shell – all we had at the stage of lifting the shell off the plug was about 5 per cent of the finished boat; this was because in our case the finished boat

North Channel 29 *(Garland of Howth)*. *Designed by Billy Brown for ultra-light construction in cold-moulded silver spruce, this little yacht has been successful in local passage racing and has also cruised extensively. LOA 28 ft 3 in, LWL 23 ft 9 in, beam 10 ft, draft 5 ft 7 in, displacement 6,000 lb, sail area 455 sq. ft.*

was supposed to be a racing machine, and though we did not put in as much interior furniture as is found in a cruiser, we still had a long way to go once the boat was afloat with the necessary tuning.

In fact the tuning was never really completed, and the first season was unsatisfactory, although we managed six firsts in nine starts. The boat herself had considerable potential, and *Garland of Howth* as she was called, was built with due regard for seagoing requirements, having a mostly flush deck though with a jarring effect struck by the rather high little coachroof amidships (which fortunately did not look as bad as it did in the drawings, and it was all my fault, as I wanted headroom in at least one small area. Billy Brown's design had been for a flush deck boat). But we had a proper self-draining cockpit and a really strong bridge-deck amidships.

She was barely afloat before we had to sell her, but subsequently in Dick Richardson's ownership and re-named *Blackwater* she took part in the Half Ton Cup in La Rochelle in France; being somewhat overtaken

A 28·5 ft cruiser/racer under construction for the author, using three skins of cold-moulded silver spruce. The first skin is in place on the plug, glued only along the backbone, while the second skin, glued and temporarily tacked throughout, is progressing from the stern.

The shell has been finished and lifted from the plug, which is having residual glue removed from it for future use in the moulding of another hull.

Laminated frames have been fitted, producing a hull of lightness with strength.

After fitting of bulkheads and the larger units of the internal joinery, serving the double purpose of providing seagoing comfort in addition to further strength for the hull, the deck — two skins of plywood — has been glued and fastened in place.

by the more modern Doug Peterson and Ron Holland designs which
swept the board, she finished in the middle of the fleet, but for seagoing
she was one of the stars, as she had sailed down from Holyhead to take
part, and cheerfully returned in the atrocious weather which persisted
during that September of 1974. For both of these long passages she was
skippered by Dick's son Willie, who being nineteen was still considered a
junior member of Holyhead Sailing Club, and officially speaking under
the rules of the club he should not really have skippered the yacht
beyond the end of the breakwater! In 1975 the boat was up in Norway,
and so in her first three seasons afloat, although an offshore racer in
concept, she had cruised in comfort over a much longer distance than
many similarly-sized pure cruisers could manage in twice the time.
Throughout it all her extremely light hull, with shell thickness of only
three-eighths of an inch, showed no signs of strain.

While the aesthetic attractions of multi-skin timber construction are
undeniable for general use there are several definite drawbacks. The
most immediately apparent of these is the problem of repair in the event
of the hull being holed: straight away, you can double or even treble the
number of planks damaged by comparison with the situation in a single-
skin craft of orthodox construction. With multi-skin, the layers have to
be cut back, not only to find undamaged timber, but also to expose a
large enough area to give proper support to the new layers being
inserted – not surprisingly, owners of holed multi-skin craft have been
known to call upon the possibilities of GRP when making their repair.

In addition to the extra repair problems posed by multi-skin, the
owners of such craft have all the maintenance involved in orthodox
wooden craft, of which it has been rightly observed that if you look for
trouble, you can generally find it. There is, for instance, that
preoccupation of whether one's keel is going to stay on at all.
Admittedly with some of today's racier GRP designs, the keel is just a fin
relying totally on the keel bolts for its continued presence, but in many
cruiser designs in GRP the keel is an integral part of the total hull
moulding: ballast is poured in and glassed into place, for structural
strength and peace of mind, the best solution.

Even with stainless steel keel bolts there is a constant worry, for
though stainless steel may not corrode, it has elements of fatigue which
are still not completely known, and thus many owners of wooden craft
or yachts with externally hung keels prefer to have mild steel keel bolts,
for though they may rust, at least you know where you are with them,
while corrosion resistant metals such as stainless steel and bronze may
hide a rotten heart under their shiny exteriors.

But enough of the gloom; there are many wooden yachts afloat which
give their owners every satisfaction and have years of use ahead of them,
while others are still being built. No one would deny that they cost a little

more to maintain than yachts in GRP, or steel or ferro-cement, but with marina charges and sail costs and engine maintenance and insurance and whatnot common to all types of yacht, the extra expenditure on a wooden boat can be very little when seen as a percentage of total cost.

A sailing cruiser in steel

The Dutch have a deserved reputation as the world's leading builders of steel yachts, a reputation which has if anything been enhanced in recent years with a proliferation of large steel clipper-bowed ketches, of which the best known type is the Trewes range designed by S. M. van der Meer.

The advantages of steel for the construction of larger yachts are many; with skilful welders and finishers, a surface can be obtained in the topsides as good as with timber or GRP; as we will see with the ketch *Verna*, it enables greater flexibility in design; its elasticity and tensile strength is a positive advantage in today's crowded and hectic harbours; and it can offer remarkably good value for money.

Against this steel is heavy, which precludes its use in most sailing yachts under 35 ft, unless they are of a very heavy displacement type; and there is the problem of corrosion – rust, electrolysis, whatever – such that anyone coming to it for the first time is bound to share to some extent Eric Hiscock's feelings on acquiring the steel 49-ft ketch *Wanderer IV* after more than three decades of ownership of wooden yachts, waking up at 03.00, worried that someone might accidentally have left a snippet of copper wire in the bilge.

Be that as it may, steel yachts make up a significant proportion of the many handsome larger cruising yachts which have appeared throughout the world during the past twenty years, and perhaps the story of one of them will go a long way to explain the popularity of this method of construction. The ketch *Verna* was launched in April 1973, and during her first year she cruised from her builders, Jongert of Medemblik, round much of the British Isles and then south via Spain to her winter base at Palma, Majorca. In 1974, she headed out into the Atlantic once more, and bound north, crossed the Bay of Biscay in heavy weather with no bother; after cruising the Hebrides she took part in the Royal Northern Yacht Club's 150th anniversary celebrations in the Clyde, and then headed south once more, eventually returning to her home port in the Balearics after a summer cruise of more than 4,000 miles. By this time her owner and his crew had fallen into the way of using the yacht during leave periods in the winter, and in the summer of 1975 they stayed in the south, visiting a number of Mediterranean islands.

Throughout all this the handsome big ketch has given complete satisfaction in every way, and yet Peter Odlum, her owner, is someone who prior to building *Verna* had been an enthusiast for wooden yachts, notably elegant craft from the board of James McGruer, one of which,

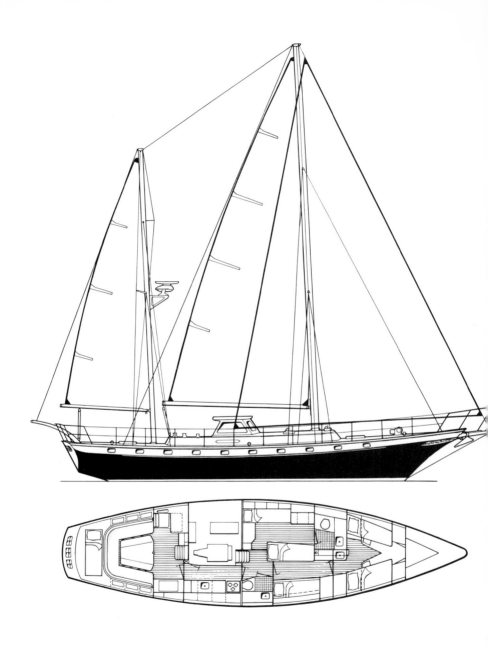

Verna. *An excellent example of the steel building techniques of the Dutch yacht-building industry, the ketch* Verna *has given good service in a wide variety of cruising.*
LOA 59 ft 6 in, LWL 41 ft, beam 14 ft 9 in, draft 6 ft 6 in, sail area 1,699 sq. ft.

the 8 Metre Cruiser/racer *Inismara*, was the holder of the Lloyd's Trophy for her superlative construction when she was launched from the designer's own yard on the Gareloch in 1963.

The conversion to steel came about through a realistic assessment of cruising requirements; with a subsequent yacht, the beautiful 48-ft yawl *Rinamara* also from McGruer, his cruising grounds, formerly just Scottish and Irish waters, were expanded, first to Norway and then to north-west Spain. Inevitably the Mediterranean followed, and in its heat *Rinamara*'s woodwork suffered. There could have been a partial compromise, for instance her dark green hull could have been painted white, but there were other factors; her layout, designed in the light of experience off the coasts of north-west Europe, was not entirely suited to constant hot weather, while her auxiliary engine was inadequate for the long periods of motoring into a lumpy sea which is inevitable in the calms of the Mediterranean.

Though wood now seemed to be out, personal preference was against anything plastic; in any case, having decided to change to a larger yacht of a distinctly different type, the requirements of so many special features were beginning to emerge that even a basic GRP hull seemed too limiting, and the flexibility of dimensions in a steel hull, plus the fact that it seemed to provide a great deal of boat for the money, made it seem the inevitable choice, a feeling which was confirmed by a convivial evening aboard the Trewes ketch *Wolfhound* in a small Mediterranean harbour in September 1971.

So *Rinamara* returned to Scotland and was sold the following year, and Peter Odlum started to bring his talents as a very successful businessman to bear on the problems of getting a much larger yacht built in a new material in a foreign country by people he had never met. Such things are part of the everyday experience of high-powered businessmen, for the rest of us they seem formidable tasks, and the way he went about it is a model of its kind for anyone having a boat built, of whatever size.

Fairly quickly he decided that a Trewes it would be, and then he started dealing with S. M. van der Meer direct; a number of meetings took place in Holland in order to establish that personal contact which is so vital to ensure that everyone is thinking on the same wavelength, and trials were arranged aboard the Trewes 56 *Lazy Stroller*, as she seemed most nearly to correspond to requirements.

It was felt that a slightly longer than standard craft would provide the good looks which the former McGruer yacht owner found indispensable. So preliminary drawings were prepared for a yacht of 59 ft 5 in. From the building point of view this would add proportionately little to the cost, as all the larger Trewes ketches have the same midship section and draft, and the builders were highly experienced in coping with extensions from this standard shape.

In fact, most of the extra length was above the waterline, and produced a clipper bow and stern of so much more elegance than the usual slightly dumpy look of the breed that everyone involved was delighted to make her the prototype of the Trewes 60. By this time, the renowned yard of Jongert at Medemblik had been appointed builders, a yard so busy that building space had to be reserved in March 1972 although the actual work was not scheduled to begin for some months.

Meanwhile the owner now had from the designer the basic plans of the yacht with the three watertight bulkheads – fore and aft of the engine, and at the mainmast – marked in, and working in conjunction with the designer he filled in the accommodation in line with his requirements. As a split-up sail-plan which could be handled by one man was envisaged, there was no need for crowding. The yacht is big enough for a proper great cabin aft, and this is the main feature of the layout; access to the rest of the accommodation is via the galley passage along the starboard side of the engine room – well ventilated with its own hatch above the cooker opening into the cockpit – and as the cockpit is half covered by the substantial shelter over is forward end, the direct companionway to the aft cabin is usable in practically all weather.

The great cabin is a gracious place, pleasantly laid out and yet, in the best yacht design manner, incorporating in its elegant furniture many things vital to the running of the ship; for instance, the emergency steering arrangement connects directly to the rudder head just under the athwartships seat, the extension if need be emerging on deck through the hatch above; the substantial saloon table, too, apart from including the support pillar for the mizzen mast, also includes a special locker for the spare parts for the generator, as *Verna* became an all electric yacht, and while the 12 kw G & M generator has yet to give trouble, easy access to it and immediate availability of spare parts is felt to be of prime importance. The engine-room really is a room, containing a 150 h.p. Mercedes OM 360 diesel, which would make the yacht a motor-sailer if she did not sail so well; as it is, the engine-room is fire-proofed and heavily insulated against noise and vibration.

Returning to the saloon, the berth athwartships in the stern is for the watch on deck; with her effective auto-pilot, *Verna* can be sailed by one man, but the bunk in the saloon is provided for a second hand on call; he can be on deck in seconds, but in the meantime that aft bunk is a delightful place for a snooze, and it is very heaven to lie there watching through the transom windows as the dawn comes up and the wake stretches towards the horizon.

The chart-table is conveniently located beside the companionway; to starboard, the large refrigerator, which has a deep freeze section, is top-loading, undoubtedly the best arrangement for seagoing use; with the emphasis on electric power, a large fridge makes sense, but the interesting thing about *Verna*'s is that it is specially built to fit in with the shape of the yacht at that point; accustomed as we are to buying standard fridges for domestic use, it is interesting to find that a tailor-made refrigerator is relatively inexpensive.

In a yacht of this size, it might be just possible to have a corridor running through the accommodation, but in reality such a feature would be something of a vanity, unnecessarily using up space. Thus the corridor to the great cabin aft also incorporates the galley, and equally the corridor to the fo'c'sle is also the guest cabin; this is not such a loss of privacy as might at first appear, as the fo'c'sle can also be reached through its own hatch to the deck, and the extra space which is available all round makes this compromise arrangement the best.

As for the fo'c'sle, four berths were fitted into it; it is rarely that all four berths are used, but cruise planning is greatly eased by knowing that if need be *Verna* can sleep nine without anyone having to use the settees in the aft cabin.

While there is also some sail stowage in the fo'c'sle, much of it is made available through one of the best design features in the yacht. The deck plan indicates what looks like a long coachroof, and yet all the accommodation is below deck level – that long coachroof is made up entirely of lockers, and one of the most attractive features of a yacht of this size is that deck gear really can be stowed like this on deck, instead of cluttering up the accommodation in often inaccessible lockers.

When building started, it was an impressive operation; Mr. Jongert's training is as an engineer rather than a boatbuilder, and his engineering training has resulted in a refreshing capacity to see the real possibilities of steel construction, provided you have the operatives to carry it out in the best possible way. Very quickly the backbone was assembled, the frames – 'S' frames of steel bar, section $2\frac{1}{2}$ in $\times \frac{5}{16}$ in – went into place, and then plating started using $\frac{5}{32}$ in sheet steel. The shape of a yacht appeared rapidly, but this was only the beginning of a remarkable co-ordinated process, as pressure on the building space and the economics of it all meant that everything had to come together at the right time, with standards being maintained in every department. Experience of building previous yachts showed through, as specialized work such as the electrics was sub-contracted, and indeed the whole operation was based on a price agreed at the finished plan stage.

Interestingly enough, for a man who had won the Lloyd's Trophy for a wooden yacht, Peter Odlum was happy to accept the supervision of Bureau Veritas, as Dutch yacht builders feel that Lloyd's scantling requirements for steel craft are excessively heavy; as it is, the resulting hull, having been shot-blasted and treated, and coated with an insulation which included fire-proofing was guaranteed for 30 years.

While steel was the basis for all the construction, including the deckhouse, extensive use was made of superbly worked teak to provide a pleasant finish both below and on deck, a teak-laid deck on top of the steel completing the effect.

Exhaustive trials were held as the hull poses problems for compasses and electrics. *Verna*'s main compass is in fact attached to the forward side of the mizzen mast, and is a Neco with repeaters strategically placed for both helmsman and navigator. RDF bearings with a steel ship are sometimes difficult, and so the Sailor VHF and RDF works through the closed loops on top of the mizzen mast. The Decca 101 Radar, whose scanner is located on the mizzen mast, has proved increasingly useful with experience, the point being made that such experience is best acquired in clear weather when screen observations can be checked visually.

The rig is a classic modern ketch with a cutter configuration in the foretriangle. With a steel built ship, a deck stepped mast can be fitted with confidence, and both *Verna*'s sticks are set up in this way. Being an out-and-out cruiser, there has been no compunction about using extra-heavy sections for the aluminium spars, and on the mainmast this has meant that a permanent shroud led slightly aft from the hounds is sufficient to withstand the strains of the inner forestay, thus obviating the nuisance of runners. A large genoa is available, and is frequently used as the ample deck space makes its handling an easy job, but when the cutter rig is used there is no boom on the staysail as it is felt its inconvenience outweighs its slight advantages. No spinnaker is carried, but poles which stow against the foreside of the mainmast can be used to boom out the headsails off the wind.

The mizzen is particularly well stayed, as the provision of permanent aft davits for the fast inflatable also provides support for a permanent backstay. A triatic stay is shown from the top of the mizzen mast to the mainmast; purists might think this an undesirable feature, as the loss of the mainmast would inevitably bring down the mizzen, but it could be done away with by a slight shortening of the mainboom, and locating the mizzen middle shrouds a little further forward.

When *Verna* finally sailed away from Medemblik across the North Sea, it was felt that she was as good as builder and designer could make her, and subsequent experience has shown the quality of their work.

On slipping her eighteen months later, the only work involved apart from re-antifouling was the replacement of the anodes, an easy job which in fact the owner feels if need be could be done with the boat afloat, using an aqualung. Otherwise with just the usual regular maintenance and cleaning she shows little sign of the many miles covered in all sorts of seas and weather in being continually afloat in more than four years since launching.

Ferro-cement

Ferro-cement construction somehow seems the most peculiar of boatbuilding methods, perhaps because a stone boat is even more at variance with popular notions of buoyancy than one in steel, but despite its air of novelty it has been around for much more than a century. In France there were ferro-cement boats in existence in the middle of the 19th century – one is reputedly still afloat. Early in this century the great yacht designer Charles E. Nicholson brought his formidable intellect to bear on the possibilities of the material and supervised the building of small ships in it. Some of these barges of this period are still around, making handy breakwaters for small boat yards and docks; they are remarkably well preserved, and a fine advertisement for the building method. I know of one that is being converted into a floating home which will in time, so it is planned, actually sail with the use of leeboards.

During the 1940s ferro-cement was developed in Italy and by the end of that decade a cruising ketch built this way was sailing the seas. However, as the boats thus constructed are built from a basic structure of truss frame and chickenwire plastered with sand and cement, standard housebuilding materials in other words, it is in some of the more pioneer-minded parts of the world that the method has really caught on, with New Zealand leading the way, Western Canada being another development area. The ultimate qualification of ferro-cement as an accepted boatbuilding material probably came about with the voyages of Dr. Bob Griffiths' 53-ft cutter *Awanhee* which sailed round the world during the 1960s, a voyage which included an east–west rounding in winter of Cape Horn, and another winter voyage from Japan to the Aleutian Islands, Alaska and Vancouver.

For the home builder, ferro-cement undoubtedly is one of the

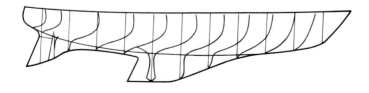

Helsal. *Lines of the mighty* Helsal, *an outstanding large cutter built in ferro-cement which, despite being fitted with every cruising comfort, won line honours in a Sydney–Hobart race.*
LOA 72 ft, LWL 62 ft, beam 19 ft 1½ in, draft 10 ft, displacement 91,000 lb, sail area 2,921 sq. ft.

cheapest methods to produce a hull, but as ever be warned that the bare hull is only a first step towards a completed seagoing yacht. The details of the methods of construction are well covered by the manuals produced by the leading ferro-cement specialists, and all that is needed is the usual giant helpings of will power.

Until recently, it had been generally accepted that only hulls of at least moderately heavy displacement lent themselves to ferro-cement construction, but this notion was challenged at the beginning of 1975 when the mighty *Helsal*, a 72-ft cutter, was first to finish in the Sydney–Hobart race. *Helsal* – nicknamed 'The Flying Footpath' in the best Australian manner – had been built with a new twist to the ferro-cement method; her basic structure was made up from light tubes held together with $\frac{1}{4}$ in high tensile rods and the usual chicken mesh. Each tube contained a steel cable, and after plastering the cables were hydraulically loaded to about 40,000 lb. It was calculated that this method of producing a post-stressed hull in permanent compression led to much greater strength, this being a property of ferro-cement, and so less material could be used in the building in the first place, such that in places *Helsal*'s skin was $\frac{1}{2}$ in thick and weighed less than 9 lb per square foot, a thin skin in almost any material for a 72-ft yacht.

Obviously at this stage of development, such a method is rather specialized for application to general use; not everyone would like to rely on such seemingly small margins of safety, for all the scientific evidence to the contrary, and so the basic method of strength through weight is still the most generally used by ferro-cement boatbuilders.

Increasing knowledge of the material has enabled Lloyd's Certification since 1965. With commercial involvement the rather crude methods have been refined to produce hulls which can stand comparison in their finish with any other material, and in recent years the 'Seacrete' process developed by Windboats of Wroxham in England has been gaining popularity, with more than 500 hulls completed.

Appropriately, the yachts built by Windboats are called the Endurance range, and the hulls are either sold to individual owners for their own completion, or are finished by Windboats associate company, Culfor Marine in North Wales. Designed by the Paris-based naval architect Peter Ibold, the Endurance range are hefty yachts featuring clipper bows and robust sawn-off counter sterns; often they have exotic sail arrangements such as brigantine rig, even down to as small as 45 ft, but generally they are powered by a straightforward ketch configuration.

The range is from 30 ft up to 55 ft, with larger craft in the offing, and one of the most attractive is the Endurance 35, which is just large enough to allow the flush deck arrangement favoured by the designer, and yet small enough to be a handy family cruiser. Already a number have

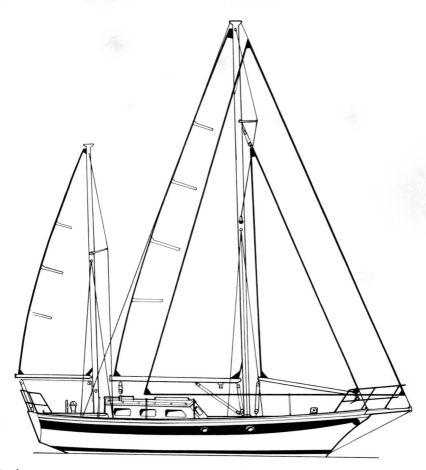

Endurance 35. *One of the most successful ferro-cement designs, the Endurance 35 designed by Peter Ibold is remarkably roomy for her size. With a snug cutter rig available on the mainmast, she avoids the nuisance of runners with a jackstay at the head of the inner forestay.*
LOA 35 ft 4 in, LWL 26 ft 8 in, beam 11 ft, draft 5 ft 3 in, displacement 20,000 lb, sail area 780 sq. ft.

completed long ocean voyages, but their usefulness for cruising shorter distances and in coastal waters has often been demonstrated, a notable example of this being Bill Bartlam's *Aiva II*, which was completed by Jones Buckie Shipyard Ltd at Lossiemouth on Scotland's east coast from a Windboats hull, and has since cruised extensively in northern waters, particularly to lesser known spots and winning her crew cruising club awards for pilotage notes.

In her first year she went to Norway with the Clyde Cruising Club's

Who'd think she was ferro-cement? — a traditional teak laid deck on an Endurance 35 belies her relatively unusual basic construction material.

race for the Bergen Yacht Club's Centenary; the fleet weathered a severe gale on the way, and aboard *Aiva II* they were pleasantly surprised by the quietness down below at the height of the heavy weather, as well as the confident way in which she coped with the conditions. As a result of this crash course in seagoing, they made some minor modifications to the accommodation the following winter, turning her into a 'go anywhere' boat, and have since comfortably cruised from their home port of Findhorn on the Moray Firth to places like St. Kilda, Loch Roag, the Faeroes, and Orkney and Shetland. At Kirkwall in the Orkneys they were bumped into by an old landing craft; *Aviva* suffered only a small chip out of the gunwale which was easily repaired, the landing craft was more than somewhat battered, all of which supports ferro-cement fans' enthusiasm for their product.

In a race to Norway in her first year afloat, she had revelled in the heavy going so much that she was placed second in her class in the cruiser division.

A number of design variations are available with the Endurance 35's accommodation, all based on the concept of the saloon, galley and navigation space being in the raised deckhouse, with the engine underneath, while the heads and sleeping cabins are at a lower level forward under the flush deck. The deckhouse is a particularly robust affair, as it should be in view of the yacht's heavy displacement. The compartmentation of the cabins forward may not be to everyone's taste, but against that one can easily overdo the open-plan notion, and the separate cabins give an attractive big-ship atmosphere in keeping with her character.

The cockpit is deliberately kept small and well aft, and on deck the effect is of a much larger craft. The mizzen is independently stayed, while the mainmast carries a masthead genoa, though it can also carry a double-head rig with the inner forestay supported by a fixed intermediate shroud. This avoids the nuisance of runners.

The success of the Endurance range has done a great deal to make ferro-cement 'respectable', for even the very best new method of building yachts inevitably attracts a somewhat idiosyncratic adherent during its early years. In time the new methods, where sound, become adopted by the cruising community at large.

Sailing in light airs, the Endurance 35 Susie G *demonstrates the heavy displacement yacht's almost uncanny ability to keep moving in such conditions once way has been built up.*

5 Accommodations

The cabin layout is the part of a design which a cruising man can most easily plan for himself, but even starting from scratch the most experienced person can make omissions. The great Carleton Mitchell, for instance, when building his dream ship *Finisterre*, made an adjustable mock-up for the interior before any joinery was fitted; the mock-up was moved around and altered until it was thought that everything was right for seafaring, and the yacht's subsequent career – successful offshore racing, delightfully varied cruising – seemed to indicate the rightness of her layout. But going aboard an exact sistership, I was surprised to note the lack of a worth while oilskin locker, and to find a chart-table which in use seemed acutely uncomfortable.

In most yachts, the eventual layout below is dictated to a certain extent by the deck layout, particularly the coachroof and cockpit arrangement, and one of the most welcome developments in standard cruiser design has been the general acceptance of the need for a self-draining cockpit. Partially this has been because, with GRP moulding, it is more convenient to produce such a configuration, but it is a welcome development just the same. What has been less welcome is the occasional elimination of the bridge-deck from this layout; in times past, a really solid bridge-deck amidships was the hallmark of the proper cruising yacht – it was an inevitable concomitant of the self-draining cockpit, it provided much needed strength athwartships in a potentially weak part of the yacht, and it guaranteed dryness below with a ideal place for lockers handy to the companionway. You do not have to go to the lengths of designs such as the Swan 44, where the bridge-deck has been emphasized to such an extent that the main companionway has been pushed forward to become a hole in the deck amidships. It is bad policy continually to enlarge the companionway, lowering its step such that even a bucket or two of water in the cockpit will find its way below. For thoroughgoing seafaring the cockpit should be able to fill completely without the water level reaching the companionway step.

Such theorizing may be of little enough interest to someone with a standard cruiser, but even with such a craft some modifications are possible, both to personalize her a little more, and make her more seaworthy above and below. No standard yacht is perfect, and more than a few – including some reckoned the very best – could benefit from alterations.

Priorities

The priorities for accommodation are as follows:

1. Shelter for the crew.
2. Means of storing and preparing food.
3. Room to sleep.
4. Facilities for keeping stores and clothing dry.
5. Space for navigation.
6. An oilskin (foul weather clothing) locker.

The galley

Inevitably, then, much of the accommodation revolves round the galley, and this is as it should be. In the midst of admiring galleys at a boat show or in the comfort of a marina, if often takes a real effort of imagination to visualize the tasteful arrangements of warm teak veneer, shining plastic surfaces and gleaming chrome being thrown about in a seaway. Some of the set-ups which look so neat in the horizontal, quite palpably just will not do at an angle of even as little as twenty degrees.

Many galleys fortunately *can* function fairly well under such circumstances, but there are very few which are successful throughout the entire spectrum of conditions. It must be remembered that not only does the angle of heel vary continually, but the cook has to cope with pitching as well; when sheets are eased and the boat starts to roll downwind, then come the conditions which sort out the seamanlike galleys from the 'tasteful arrangements'.

Minimal motion and good ventilation are important requirements in galley location, so inevitably it should be near the main companionway: indeed the traditional place, on your port hand at the bottom of the companionway ladder, still has much to recommend it. The port side is traditional because it was thought that in a gale, you could heave-to on the starboard tack, so that in theory you had right of way over everything

Although standard production yachts are generally sold in an almost totally finished condition, an enthusiastic owner can often find minor improvements which he can make. For instance, in most galleys the cups are housed one on top of another in a single stowage box. Far more useful is stowage like this, where mugs of worthwhile size can be filled before removal from the holder.

afloat except lightships: with the yacht heeling to port it was considered easier and safer to have the galley on the lower side.

For all its limited use in today's crowded seas, it is a charming notion, so we will have our theoretical galley on the port side beside the companionway, though provision will be made for shelter from solid water, should it ever find its way down the hatch. There will be alternative ventilation, including an extractor fan if we have a yacht with elaborate electrical equipment.

More than in any other part of the ship, the golden rule for the galley is a place for everything, and everything in its place, but it must be remembered that the place should not be hung on a hook. Sometimes, in standard galleys the spark of owners' individuality consists only in filling the deck-head in the galley with cuphooks, and the minute the boat puts to sea anything hung on the hooks begins bashing around, wearing holes in that lovely warm teak veneer, with that charming row of colourful mugs in bright array weaving in vague unison like a line of drunken guardsmen, a sight guaranteed to induce seasickness.

By all means have your favourite cooking knick-knacks aboard, but be sure that the handy place you keep them convenient to the cooker is

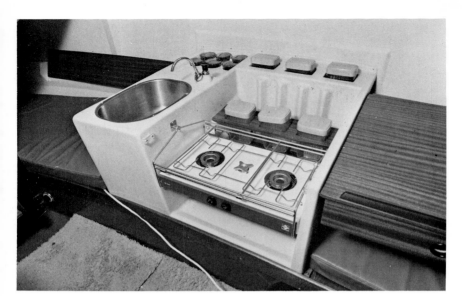

The Ecume de Mer's galley is located in a single GRP module integrated into the yacht's construction on the port side in the roomiest part of this small cruiser's saloon.

also a place where they will neither rattle nor roll, and indeed the entire stowage arrangement of any galley should be based on this. Until you have experienced a long run, with the pride-and-joy rolling her way elegantly across the sea, it is difficult to imagine the sheer hell of a rattling galley. After the transatlantic passage of the minute *Sopranino*, Colin Mudie who was one of her crew remarked that he was able to tell the difference between the clink of a jar of Bovril and the clink of a jar of Marmite, while those of us who have made the more modest passage south to the Mediterranean remember the glorious swoop down the Portuguese trades, with the lasting memory of each watch coming below and spending half an hour in the galley stuffing little bits of kitchen roll into each and every clunk and rattle until there was enough peace for some sleep – but only until someone makes a cup of coffee!

So during the winter, when you bewail the fact that GRP boats leave no room for good old-fashioned fitting-out, remember those irritating rattles and at least line the lockers with felt or synthetic foam, and make up individual holders for all those noisy little jars which are in constant use. One particularly useful item in this line which is a favourite of mine is a mug holder of the type shown in the sketch. There is nothing more

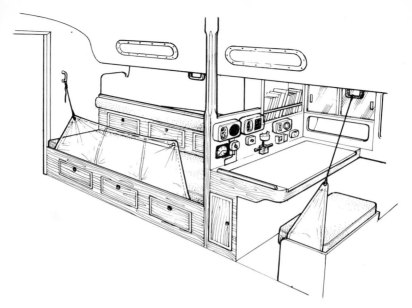

Starboard side arrangement of an average cruiser in the 28 to 40 ft size range. Although the development of this layout owes much to the evolution of offshore racing accommodation, for serious seagoing in any cruising yacht this arrangement has much to offer as it provides comfortable off-watch berths with first-class navigation facilities.

annoying than the miserable little cups which are often provided with standard sailing cruisers. They are often stowed one on top of another in inaccessible holders. With the holder shown, I use mugs of at least half a pint capacity, preferably a pint. The mugs can be filled without removing them from the holder and in heavy weather a useful diet of instant soup or other hot drinks can be kept going with minimal effort.

It may seem a little extreme to have individual stowage for virtually every item in the galley, but at sea such a system is wholly worth while. Going on to more general requirements, useful work surfaces around the cooker are essential, but many standard boats have inadequate fiddles; my own preference is for all fiddles to be a minimum of $1\frac{1}{2}$ in deep with at least one work surface surrounded by 3-in fiddles, the best place for this extra height being between the galley and the saloon, a sort of seagoing sideboard. It is all part of the policy of keeping things in their proper place, and in line with this a draining board with the sink is of limited benefit – much better to have double sinks, which will stop dishes and so forth falling around.

Inevitably there will be compromises; often the only way to fill the space behind the cooker is with lockers of some sort, but their usefulness will be limited by your ability or otherwise to get at them when cooking is under way. In theory, locker doors opening athwartships should be avoided, in practice this is impossible, but such lockers should have high fiddles – preferably in clear plastic – along the front of each shelf. And with lockers, drawers and anything else that opens, do check that it will stay shut in all conditions. The growth of the marine industry has led to vast improvements in cookers, iceboxes, deep freezers and so forth for boats. Most of us now accept gas (propane or butane) as the most useful cooking fuel, though in larger yachts electricity is being seen more frequently. Gas may be potentially dangerous, but its danger is limited if everyone aboard is aware of it, and its convenience is undeniable. Many yachts have an on-deck installation for the cylinders as standard, but a growing body of opinion reckons that a locker convenient to the cook is best, with that most important personage being wholly responsible for the galley and all its safety requirements. A small cylinder swinging with

Seagoing galley in the 'orthodox' port side aft position, in this case on a Nicholson 31. Note sound design features such as the high fiddles and the rounded corners, as well as the laminated shield to protect the occupant of the pilot berth and the double sink arrangement which proves invaluable at all times, especially in a seaway. One possible useful addition would be a pillar/handhold from the forward inboard corner of the sink worksurface to the deckhead.

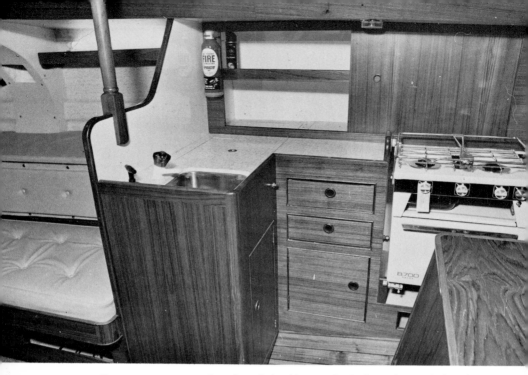

Galley on a more race-oriented craft, in this case the Holman & Pye designed UFO 34 Three Quarter Tonner. With the need for a performance yacht to have all interior weight as far as possible amidships, the galley space has to be shared to a certain extent with the engine box in the foreground, and foot-room is restricted by the curve of the yacht's hull.

the stove itself – Camping Gaz for instance – is increasingly popular.

Even in some very small cruising yachts, a cooker complete with oven is often standard. The necessary gimballing of such an arrangement is very space consuming, and ingenious alternatives are available, including having a fixed oven with just the burner-grill section gimballing. But even where the yacht is large enough to enable the whole unit to be gimballed, provision must be made for easy position-locking of the cooker, as opening the oven door unbalances the gimballing. From the safety point of view, a 'crash bar' across the front of the cooker, firmly attached to the furniture on either side, seems a sensible notion, but be sure that it provides sufficient clearance to allow use of the cooker when heeled.

With larger yachts where space permits, a gimballed surface can also be useful, in fact I have seen at least one boat where the entire galley was on gimbals, and she was big enough to make it a realistic proposition. In smaller craft, a chopping board with asbestos on the underside made to fit into the top of the cooker provides a handy gimballed surface when the going is really rough.

Being a simple soul, I find that an icebox is quite enough to be going on with in the food preservation department, indeed for long enough we cruised without even this, relying on such things as a side of bacon hanging in the fo'c'sle to provide what we needed in the way of fresh meat. The theory was that the bacon was sliced off the entire exterior surface just a little quicker than it went bad.

But nowadays I will concede that iceboxes have proved their worth in every way, and the developing market has meant that seagoing fridges and deep freezes are now realistic propositions.

It is surprising how many boats go afloat without adequate provision for convenient stowage of a gash bucket. The best arrangement is one where the bin, bucket or whatever slips handily out of sight when not in use, and the usual system is through having it attached to the inside of a lower locker door.

Handholds
In the rest of the accommodation, strategically-placed handholds continue to be a first requirement; a number of different types are available – handgrips can be easily located anywhere, but when the going is rough the fact that they are just in one single place limits their usefulness – a solid 'drip-catcher' running along the side of the coachroof provides a sort of universal handhold, without having to search for it. It also catches condensation. Perhaps best of all is one or two, or more, vertical pillars; these seem to be the most 'grabbable', and have the advantage as well that you can hold yourself with the pillar in the crook of your arm, thus leaving both hands free. The most useful place for such pillars is between the navigation/galley area and the saloon, where they can provide structural support.

The saloon
Moving into the saloon itself, many of its requirements have been discussed in the chapters on designs of standard yachts, and its best layout depends largely on your use of the yacht. A dinette, for instance, is an excellent feature if you anticipate spending a lot of time in port, as it allows convenient access up and down the boat even when people are at table; let us be honest about it, most of us spend the most of our cruising time comfortably upright in port, but nevertheless if we at least aspire to spend as much time as possible at sea we should favour the more traditional layout of settee berths fore and aft with a table in the middle, also fore and aft.

Perhaps the best compromise is an L-shaped settee on one side with a settee berth and pilot berth on the other; I have already stated my personal preference that the 'thwartships arm of the L-shaped settee should be at the for'ard bulkhead. The disadvantage of this arrangement is that it uses up important space along that forward bulkhead; often this is already limited by the presence of the mast. The area can be used for location of a cabin heater if you do not have a warm air system such as the Webasto, which works through ducts, such as under the bunks. The space available on the for'ard bulkhead provides useful stowage for a folding table.

Looking aft in the saloon of the Mirage 37. The skilfully incorporated corridor under the starboard side of the cockpit obviates the need for the usually inevitable forward facing hatch in the aft cabin.

Bunks

Bunks should fit people and not vice versa as is so often the case, but even with bunks requiring some element of standardization certain basic rules of seagoing requirement are ignored. If at all possible, for instance, bunks should run fore and aft. Making them follow the waterlines of the ship may seem to provide more room down below, but alters head against foot level when heeled.

Most bunks are far too wide for seagoing; I have heard it argued that twenty-one inches is quite enough in width, and certainly the pilot berths on an Arpege, which we mentioned earlier, are no more than this at their widest point, and yet the pilot berths of an Arpege are really comfortable at sea. Perhaps an inch more is permissible, but no more. If a bunk can be made 6 ft 6 in length, it is most comfortable.

Settee berths should be no more than 22 in wide, and the canvas leeboards can be used, even in port. If you insist on having wider settee berths, then for seagoing the best solution is to have the bunk cushion in two parts, with a fore and aft divide through which the leeboard emerges. Leeboards on standard boats are also often flimsy affairs which would inspire no confidence in anyone trying to sleep in rough conditions – they should be to sailmaker's standards, and should be at least two feet deep, preferably three, with their attachment points located to have the leeboard coming in over the sleeper. This may seem claustrophobic, but there is nothing worse than feeling the next good lurch of the yacht is going to pitch you out on the floor. As for it delaying your rapid exit to the deck in case of emergency, it is most doubtful – I remember once sailing on a very nice sloop in which the owner had insisted on enlarging the chart-table to such an extent that the quarter berth was almost inaccessible, and during a cruise the man in the quarter berth used to complain that it took him at least five minutes to get in or out of it. Very early one gentle morning we were sailing close inshore to avoid a foul tide and – despite the facilities provided by the new chart-table – we biffed a rock; man in the quarter berth was on deck in three seconds!

Pilot berths are a complete study in themselves; back in the old days aboard your actual pilot cutters, each pilot's berth was his little cabin, and personally I am inclined to think there is still a lot in favour of this, indeed a harmonious cruising yacht is often one where each crew member has his own permanent berth used by no one else. In the otherwise rather crazy design of the accommodation of my little half tonner (I did the layout myself) I made a point of having the pilot berths deep enough that whoever was in them could sit up without bashing their heads on the deckhead. Thus of a morning they could get dressed without having to get out of the bunk, which made the boat seem twice as roomy in those vital first moments of the day, and indeed so much room was given over to those two pilot berths that in effect they did serve as little separate cabins. To do this, however, 3 ft 3 in of headroom had to be provided over and above the mattresses, and this consumed a lot of space which might otherwise have been used for lockers along the back of the settee berths.

Gimballed bunks are sometimes found in large offshore racers. As with anything gimballed, inevitably extra space is used up, and so this feature can scarcely be applied in smaller craft, but if you insist on sleeping on a level surface another solution is adjustable cots on either side; peronally I find that a properly designed and installed leeboard in a bunk of the right width gives all the comfort and security needed, the only other proviso being the ironic one that mattresses must not be too thick, or you will bounce around on them. A two and a half inch thickness of foam rubber is often as much as you will need, even on a wooden surface, when in a seaway, and anything above four inches thick is undoubtedly counter-productive in the sleep department on the rolling ocean.

Lockers

The primary need is that lockers for clothes and other gear should be dry. Often in a production boat they are not, because the water can run along the hull or internal modules from a source a long way away, getting at the lockers from a direction which the builder did not think needed waterproofing. So until you know the lockers really are watertight, assume they are not and have everything that goes into them in watertight plastic bags. The further away from the actual skin of the boat a locker is, the dryer it will generally be, so your stowing plan can be designed accordingly, with non-perishable items stowing against the hull under the settee berths, while things that will suffer from damp get a more protected home.

As to allocation of lockers, every crew-member if possible should have a personal one which is readily accessible, and then extra space for less immediately required gear can be found in lockers elsewhere. A nice variation to this system was once seen aboard the Finnish Swan 43 *Runn* for a transatlantic passage; with a crew of nine, everyone aboard was given a number and this was then put on the lid of each of his personal lockers. All items of clothing had to be numbered as well, and then if some unclaimed clothing was lying about – something which happens on even the best-run ships – all that had to be done was the number was read off, and it was put into the nearest appropriate locker. This may all seem a little complicated for an apparently trivial problem, but in the relatively confined space of a yacht's cabin prior effort towards future harmony pays wondrous dividends, and the *Runn* approach is surely better than that of some other skippers who gradually accumulate piles of unclaimed clothing.

Some lockers close with fancy little catches which frequently seem to involve the near-breaking of one's finger as the catch is on the inside of the locker door and is activated through a hole in it. An alternative – it is seen on a variety of yachts, including ones at the luxury end of the market such as the Frers 39 – is to have the locker held shut with shock cord, attached internally and visible only when the door is open. This has the disadvantage of the door having to be held open when you are getting things in or out, but with some of the more inaccessible locker doors where the catch can be a real hazard the shock cord may be the best solution, and the overall effect is very neat with any locker, especially where the door is upholstered – as along the back of a settee berth – and no handle is needed to open it.

The table

Solid simplicity seems to be the answer for cabin tables, a solidity which can be added to by having at least one end of the table supported by a pillar. In almost every yacht, even the very biggest, the table will need to fold partially away, and a simple central structure with fold-down flaps

Dinette arrangement in the Salar 40.

either side serves very well, though do ensure that the fold-down flaps can be made rattle free when the table is not in use. One extremely sensible notion is to have one of the flaps folding over on top of the table as shown, see page 146, providing a seagoing smaller table with really high fiddles.

There is no doubt that a gimballed table has great attraction – I did much of my early cruising in an old yawl with a huge swinging table which dominated the saloon, and took up lots of room, but we would not have removed it for the world. But it must be remembered that to be effective such a table needs lots of weight, and must be balanced perfectly; perhaps a useful compromise here would be an adjustable table which can be set at different angles with fiddles of a good height round it.

It does not take up as much room or weigh as much either. Whatever your choice, do have a table of some sort – out-and-out racing boats in

A really solid saloon table is the heart of many a cruising yacht. Aboard this Nicholson 31 the table, with robust supports, offers a number of different configurations. In heavy weather at sea, the central portion with its high fiddles would be in use, while the starboard flap shown here in place would be folded away, attached to the table to prevent it banging. In port, the seagoing section folds over to become the portside flap, and a large table is available for use.

which the table has been left out for weight-saving reasons are depressing in the saloon.

Most production cruiser-racer builders have got their finishing down to such a fine art that the interiors of their craft look very complete, and there is no doubt that making modifications can be difficult when coping with double-skin foam-filled decks or head liners that have been fitted by master upholsterers. Nevertheless, there is always some scope for individuality, and one addition which might improve the accommodation is the addition of 'sideboards' at the forward end of the settee berths where the entire length of the berth is open. With a couple of little sideboards you get some handy shelf space and you also have underneath some useful stowage for sleeping bags and pillows (you may not believe in pillows on a cruising boat, but personally I loathe resting my weary head on a couple of damp jerseys). With an upholstered board to fit over this bedding locker, the effect of easily-achieved neatness is most attractive.

One last little point before we leave the saloon, in fact it may be several little points – look around critically and see if there are any sharp corners jutting out. If you have ever had a seaborne rabbit punch to the kidneys from such a corner, there is no need to advise you to round it off.

Heads

As was pointed out in the reviews earlier, ideally the heads and washroom should be located aft, but this is not practicable in smaller craft, where the best location is usually immediately forward of the mast. It is an area of brisk motion with less than complete headroom – sounds horrible, and often it is. Adequate handholds are seldom provided, and while the reality usually is that you shave while seated on the loo, the mirror as often as not cannot even be seen from this throne. Indeed, I have been on yachts with seemingly fancy little washrooms where you cannot see the mirror while thus seated, and yet if you sort of crouch over the ludicrous little washbasin for that vital morning shave the mirror is somewhere under the side-deck and you are still stymied. In other words, there is scarcely a toilet compartment which could not be improved by a thoroughly realistic assessment of its possibilities and limitations.

Stowage in the heads seems to be best provided by a separate little pigeon-hole for each crew-member's washbag, a little complex but worth it. As for fancy equipment, such as pressurized water-systems and showers, by all means have them if 'gadgeteering' is what you enjoy, but one owner I know who had a 42-ft sloop with pressurized hot and cold water, and a shower and all sorts of other goodies, became so fed up with breakdowns that when he moved up in size to a new 47-footer the heads just had the very simplest Lavac vacuum w.c. and a washbasin with one hand-operated cold tap. Anyone who wanted hot water just got a kettle from the galley, and while it sounds somewhat crude when related to the size of the boat, at least everything worked and there was no crawling around the bilges chasing up the electrics.

Fo'c'sle

In most cruising yachts the forecabin leads a double life. At sea it is the fo'c'sle, where sails are dumped direct from the foredeck and all is damp discomfort. Once into port, the sailbags are on deck clustered round the mast and the fo'c'sle is being dried as quickly as possible in order to revert to being the 'separate double cabin' as described in the glossy brochures. Unless conditions are remarkably calm at sea, or you are spending all your time sailing with sheets very free, the motion forward makes the forecabin untenable for all save the strongest stomachs, so its sail bin function offshore seems the best compromise.

Discussing the plans of the Tradewind 33, the logic of having a double berth, if such is required, in the fo'c'sle seemed inescapable – double berths are unusable in a seaway, the forecabin is unusable in a seaway, so have the double berth in the forecabin and make it a honeymoon suite in port. Inevitably the double bunk is often the owner's perk, but if you are interested in serious seafaring be sure that the double mattress is in two parts: then an effective leeboard can be hauled out to make a single berth for offshore work.

Also around the forecabin, or between it and the saloon, there is usually a hanging locker; unless civilization is being abandoned altogether, it is only good manners for every crew-member to have one reasonably presentable set of shoregoing clothes, but in even the best of yacht's wardrobes they should be hung up in special protective bags. Indeed, after a rough passage it has been known for the reefer jacket to emerge from the wardrobe with holes worn in it by the rolling of the ship.

Chart table

Unless you can have a full size chart table with all the navigator's paraphernalia around it in usuable array, then a better solution is to design the 'navigatorium' around the saloon table and work from there. In an out-and-out small racer, you probably would do away with the saloon table rather than do without a workable chart-table, but in a cruising yacht you would not dream of doing without a saloon table and in most boats under about 28 ft LOA this could also serve duty as the chart table. Navigation gear should be installed conveniently to it.

A chart table just ahead of a quarter berth beside the companionway can be wet, but with a sheet of clear perspex or some such plastic fitted between it and the companionway, light gets in and damp is kept out. The navigator here is in close contact with whatever is going on in the cockpit, as well as making it only a short step for him to take a hand bearing or visual check from the hatch.

The large space under the bridge-deck is particularly desirable if one of the more complex radio-telephones is fitted, as these are items which seem to fill up half the boat if they are attached to the semi-bulkheads which usually front a forward facing chart table. In this case an aft-facing chart table can be better, as it gives the navigator peace to get on with his work while at the same time keeping him as much as he wishes in tune with the running of the ship.

Most chart tables nowadays are horizontal, for though a desk-type may have some advantages in theory, at sea it proves to be something of a nuisance. The chart table itself will also include stowage for the charts within it, but all too often as a cruise progresses it is found that this handy stowage space gets cluttered with everything else. If such space is fitted, it should not become the ship's safe. Yachts are notoriously difficult to make thief proof, so the fitting of a safe locker, placed somewhere that only prolonged searching will reveal, is another of the owner's responsibilities.

Companionway

We now seem to have travelled clockwise around the entire accommodation of the average seagoing cruising yacht, and having started on the port side aft with the galley in its traditional location, have arrived at the starboard side aft at the chart-table, shrine of arcane procedures. In between will probably be the engine box, discussed in Chapter 7, and there will also be the companionway. A separate companionway ladder is an attractive feature, indeed in some yachts it has been made a highlight, a masterpiece of the shipwright's art, but in smaller craft such a ladder takes up precious space, and it is perfectly valid to use the engine box and part of the galley work-surface to contribute parts of the companionway ladder, provided adequate handholds are available, the two most important being a couple of handgrips at either side of the hatch itself.

Hopefully, despite all this accumulation of interior joinery-work, space will still be available beside the companionway for provision of an oilskin (foul weather suit) locker; indeed, some old salts would insist that the oilskin locker should be designed first, and the rest of the accommodations fitted afterwards. The locker should provide space for the jackets at least to be hung up, as there is nothing more unpleasant than hauling on a damp oilskin top which seconds before was a wet bundle; the locker itself should be well drained; it should have room for seaboots where they will not be dripped on. A separate locker for seaboots would be better. Further, to prevent damp from oilskins spreading, a grating at the foot of the companionway where people can stand while they are stripping off wet clothing is a real boon.

Ventilation

The importance of good ventilation cannot be overestimated – apart from the usual provision of waterproof ventilators such as the Dorade type in strategic locations, electric extractor fans in the galley and toilet areas can be helpful. An opening skylight above the saloon can also be a boon, and nowadays there are a number on the market which really are watertight when shut.

Decoration

With many yachts nowadays thankfully having low seamanlike coachroofs, or even flush decks, there is a real art in imparting an air of brightness in the accommodations. Too much use of dark woods, while it may lend an atmosphere of opulence in port, can cause gloominess at sea. There are plenty of attractive light coloured wood veneers available, and a bit of good old white paint can work wonders. Fabrics of cheerful colours can help, and one of the benefits in the development of waterproof synthetics is that we no longer have to have nasty shiny material on our bunk cushions for them to resist damp. Something in the line of watertight tweed — such materials do exist — can work wonders.

While the cabin sole may look very dignified if it is beautifully laid in oiled teak, nowadays many cruising men find it more comfortable to have a carpet at least in the saloon part of the yacht. As it will be of synthetic material, if it does happen to get wet it will dry very quickly; certainly by the end of the season it will look a bit the worse for wear, but do not forget that in fact the sole area is very small, so it is only a very small piece of carpet, and it costs relatively little to replace annually.

Water tanks

The overall performance of the yacht can be improved by having the water tanks located well down in the ship, even down in the keel if need be. There are some yachts afloat whose designers, for reasons best known to themselves, have put the water tank in the bows, right in the eyes of the ship where the space admittedly is scarcely otherwise usable, but where a considerable weight of water will be dreadfully detrimental to the yacht's performance. Even the most easy-going cruising man likes to think his yacht is giving of her best when sailing, and performance is often decidedly improved by filled water tanks as low down in the ship as possible. The amount the tanks will hold depends on the general use of the yacht; obviously for ocean cruising you will, in the case of a larger yacht, be thinking in terms of tons of fresh water, but with port-hopping it is often the case that water is used more quickly than on long hops, and so an absolute minimum of ten gallons per person aboard in the main tanks is required, and preferably much more. A couple of portable emergency tanks, stowed somewhere safe to ensure they will not be casually used, are a sensible insurance.

6 Rig, sails and deck gear

Masthead rig

The masthead sloop is the most commonly seen rig and becomes most effective as we move up the size scale.

Hefty cruisers such as the Twister or the Trapper 500 seem to belong under their no-nonsense masthead rig, but the H Boat, of similar length, looks just right with her attractive split level rig. Moving into smaller performance craft such as the Sonata 7, this rig fits in nicely. In these smaller boats no jumpers are fitted, because the support for the forestay comes from swept back main shrouds. For general use this has to be watched, as it can cause chafe both to the mainsail and the mainboom.

Once we get above about 30 ft LOA in all craft, the masthead rig is inevitable for cruising use, and rightly so, for we have a craft large enough to provide the deck room for the sail handling involved in the substantial genoas and spinnakers. Getting beyond 40 ft LOA, new problems arise with the sails becoming so large that a couple of people cannot handle them comfortably. For cruiser-racing purposes, the masthead sloop continues to be a practicable rig until at least 50 ft LOA, but for cruising only with a small crew a real necessity arises for splitting up the rig.

Ketch rig

Nowadays rudders are so far aft that the yawl is a rarity, so a second smaller mast aft usually turns the yacht into a ketch. Somehow or other, the ketch rig symbolizes the spirit of cruising for many people, but despite this it is not perfect. The extra cost involved in fitting that small

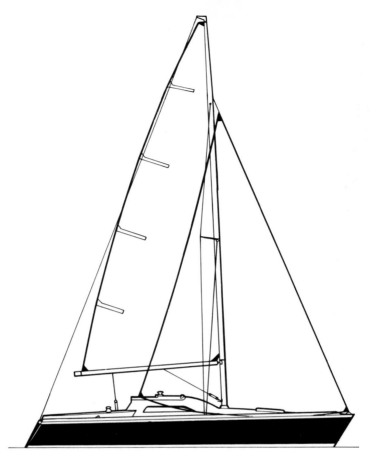

Farr 727. *An interesting recent development has been a distinct swing back to three-quarter rig, particularly among small craft. Such a rig is cheaper to run as the headsails are proportionately smaller and less expensive, and they are the sails which most often need replacement. As well, a skilled helmsman can manage such a yacht with a less able crew than is needed to cope with a large foretriangle.*

mast is usually astonishingly high, almost invariably it clutters up the cockpit, or at least the afterdeck, and the usefulness of the sails set thereon is decidedly limited. Whereas the sails of a sloop work together to drive a yacht along, the sails of a ketch often seem to work against each other, hindering her progress. A ketch going to windward will almost invariably be rigged with mizzen stowed, though when sheets are eased the rig may come into its own. A mizzen staysail can prove a fine driving

The Ericson 36 cruising cutter from California has her mast stepped well aft in order to equalize sail sizes, for ease of handling.

sail, particularly in light airs, nevertheless many ketch owners have a sneaking suspicion that the rig is not worth the trouble and expense involved, at least until you get up to a yacht around 55 ft LOA.

On real advantage of the ketch configuration is that, in the event of a dismasting, provided the two masts are not stayed together, at least one stick should remain standing. For many people such a safety factor alone is sufficient argument in favour of ketch rig, but a number of ketches afloat these days cancel out on this score as the designers of the rig have failed to resist the temptation to have a triatic stay from the head of the mizzen mast to the head of the mainmast. One other argument in favour of ketch rig is that the mizzen provides a handy place to locate the scanner if the yacht has radar, as it provides the height necessary to get above the clutter effect invariably caused by waves. In some cases you get the feeling that the sole *raison d'être* for the mizzen mast is to provide this, which seems a case of misplaced functions and will be further investigated in the section on instrumentation.

Eric Hiscock's rig

During the summer of 1975 I was fortunate enough to meet that remarkable cruising couple Eric and Susan Hiscock on their arrival in England to complete a 46,000-mile seven-year cruise round the world in their 49 ft steel Trewes ketch *Wanderer IV*. It was their third circumnavigation, the two previous ones having been made in their Giles-designed 30-ft sloop *Wanderer III*, and the conversation ranged over many topics. On seagoing rigs, I knew that many years previously, after his first world cruise, he had been in favour of masthead cutter rig, with the mast stepped well aft. At that time he thought that perhaps gaff rig for the main made most sense, and though by '75 he acknowledged that probably a Bermudian main of fairly low aspect ratio was best for the mainsail, after his lengthy experience with *Wanderer IV*'s ketch rig he was more than ever convinced that for yachts of up to at least 50 ft overall length a sensible cutter rig provided the most seaworthy and most economical rig. With such a rig, he reckons that the staysail is allowed to fulfil its proper role as the best driving sail in the ship, an opinion shared by other experienced sailors. We further concurred with the opinions of others in agreeing that such a sail should not be fitted with a boom, which is a nuisance in every way.

There have been cruisers with masts well aft as he advocates. Indeed, the influence of rating rules has been such that most standard sloops nowadays have their masts well aft, and the larger ones such as the Swans generally provide an alternative cutter rig. One less welcome contemporary feature is that with the limits of lightness being explored, often production sloops have to be fitted with runners and an extra inner forestay in order to prevent the mast bucking alarmingly in a lumpy sea. Runners may be all right if you are fully crewed up for racing, but in a cruiser they are a menace.

But in any case, the latest sloop rigs which are common today, even when cutter rigged are of too high an aspect ratio to be the practical seagoing proposition which is advocated by Hiscock and others. The kind of rig he has in mind is more on the lines of the famous cruising yacht *Angantyr*, designed by MacLear and Harris of New York for an experienced owner who clearly knew exactly what he wanted, and who imposed his requirements on every aspect of this unusual design. Her sheer individuality means that *Angantyr* will not appeal to everyone, but there is no doubt that she sports a rugged seagoing rig which gives maximum crew effort.

Admittedly her staysail has a boom, and is not of the semi-genoa type

Angantyr, *a 60-footer designed by MacLear and Harris, is an advanced development of the cutter rig, so much so that she seems to be a 'one masted schooner'.*

which will really haul the yacht along; also her mast if anything is *too* far aft; but nevertheless it all speaks of a refreshingly determined approach to dealing with the problems of having a worth-while cruising rig.

Given a free hand in fitting a cruising rig to a yacht between 40 and 55 ft LOA, I would go for a cutter rig of moderate aspect ratio with the mast fractionally further forward than *Angantyr*'s. Inevitably with such a rig a double spreader arrangement will be necessary, which involves some extra expense, but with a boat of this size and above for cruising the cutter rig is unavoidable unless you do not mind seeing crew-members being lifted off the foredeck by billowing genoas, so the expense will just have to be borne. With *Verna*, for instance, a mast section of sufficient strength has been selected to obviate the need for runners, with further support being given by an aft-led shroud direct from the hounds, by-passing the lower spreaders. This must give a little support, but more direct aid can be given by a jumper stay on the forward side of the mainmast. *Angantyr* is shown with a rather complex arrangement of jumper diamonds, just a single jumper is nearly as effective, and with properly fitted anti-chafe gear it will do very little damage to the leech of the headsail on the topmast forestay.

Going Chinese

While the Bermudian sloop rig and its immediate variants is the standard sailing cruiser rig, there is evidence of a reaction against it, not just because of its almost total universal spread, but because thinking sailors feel that there could well be alternative viable methods of setting sail, and more especially of taking it in. Already we have seen the unusual rig of the Freedom 40 but there is another rig, half as old as time, which has become increasingly popular in recent years. This is the Chinese junk rig which has had a number of devoted European adherents for many years, but which really sprang to prominence with the work done by the inventive Colonel Blondie Hasler and his junk-rigged Folkboat *Jester*.

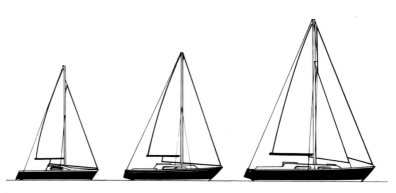

Progression of rigs through sizes, using variations of the Bermudian rig to give as much efficiency with relative ease of handling as economically as possible. The choice depends on the type of yacht hull involved, the kind of cruising planned, the number of crew carried, and the owner's personal preferences.

Despite the proven seagoing and handling capacity of *Jester* and other junk-rigged boats like Jock MacLeod's two-masted *Ron Glas*, the rig had always had a slight but unmistakable crank image, so during the summer of 1976 I was intrigued to meet up with a highly experienced yachtsman from the mainstream of cruising who had become converted to the virtues of the Chinese rig. Admiral Fisher's experience of seagoing under sail is remarkable – as a youthful lieutenant, he skippered a yacht in the 1928 Fastnet, but it is as a cruising man that he is most renowned, and although when he retired from the Navy in 1957 he had also found time to make cruises of which anyone would be proud, he regarded his cruising career as only just getting properly under way, and he bought the 20-ton Uffa Fox designed sloop *Fresh Breeze* and every summer ranged far and wide. However, eventually his family crew grew up and went away, as family crews do, but being determined to continue cruising with his wife, he hit on the idea of going Chinese, for even he was prepared to admit that he was past the age when most people regard a bit of gentle gardening as the limit of their activities, and *Fresh Breeze* was a bit of a handful.

Having made his decision, he saw it determinedly through to the end. The beloved *Fresh Breeze* was sold, and he set about looking for a builder of a wholly glass fibre 30 ft or so cruiser who would be prepared to modify one of his boats to become a junk-rigged schooner. Being the early 1970s when the marine industry was booming, it was difficult to get any attention at all for possible deviations from profitable production lines, but with R. A. G. Nierop of Westfield Engineering of Poole, who was already producing a Chinese-rigged variant of his long-running

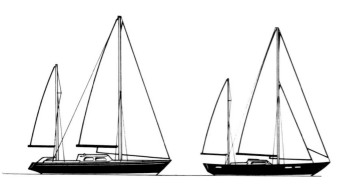

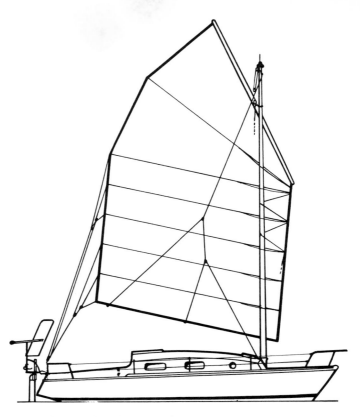

Chinese lug sail as fitted to the Kingfisher 26.

Kingfisher 20, he found a designer-builder who could not resist the challenge of innovation, and they set to work modifying the popular Kingfisher 30 for the job. A classic Chinese schooner rig with mainmast amidships and a forward raked foremast was designed, and Jock MacLeod of *Ron Glas* produced drawings for the masts which were built as substantial hollow spars, glassfibre sheathed but retaining their attractive light wood appearance, by Souter's of Cowes.

As the Kingfisher 30 is strongly built in the first place, relatively little extra glassing was needed in the coachroof and foredeck to carry the weight of these unstayed masts, and with the standard head-liner in place the reinforcement is in fact invisible, with no alteration having to be made to the location of cabin windows and so forth. To strengthen the support given to the mast, large glass fibre collars were bonded on to both masts half an inch above the deck level at the mast partners, and these were then bolted down to the deck, the masts thus being in compression between the deck and the mast-step, resulting in an arrangement of great strength such that although movement in the masts was expected between deck and keel, none has so far been observed. The new yacht was named *Yeong* – Chinese for 'Kingfisher' – and in 1972 she started her sailing career, her subsequent success delighting her owners, while the obvious effectiveness of the Chinese rig generally has not only led to remarkable sales of the Chinese-rigged Kingfisher 20, but has also encouraged the builders to bring out a Chinese-rigged variant of their larger Kingfisher 26.

As was expected, *Yeong* has not proved quite as fast to windward as her Bermudian rigged sisters, but off the wind she goes very well indeed, running being specially easy as the forward rake of the foremast facilitates goose-winging, and in ease of handling she is light years ahead. The Admiral has arranged for all controlling lines, halyards, sheets, the lot, to be led to the cockpit, and with the use of self-tailing winches any heavy work is made into an easy single-handed task.

Not that heavy work is a feature of the Chinese rig, as it has its basis in the distribution of loads, such that almost nothing involved with it gives an impression of weight or strain, and it takes very little effort to hoist sail, while reefing is of course just a matter of folding it away. Admittedly with the spreading of loads in the sheet arrangement there seems to be rather a lot of light lines and blocks, but coping with these is a matter of experience in use, and it took two or three seasons cruising before *Yeong*'s skipper reckoned he had his rig just right.

When I met him, he and his wife were homeward bound on their most ambitious cruise to date, from his home port of Tarbert on Loch Fyne

Admiral Fisher's junk rigged schooner **Yeong** *is based on a Kingfisher 30.*

The deck arrangement on Yeong, *showing the GRP collars which are bonded to the masts and hold them in compression between keel and deck.*

down to Spain. *Yeong* had performed well throughout, and her speed had been amply demonstrated by averaging more than 6 knots on a reach across the Bay of Biscay from Benodet to north-west Spain, a passage time which had included sitting out a calm at the start. The little schooner had a very workmanlike air about her, and it was clear that with her, the Chinese rig had become an accepted part of the cruising world.

Dismastings

It might be thought that by now the sizes of mast section and rigging could be known fairly closely by builders and designers, but so many variables are involved that it is still as much an art as a science. Thus some yachts sail happily for years on end, while others drop sticks at frequent intervals. Some friends of mine sailing offshore in an S & S 34 one brisk night remarked to each other how well the boat was going, and she might go even better with just one more turn in the backstay wheel to straighten the forestay that little bit further? So they put in just one half more turn than they had ever had before, and in seconds the mast collapsed; no rigging had broken, it just gave under compression.

We look into dismastings in Chapter 9 on Safety; in the meantime it does well to reflect that although the sparmakers and riggers can make judgements based on data a little more scientific than that obtained from studying the entrails of a chicken, at times they too are very much feeling their way. For cruising it is always good policy to err on the side of caution and get everything a little heftier than standard. Once upon a time a racing helmsman upset the trends towards lightness aloft by having his new offshore racer fitted with a rig much more robust than most others were going for, which worried the designers and builders. But this helmsman said that he wanted to enjoy sailing the boat without having to worry about the mast every time there was a breeze, and he did not want the nonsense of runners every time a sea started getting up. So they made him a stout rig just as he wanted, and as the boat was called *Stinger* and her owner was Dennis Conners and he went straight out with her and won the 1975 SORC series outright, it seems to me that not just cruisers, but also cruiser-racers, could follow such a sensible example with benefit, and not go around filling the sea with broken rigs.

Setting up rigging

Admittedly if you use hydraulics to set up rigging, experienced engineering attention will be needed from time to time, but for straightforward cruising if it is felt that adjustment is needed then a wheel on the backstay and possibly the inner forestay should be all that is required. There is a lot to be said for the point of view that for cruising the rigging should be set up at the start of the season and kept so, because continuous adjustment of rigging inevitably causes changes – however minute – in yachts' hull shape, and over a number of seasons this can only accelerate materials fatigue.

It is surprising how much movement can be induced in the hull of a yacht by the setting up of the rigging; it is obviously preferable that once the mast is tuned, further movement should be minimized, and at the basic design stage it should be ensured that strains from the mast are properly distributed through the hull. In smaller yachts it is possible to have a deck-stepped mast supported with real strength, and the extra space available in the accommodation is most welcome. The rigging strains should be absorbed in a complete bulkhead unit located directly under the mast, but if this cannot be done it is much better to have the mast going through to a proper mast-step on the keelson. Such an arrangement makes it easier to get the mast into proper tune, such that under pressure the middle part of the mast tends to bend forward, but do not assume that just because a mast goes through the deck, all is well no matter how much you tension the rigging. I remember once sharpening up the performance of a cruiser-racer with continuous rigging adjustment until the stick seemed to be sitting very nicely on all points of sailing, but then with the boat sailing along like a dream, we found our fresh water starting to taste brackish. The mast was stepped on a steel plate above the fin keel, and the fresh water tank – of GRP – was located in the hollow top of the keel. With our tensioning and tuning, we wound the mast down until the steel plate had bent so much it fractured the top of the water tank, and the bilge water trickled in. In other words, while the through deck set-up is preferable, it can have its own problems.

Some cruising men may give only the most perfunctory attention to the setting up of their mast, thinking that tuning is strictly for the racing brigade, but when you think of nasty circumstances of being embayed, or having to perform efficiently when beating through a narrow channel, it is clear that any seagoing yacht must be rigged to give of her best. The tuning of a mast starts with the most basic things, with free-turning rigging screws in good order, effectively locked with high-quality split-pins (cotter pins).

Everything that should move, ought to be able to do so freely, while everything that should not move ought to be properly seized with split pins or wire, and afterwards sealed off against tearing sails and ropes. Nowadays you can get attractive plastic covers for rigging screws, but in any case wrap up any sharp points in plastic adhesive tape as an extra precaution. Aloft, all shackles permanently installed should be seized with wire: remember to seize them with a wire of the same metal as the fittings, and here again make sure that sharp points are made harmless.

Do-it-yourself spars

A number of firms now provide kits specially for such enthusiasts. Typical among them being Sailspar Ltd of Brightlingsea in Essex who have made a speciality of this kind of thing. They have not heard of anyone who has had a serious problem in putting one of their kit masts together. The usual kit comprises the mast section 'as milled' (that is without any cleaning up) with the masthead box sheave welded in and the sail entry cut and all the fittings including sheaves, tangs, pins, spreaders, cleats, winch pads, and fastenings supplied loose, the fastenings consisting mainly of stainless steel bolts and nuts and monel pop-rivets. The only additional tool required extra to the usual handyman's equipment is a pair of lazy tongs for these $\frac{1}{4}$-in rivets.

A friend of mine made up a Sailspar mast for his 1938-built 39-ft Robert Clark-designed Mystery class sloop, and with a friend helping it took about a week's full-time work. The cost was only about a third of the price of a complete mast, but of course such a mast would be properly anodized and be tapered towards the head, whereas the Sailspar mast is the same hefty section throughout, and has to be painted, using protective paints developed in the aircraft industry. The effect can be a little rough and ready, but properly done, with the

The 1912-built yawl Ainmara *is an interesting example of how a well-cared for older yacht can continue to cruise successfully, as her cruises in the 1970s have included ventures to Norway, the Outer Isles of Scotland, and southern Brittany. One particularly notable feature is her alloy mast, which was built by her owner. The retention of her three-headsail rig is of interest – older craft can be unduly strained by a modern masthead rig with alloy spars, but in* Ainmara*'s case the strains are effectively distributed by the divided rig.*

painting completed before the smaller fittings are put in place, the finished mast is attractively robust in appearance.

If you are really determined to have a new alloy mast at minimum cost, it is possible to do this starting from scratch with extrusions bought direct from the manufacturers. This can involve ticklish negotiation, as the dies for the extrusions are often owned by the sparmaker to whom the extruder is supplying. But it can be done, and Dick Gomes who

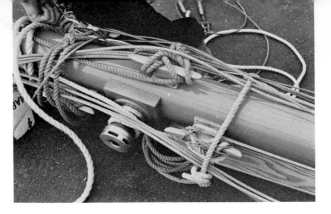

It can be done! Detail of Ainmara's *mast, which was owner-built from bare extrusions without a mast-building kit to begin with.*

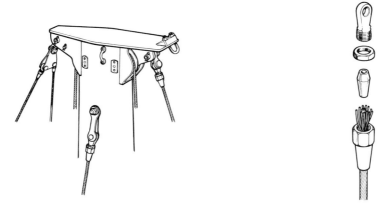

Standard masthead fitting. The vast majority of today's cruising yachts carry a straightforward masthead sloop rig which has led to the development of sensible no-nonsense fittings.

The swageless terminal enables the amateur to make a neat end-fitting for standard rigging.

cruises far and wide with his 1912-built 9-ton yawl *Ain Mara* did it all with an alloy mainmast which he made, starting just with two bare extrusions. Admittedly, he had the assistance of a friend who was a foreman rigger in an aircraft factory, and this greatly facilitated the making-up of the various parts, but it was a formidable achievement nevertheless.

For most of us, however, the most advanced do-it-yourself that we will do around a new alloy mast is the fitting of something like Norseman Swageless terminals to the lower ends of the standing rigging. With new craft, yacht designers are notoriously reluctant to specify an exact length for rigging, and masts in this case will arrive with the lower ends of the rigging bare. I have been involved with rigging new masts in this way three times. Strangely, with two year gaps between each, I found that everything learned the previous time had been forgotten; the relatively easy knack of fitting the swageless terminals had to be re-learned.

If you happen to be doing this, the best thing is a bit of practice beforehand with a spare piece of wire, and the expense of an extra terminal is well worth while. When it is all finished, it looks very neat – much neater than amateur eye-splicing, for instance – but inevitably someone will remark that ideally another mast should be done right away, because with the experience acquired with the first one, the second is easier.

And this if course is the problem with every aspect of do-it-yourself around boats – everyone I know who has made masts, or indeed built boats, has bewailed the fact that they had to stop with just one; with what they learn with the first one, they reckon the second would be much easier. Inevitably, with the huge expansion of sailing and cruising, the marine industry has become more specialized, and with that specialization there has come a development of processes and an efficiency which tends to push the amateur worker to one side.

But equally inevitably, with every world financial crisis raising prices, there are people still so determined to get a boat that they will explore every avenue, and so do-it-yourself will always be with us, and if you have time it is quite remarkable what can be done, not only building boats, but making up masts and even assembling your own engine. However, if you are a busy person who thinks that boats are for sailing and things like mast-making are strictly for the experts, that too is a perfectly valid point of view.

Sails

The kind of sails that a yacht carries tells us more about her usage than almost any other aspect of her. Some cruising men for whom racing is a dirty word manage to make do with remarkably few sails, and provided that these sails retain a vaguely triangular shape, they continue with them for years. At the other extreme, there are racing men who buy sails at such a rate that you begin to think that is the only way that they know they are alive.

What you need is enough sails in order to get a reasonably efficient performance from your boat and a reasonable selection of stout heavy weather cloth so that in strong winds there will be no undue anxiety about tearing sails. Equally one or two light weather kites are useful so that you do not have to disturb the peace of the sea with engine noise when the breeze goes light. Against this, you do not want to have so many sails that they use up much of the accommodation when stowed.

Despite its reduced status in today's masthead sloop rigs with their large foretriangles, the mainsail still is the 'main sail' if only because it is the sail most continuously in use. Although headsails and spinnakers attract all the attention, in many ways the mainsail most tests a sailmaker's ability, as it has to function in winds of every strength from the lightest zephyr often to above forty knots. It has to withstand brutal treatment from luff, foot and leech tensioning in order to assume the best shape for conditions prevailing, while reefing can be very hard indeed on cloth.

The advent of synthetic fibres, usually terylene, has revolutionized our views on the potential of mainsails; nowadays it is remarkable the abuse they can withstand, and even the most dyed-in-the-wool cruising man is aware that the ferocious competition of offshore racing has shown how better performance can be obtained from any sailing boat by fairly elementary rules of sail adjustment. It is a great benefit to alter the draft of sails by the luff and foot adjustment as the wind falls away or sheets are eased, to flatten the sail as the wind is brought ahead and as it freshens, using a leech cringle to induce instant flatness and then a Cunningham hole to further the process.

The complexity of your sail controls depend to a large extent on the type of person you are. Going off on a fortnight or three weeks' cruising in a fully-crewed boat, it is all part of the fun to keep the boat moving to best effect, using 'go-fast goodies'. On the other hand, a pure family cruiser, sailing a little less energetically, probably short-handed, using the simplest of rigs, will have a minimum of gadgets and will have her performance emphasis elsewhere.

Sail cloths vary enormously in their ability to retain shape under tension; some of course are meant to stretch, but it is worth while to discuss your requirements with the sailmaker, because it could well be that slightly more expenditure in the early stages could provide a sail that lasts much longer. Unfortunately, when delivery is being taken of a new craft, the sails often get less attention than anything else, but in a proper sailing yacht they are one of the prime components and any skipper doing his job properly will make it his business to get to know the sailmaker and find out everything he can about sails, sailmaking, sailcloth and sail care. The autumn is a useful time to do this, as sailmakers are usually having a quiet period, and they even offer quite substantial discounts for orders placed before the end of November. Unfortunately for most cruising men the autumn is usually a time of drawing-in, there is the instinctive tendency to hibernation and the last thing you want to think about is new sails for next year, but if you can make the effort you will get far more attention from the sailmaker than would be the case in the hectic springtime.

The genoa

Perhaps cruising men expect a little too much from one general-purpose genoa. After all, most of our sailing is done in winds between four and twenty knots, and it seems a little unbalanced to have just one headsail for this, and then four or five smaller jibs for winds which are fresher. Admittedly, in the fresher winds there is an urgent need for a sail which exactly fills the bill, but my own preference would be for a genoa which suits from 0 to 12 knots, and then another of the same size but in heavier cloth which will do the job from 8 knots up to 20. The extent to which your yacht can tolerate variations in wind strength will to a large extent depend on her displacement; the lighter her relative displacement, the more closely defined will be her sail area limits, but in a cruising yacht of moderate displacement genoas of overlapping power as suggested will allow considerable flexibility, and your long-suffering crew will not be running up and down the deck changing headsails every time the wind flukes about.

All this assumes that your headsail reduction is in the usual manner of changing down to a smaller sail; we will shortly be considering all aspects of reefing, but continuing with a straightforward selection of smaller headsails, one welcome development in recent years has been the reappearance of headsails for brisker breezes which look very like the good old working jibs of yore. Such sails have almost as much luff length as the working genoas, something which gives them the power to haul a yacht along to windward, and yet because they do not have the body of a genoa, they are safer in rough water as there is relatively little of them for the seas to crash into, while the improved visibility forward is a further distinct advantage. In larger yachts, such sails can also double as the No. 1 jib – not the yankee – when the change-down is made to cutter rig. When running in heavy weather, this working jib booms out better than a genoa, which bellies too much.

Storm sails

In the smallest headsails, it is essential to have a strop fitted at the head and clew, the one at the clew to lift the sail above the deck to keep it clear of breaking water, and the one at the head to ensure that the halyard is functioning properly, with the heaviest strains being taken by the wire part, while the rope tail should be only active on the winch.

Nowadays many smaller cruising yachts are fitted with luff grooves not only for the mainsail but also for headsails. Provided a proportionately large enough crew is carried, such a system can also work well enough even with larger yachts, but as with all specialized equipment it can go badly astray with inexperienced handling, and if there is any doubt at all about your crew's capacity to cope in all conditions with a headsail groove, then it is much safer to stick to the traditional arrangement with hanks. Even where a groove is in use, storm jibs should be fitted with some fail safe device to hold the sail to the forestay if the luff rope fails – a toggled loop is one suggestion. Until you have actually experienced real storm conditions at sea – and few of us ever do, even in a lifetime's cruising – it is impossible to have any conception of the incredible strains inflicted on sails and gear *in extremis*, and both luff ropes and ordinary hanks are liable to give out in very heavy weather. Traditionally the feeling is that shackles are the only things which will hold a storm jib to the forestay in a proper storm, but this notion dates from the period when galvanized steel shackles were the norm. These days our fancy pleasure yachts are covered with a plethora of stainless steel equipment, including shackles which turn much more freely than the slightly rusty and stiffer shackles of days past; thus I have a notion that a few seconds' flogging in a Force 12 would soon undo a storm jib's stainless steel shackles no matter how tightly they had been screwed up by spike or shackle spanner, but perhaps the tension induced by heavy weather might make one give them that extra twist which would hold against anything.

We return to the matter of storm sails in Chapter 9, but it should be pointed out at this stage that though storm sails very seldom appear, when they do they are absolutely vital, and thus the storm jib and the trisail deserve as much attention as the rest of the sails put together. Needless to say they seldom get it, but the trisail in particular is a sail of great importance, because with most yachts carrying only one mainsail it offers the only alternative way of setting sail aft of the mast in the event of substantial damage to the mainsail itself, while in really heavy weather the extra drive of a trisail may make the difference between success and failure in extrication from a tricky situation. Despite this, an astonishing number of yacht crews have never even removed their trisail from the bag, and when they come to set them total confusion is often the result – the sail may not even fit the track, and sheeting positions are unknown.

Reefing

Any consideration of today's reefing systems leaves one with an inescapable feeling that there is really nothing new under the sun; certainly it all underlines the fact that what we are living through in today's cruising is very much a materials revolution rather than a design revolution. During the 1960s, refinement of roller reefing of mainsails was all the rage; to hear some people talk, you would think it had only

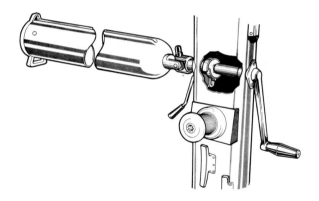

Through mast roller-reefing is neat and simple even if it sometimes fails to obtain as good a reefed shape as the slab method.

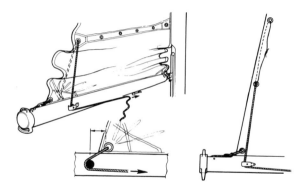

Slab reefing equipment on a small cruiser. With larger craft, winches and cam jammers will be required to deal with the loads involved.

just been invented, whereas there has been roller reefing of some sort around for at least a couple of centuries.

Then in the 1970s we had the great 'invention' of jiffy reefing. Any examination of this shows it to be good old fashioned 'cringle 'n' points' or 'slab' reefing given a new twist by the strength of terylene cloth. Further refinement is provided with roller reefing of headsails by rotating a forestay which may be in effect a separate spar; well, roller furling of headsails has been around since the 19th century, while in various parts of the world the use of a spar on the forestay to provide

A through mast roller-reefing boom modified to carry slab reefing. Note that with more wind expected a messenger line has been used to rig the outhaul for the second reef.

effective roller reefing and furling has been known for many a day. As I write this, advertisements from a leading firm of sailmakers have been appearing in which they claim to have invented a new way of shortening down on headsails – you don't roll them round the forestay, you just reef them down like the jiffy-reefed mainsail . . . just wonderful, except that like many other people I can remember sailing in ancient craft in which a set of reef points in the old staysail was looked on as a usual arrangement.

The kind of reefing selected depends on a number of factors; there can be little doubt that jiffy reefing, or slab reefing as some prefer to call it, produces a smaller sail which is generally a more effective shape than that which results from roller reefing round a boom, but against this jiffy reefing involves a number of extra ropes and lines, and other paraphernalia such as winches. People can get caught in such ropes, they can break, winches can jam, and though the basis of the system is very simple, situations arise where the straightforward nature of roller reefing, though it may often produce a somewhat wrinkled sail, is preferable.

The simplest jiffy reefing is with all lines led externally and the winches for the clew lines fitted to the mainboom just aft of the mast. Some deckhands profess to dislike working with winches which are located on something which can itself move around, but with this system the reefing line or pendant is simply led up through the cringle on the leech, down to a cheek block on the side of the boom opposite, and along the boom to the winch. The location of the cheek block and the first attachment point of the pendant is critical to the set of the reefed sail – too far aft, and the sail is too hard along the foot with a slack leech, too far forward and the leech is strained with the foot too slack, and the sail too full.

As the pendant line passes along the boom, it should be led through strategically placed eyes in order to minimize the chances of the line becoming fouled when slackened. Generally this problem of fouling in other warps, ventilators or whatever is avoided by having the line led internally through the boom, but this may cause fouling within the boom and of course there is always the danger that chafe is taking place out of sight.

Indeed, chafe is the greatest single problem with the system, and is the root of many people's objections to it. There is the chafe where the pendant leads through the clew cringle, there is the chafe, though usually minimal, where it passes through the cheek block, and there often is chafe where the line passes in and out of the boom. The situation becomes worse when the system is further refined with the reefing lines led to winches on deck, as it is often difficult to obtain a universally fair lead for lines which are led to a fixed point from a boom which can and inevitably does change its angle to the lead. The advantage of leading the lines to the deck is that the winches can be located aft at the cockpit, and thus the only deck work involved is lowering away the main halyard and hitching the tack over the hook at the boom gooseneck. But with reefing lines led aft there can be as many as seven points where the lines are being put under strain and if one breaks when the yacht is hard on the wind, the boom will crash down and heaven help anyone whose head happens to be under it. However, this reefing system is constantly being improved, and already some of the better modern variants of it have reduced chafe to a minimum, with very satisfactory results in the resulting sail shortening.

Still, there is no doubt that roller reefing can produce sail shortening possibly slightly faster, and the equipment is simpler, particularly if you are using the through-mast system which was developed by designer Dick Carter and sparmaker John Powell. With this system, it is possible to have a long handle which can be worked at with a much better mechanical advantage than the worm gears of days past, which were often exhausting to operate. The secret of roller reefing seems to lie in judgement of correct tensions – just enough tension in the topping lift to take the weight of the boom off the sail without having it so loose that the sail winds up any old way, this balance being maintained by having the halyard eased at just the right speed. Properly done, the result is quick and effective, but as with just about every aspect of sail handling, it is a good idea to practise reefing in gentle conditions, whatever kind of system you employ.

In fact, if you prefer sailing with the minimum of effort and the maximum of fun, probably the best thing of all is to have a roller reefing system on the forestay. Nowadays these sytems have been developed to a remarkable degree, and some very large cruising yachts use them successfully, so much so that the ultimate has been developed on a ketch with the jib, mainsail and mizzen being reefed in this way, the reckoning being that rolling round the luff gives a better shape to the reduced sail than rolling round the boom.

While the basis of the rolling system is simple, inevitably it involves some fairly sophisticated engineering in order to ensure that it functions with a minimum of friction and effort. Ensure that in the event of breakdown alternatives are available, and that, most important of all, the sail can be got down.

In selecting reefing gear, do be sure that it *is* reefing gear – there are some roller furling devices on the market which are just that – *furling* devices. They make no claims to be reefing gears, as this involves much more robust equipment which has to withstand considerable strains in order to get a worth while smaller sail shape.

There are certain limitations on the shape of sail which can be effectively rolled around its own luff. In a perfect world such a sail would be an isosceles triangle, and moreover there would be wire reels both at head and tack in order to spread the strains of the considerable torque involved. However, a sail of such shape would have only limited applications when in use, and a second reel at the masthead, apart from being somewhat ridiculous, would have endless drawbacks in use. So the inevitable compromise is to have a sail with a fairly high clew, but not absurdly so, and thus with the bulk of the sail in its lower half, all the rolling can be done by one drum located at the tack.

Using these criteria, we end up with a headsail looking very like the yankee of a classic cutter rig, and in fact the noted American cruising writer Don Street has taken this to its logical conclusion by having both headsails in the cutter foretriangle of his 1905-built vintage yawl *Iolaire* set on roller reefing gears; it produces a powerful yet very easily handled rig, and *Iolaire* has sailed many seas with it, including a couple of fast crossings of the Atlantic during a cruise to Europe in 1975.

Aboard *Iolaire*, they use tackles to bring home wires from the reels on the two headsails; a more usual method is to have a main-halyard type wire winch at the cockpit, led aft along the deck, usually through a series of leads around the edge of the deck. With this system the effort in shortening sail forward is minimal, but it is obvious that the strength of

Roller reefing system in use on a headsail. For the most effective application of this system, a fairly high clewed headsail functions better than a genoa of more orthodox shape.

each part of the gear must be above question, and even so in the event of a breakage it must be possible to get the headsail down with a minimum of fuss, with alternative sails readily available. Indeed, with all reefing systems some alternative is a good idea, particularly with roller reefing round the mainboom where a set of reef points about halfway up the mainsail could be a very present help in time of need.

Running sails

Many cruising men abhor spinnakers in any conditions. They get their downwind drive from high-clewed genoas which can sheet to the end of the mainboom, and when the wind comes further aft a handy system of a pole to the genoa clew does the trick. Unfortunately, there is a ten-degree sector of the wind arc where nothing is quite right – it is too far aft for the genoa to work properly on the same side as the main, and yet it is not far enough aft to fill the sail quietly with it boomed out. But it is only a very small sector, and a steady wind direction is a rare thing, so course can be marginally altered from time to time to keep the sails happy.

Booming out in fresh breezes, means the largest genoa can be carried in winds of considerable strength without the heart-in-mouth emotions inevitable with a spinnaker. It is better to have a slightly smaller genoa set as it can be flattened to give better lift without a twist

Running in strong breezes, the yacht will sail in the most possible comfort if sails are kept as flat as possible in order to prevent billowing at the head which induces rolling moment. Thus an effective boom vang is a real asset to cruising comfort, while the headsail in use should be of a size that will boom out flat.

which can cause the boat to roll. The Junior Offshore Group rules, taking note of the fact that a spinnaker pole of the size permitted by the rule was not large enough to flatten a boomed-out genoa, used to have a rule which permitted a telescopic pole for this purpose. Such a refinement is a little too complex for a straightforward cruising yacht, the best solution is to find the largest genoa which can be flattened by the standard pole and use it for running. The clew of this sail should be a high one in order to keep the sail out of the water in the event of rolling, and also to provide a better angle so that the foreguy can exert a real downward pull. I remember once running before a near gale with a large genoa set, in order to get the maximum spread the spinnaker pole was right at the foot of its track, and thus the guy and foreguy were almost in the same horizontal plane. Between them they exerted very little real downward pull, and in order to flatten the sail we hardened in on them even further; with an almighty bang the track came off the mast, and in a split second there was a track shaped hole in the mainsail, quite horrifying because if anyone had been in the way he would have been decapitated.

With a sail like a yankee being used for running purposes, it might not even be necessary to have a full-length spinnaker pole, and shorter poles can be very handily stowed vertically against the mast, leaving extra room on deck. With practice, headsail booming out drill can be refined to make for minimal effort – some old seadogs reckon that the best way is to boom out the high-clewed sail before it is hoisted, and then when everything is set up you just haul away on the halyard and hey presto! the running sail is set.

Deck gear

There is a widely held notion that a cruising yacht does not need sail control equipment of the same power as a similarly sized offshore racer. In an ideal world of unlimited funds, I would not subscribe to this theory – if anything, as a cruising yacht generally makes do with a lighter crew than a racer, her sheet winches should be more powerful. But in this distinctly less than perfect world we just have to make do with what we can afford, with cruisers generally having less powerful hardware. It is up to the helmsman to work in sympathy with his crew in order to ease their work in trimming sails with possibly inadequate winches.

Any seagoing yacht's cockpit is a compromise between a place needed now and again for hectic bursts of sail trimming, and a place needed practically all the time for sitting. Inevitably the needs of the sitters become paramount, but in siting winches and cleats it must be remembered that their occasional bursts of activity are very necessary, and their location should have due regard for the ergonomic needs of the cockpit crew.

Winch location should not be done in isolation either, but must be related to the lead of the sheet, which usually comes from a cheek block aft of the winch. The cheek block, apart from giving a constant lead to the winch, thereby greatly reducing the possibility of riding turns and other embarrassments, also helps to spread the considerable load imposed by modern headsail sheets and greatly facilitates the continuous adjustment of the sheet lead itself.

Much more variable than the fairly straightforward needs of the headsail sheets is the type of mainsheet arrangement used. The mainsheet can be led from almost anywhere between the outer end of the main boom to almost as far forward as the middle of the boom, and can be attached in at least four places – at the other end either to the top of the coachroof, to the bridge-deck, in the middle of the cockpit, or to the aft end of the cockpit. I must confess to a personal dislike of having the sheet on the boom anywhere other than the outer end. There are the needs of roller reefing, where a boom end fitting is preferable to a claw arrangement around the boom. Whenever the boom end is extended beyond the mainsheet you get a hostile piece of thrusting spar which seems bent on injury towards everyone in the cockpit. With the sheet led to the end of the boom, the furthest forward we can have the lower attachment is on the bridge-deck, and there is no doubt that this is a handy arrangement in that it takes up a minimum of room and yet permits really convenient control of the sheet. However, if you generally sail with family or inexperienced friends as guests aboard, a mainsheet led to the bridge-deck, particularly if it is attached to a traveller on a track, can be a positive menace when tacking or gybing as the less alert can get caught in the thing. A further disadvantage is that when the sheet is right down the track it gets in the way of people operating the genoa winch on the lee side.

To a certain extent this latter drawback continues when the track is further aft immediately forward of the helmsman, making for a division in the cockpit which status conscious drivers find most satisfying. With the track across the cockpit in this way, there is a clear area forward where the less experienced can linger for reassurance in the companionway area, but with smaller craft such a track takes up too much room. Generally the old-fashioned method of having the mainsheet led to the deck at the aft end of the cockpit has a great deal to recommend it.

This is only possible where there is a longer main boom than is usually the case with the latest high aspect ratio rigs, but if it can be rigged it is certainly an arrangement where the mainsail provides the minimum of personal danger for those in the cockpit. With it, as with all mainsheet arrangements, do ensure that the sheet leads vertically fore and aft when the boom is amidships – having the sheet at an angle is not only bad mechanically, but it also provides added possibilities for people to get their heads caught in the thing when tacking or gybing, particularly the latter.

Coloured ropes

A useful development in recent years has been the introduction of coloured ropes; when it is remembered that the lines leading to the cockpit can include genoa sheeets, mainsheet, spinnaker sheets and foreguys, genoa halyard and spinnaker halyard, not to mention staysail sheets if the yacht is a cutter, and reefing lines if there is slab reefing fitted with the lines led aft, then obviously anything which helps clear identification is a boon. The well-known firm of Marlow Ropes have introduced a colour code which is: genoa sheets: blue; spinnaker sheet: red; mainsheet: white. Hopefully in time this will become standardized, and though it is sound policy to have your crew aware of sheets and their function rather than thinking of them just as different coloured ropes, at hectic moments instant identification within a jumble of rope can be very helpful.

Hoods and dodgers

Before leaving the cockpit, one final item for consideration is the provision of a folding shelter over the hatchway; this comes in two forms – either a little pram hood type which justs fits over the hatch itself, or a larger arrangement which fits right across the forward end of the cockpit. The idea of them is unattractive, they spoil the line of the ship, but there is no doubt that they are a benefit in wet, windy or cold weather, keeping spray and even solid water from getting down below, and providing a certain amount of shelter for those in the cockpit, while they fold almost out of sight when not in use.

They have some drawbacks. In really unpleasant weather, the cockpit crew tend to shelter so much behind them that it is quite possible that a proper lookout is not being maintained, but against that it could be argued that a benumbed deckhand shivering in an exposed position is unlikely to be looking around with any great enthusiasm. However, perhaps the pram-hood type is the best compromise as it gives extra shelter to the accommodation while leaving the cockpit clear for action.

Spray dodgers can be fastened to the life-lines either side of the cockpit. On some yachts these are very large indeed, extending well forward on either side. One really useful function they perform is as a nameplate – with the number, and preferably the name of the yacht affixed to these in large letters, identification at sea is made much easier, indeed identification anywhere, as anyone who has looked for a strange

While we all dream of cruising in summery weather, it is prudent to take precautions to reduce the inconvenience of rain. A good cockpit cover, preferably with standing headroom underneath, greatly increases the usable accommodation at anchor on rainy days, and on this Nicholson 32 it also serves a second purpose as extra protection when the yacht is laid up afloat. Note too that both on her and the yacht in the near foreground the halyards are held away from the mast – even with alloy spars the damage done by a winter's flapping of halyards is quite remarkable.

yacht in a crowded marina can vouch for. But like the folding shelter over the main hatch, these spray dodgers look rather overpowering when set above the clean lines of an elegant yacht, and when the yacht is driving along to windward, the helmsman tends to make himself comfortable in behind both the shelter and the weather dodger, and because of the angle of heel he sees little ahead or to windward. Collisions have occurred as a result of this, and though it is easy to look out from behind a shelter alone, with a high dodger well up to windward, a proper lookout is virtually impossible. One would prefer to do without one altogether; in really heavy weather damage can be caused to the stanchions. A canvas nameplate of half-stanchion width, attached between the two guardrails and *not* between the lower guardrail and the deck, looks after the communication problem, but even that is a possibly undesirable compromise, for though by having it well raised the water cannot be caught between dodger and deck, a solid clout of spray hitting the raised canvas will exert considerable leverage.

Winches

Moving forward, we frequently find a tendency for halyard winches to be located on deck with the halyards fanning out from specially located leads just above where the mast goes through the deck. Certainly for a cruiser with a performance orientation it is a good idea to have the genoa halyard winch on top of the coachroof, back at the cockpit where the genoa luff tension can be adjusted without having to go on deck. In cruisers up to about 35–40 ft it is not a bad idea to have the spinnaker halyard, if you have one, coming aft there as well as it enables the sail to be raised and lowered by one of the cockpit crew, but otherwise the best arrangement for the average boat is to have the winches located on the mast. That way they do not take up room on deck, which is valuable around the mast, and they can also be placed at the easiest height for working, a desirable feature for those of us who are getting a little stiff in the joints, and find crouching over a deck-mounted halyard winch unnecessarily tiring.

In very large yachts where, if all winches were to be located on the mast, the upper ones would be almost out of reach, a separate console immediately aft of the mast can be used to carry some of the more frequently used winches. One yacht which has this is the Bowman 57, and the deck-house is just the right height for the crew to sit on as they operate halyards. Whatever way the winches are located, one very useful idea, particularly in larger yachts, is the provision of support bars around the mainmast; provided they are fastened really securely, they act as handy anchor points for safety harness lines, and can be leant against in comfort.

Ground tackle

The foredeck of many of today's cruising yachts would be unrecognizable to a cruising yachtsman of the old school; where formerly you had a stout samson post or a windlass to look after the anchor chain, and stowage for at least one anchor large enough to hold the yacht in all conditions, nowadays you get a foredeck bereft of everything except perhaps a rather feeble looking cleat which looks barely fit to hold mooring warps in a marina, which is all it is usually expected to do. Often we even lack a proper roller fairlead at the stemhead, and it is all a sad comment on today's cruising, or rather what passes for cruising, for many of today's standard craft would seem to be fit for nothing more than hopping from marina to marina.

For proper cruising, nothing less than a real chain with a hefty and immediately available anchor will do. To supplement that basic anchor you will need at least one fisherman kedge and sundry lines (see Chapter 9 on Safety and Emergencies) but do for heaven's sake have that basic anchor always ready to go. Another aspect is that your cruising immediately blossoms, for you discover the lost art of anchoring.

Even the most misanthropic cruising man occasionally has to come alongside, be it pontoon, pier or quay. Doing this is greatly helped by having the correct equipment – substantial fenders, not the toy things that plague many a boat, and warps that *are* warps, and not the tailend of the mainsheet or some such misapplication. Ensure that really hefty cleats are fitted fore and aft to take these, and if you have any choice in the matter do try and have the yacht fitted with closed-fairleads, Panama fairleads as they call them in big ships, because any other sort of fairlead is worse than useless.

Fortunately nowadays the full-length alloy toerails which grace many yachts lend themselves easily to the inclusion of such fairleads, but it must be ensured that the fairleads are properly throughbolted; in years of cruising you may get only a couple of occasions where you get a battering in port, but it can happen; or perhaps you may take in a canal passage as part of a cruise. In both cases really sound fairleads which do not chafe your warps can make the difference between a satisfactory conclusion and expensive damage.

If you do not have full-length alloy toerails with attachment holes at frequent and regular intervals, do ensure that such attachment points are fitted at strategic points, as they are very useful for carrying snatch-blocks and tackles which can perform a myriad of tasks, such as the tackle for a vang for the mainboom when sheets are eased, or for snatch-blocks to improve sheet leads.

7 Engine and electrics

While there is an attractive purity in the approach of a very small number of cruising men who continue to sail without sullying their yachts with auxiliary engines, for most of us the engine and all the other equipment it allows us to use is an integral part of the sailing cruiser's make-up. Certainly if ocean cruising is your interest, then the need for an engine is lessened as there are other ways of supplying the required minimum of electric power, and the ports you elect to call at can be selected on your known capacity to handle the yacht in confined waters under sail alone. In time it is quite remarkable what can be done in this way, but nevertheless doing without an engine implies limitless resources of time, something which few people have today. Increasingly too, most of us sail either from closely packed marinas or tide-ridden anchorages, when many attempts to get out under sail only prove anti-social, to say the least of it. Then we sail in waters increasingly crowded with commercial shipping, and the situation arises that an engine is needed in light winds to get out of the way of a large ship which either cannot manoeuvre, or has not seen us.

Such occurrences provide only the most basic reasons for having an engine. More generally, a reliable engine can make all the difference to planning a cruise; you yourself may quite happily sit becalmed at sea within a few miles of a port, but perhaps your crew, particularly if you are sailing with your family and have small children aboard, can quickly become disenchanted with the beauty of the evening and the ensuing night. When cruising with a weak crew, situations also arise where progress can be made close inshore motor-sailing, whereas bashing it out in open water is out of the question if you wish your family to continue to share your enthusiasm.

There is no need to fear that such an approach will result in your becoming little better than a glorified motor-boat fan. If your yacht is a proper sailing cruiser, when conditions are suitable for sailing you can be absolutely sure that she will be abominably uncomfortable under engine only, rolling her guts out or pitching herself silly.

Doing without. The 47 ft Robert Clark sloop Moonduster *was originally built in 1965 without any auxiliary engine, and for many years the then owner Denis Doyle sailed in and out of harbours of all sorts, executing neat seamanship such as this one getting away from the marina pontoon at Dartmouth in Devon.*

Diesels

The first argument put forward in favour of the diesel is the safety element – diesel fuel does not have the same potentially dangerous volatile nature as petrol, and thus the hazards of a fuel leak are not so great. But a properly installed and maintained petrol engine can provide reasonable margins of safety, and many cruisers will be using excellent petrol auxiliaries for years to come. Such engines run much more smoothly and quietly than many of the smaller diesels, and with reasonable care will continue to do so, saving their owners the expense of changing to diesel, a movement which at times seems something of a fad rather than being really essential. However, with the weight and running qualities of diesels of all sizes improving every year there is no doubt that if a change has to be made, it can reasonably be made to a diesel auxiliary, and even the traditional complaint of the obnoxious smell of diesel can now be dealt with – some of the better equipped chandlers can supply tablets which, if put into the fuel tank in the prescribed dose, can eliminate the fuel smell. Anyone who has had to endure the sick-making stench of diesel fuel will welcome this, but be warned – a cruising skipper of my acquaintance added the 'medicine' to such good effect that his shallow bilges filled with diesel fuel from a leak without anyone being aware of it; once the yacht was sailing the fuel swept over the cabin sole after tacking, giving the cabin all the seagoing properties of an ice rink.

Selection of engine size is generally related to displacement, the old ready reckoning being that in the average size yacht – say between 30 ft and 40 ft – you had 1 h.p. per ton of displacement, with smaller yachts needing more and larger yachts needing less. Nowadays the trend is to considerably more power; yachts are generally of lighter displacement, and so their greater windage relative to displacement means a greater power requirement; also it is possible to provide more power with an engine of the same weight, and so a yacht can be provided with power in reserve. Thus it is not uncommon to find a lightish displacement Half Ton cruiser-racer, a yacht of around 30 ft displacing less than 7,000 pounds, having an auxiliary of 12 or even 15 h.p., and I know of many 'pure' sailing cruisers around the 35–40 ft size, carrying auxiliaries of more than 30 h.p.

Merely having such power available is not of course enough – the correct propeller installation is vital, and is something which all too often receives no attention at all. Propeller design is very much a specialist's art, but any cruising skipper who wants to get full value from an engine which is generally a rather expensive item of equipment would do well to look to his stern gear. With power in reserve, and with it driving the yacht through an optimum screw, such skippers can be the greatest of sailing enthusiasts, confident in the knowledge that if the engine is suddenly required to get out of a tight spot with sudden manoeuvring, or to push the boat through a tortuous channel against tide and strong headwinds, then the power is there to do it.

In the very smallest cruisers, there is a lot to be said in favour of an outboard motor. The simplicity of an outboard lends itself to such small craft, but the usefulness of such auxiliary power diminishes very rapidly as the boat increases in size, and the nature of most outboards is such that virtually all sailing cruisers above at most 25 ft are better served by having an inboard auxiliary. Outboards generally are designed to provide a high power-weight ratio for small craft, and they quickly

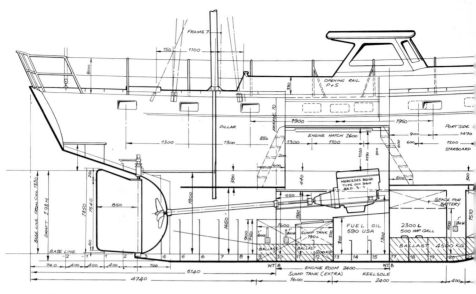

With larger yachts used exclusively for cruising, weight-saving is no longer paramount, and engine installations can be brought up to 'big-ship' standards. The heavy displacement ketch Verna *has made full use both of her size and her steel construction to have an engine installation which inspires real confidence.*

become irrelevant to the needs of larger yachts where a different kind of power, useful for moving a displacement hull, is required.

Engine space

With any inboard auxiliary, the first requirement is for total accessibility for maintenance and repair. This may seem so obvious as scarcely to require stating, but is subject to the dictates of accommodation and sailing performance, where an engine is stuck out of the way either to make room in the cabin, to make the boat stiffer by having it low down in the bilges, or to have it far away from the centre of the boat in order to avoid weight in the end. The engine should not be sitting plumb in the middle of the saloon, but with the increasing expertise which designers have in utilizing the space around and under the cockpit, it should be perfectly possible to have fairly easy access without having to lower someone headfirst through a hatch in the cockpit floor. In theory the problem gets easier as yachts become larger – the ingenious accommodation of the Mirage 37 shows how an engine can be made

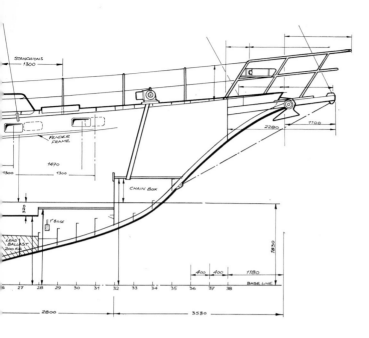

accessible. Admittedly this provides a hazard of grease and muck spreading over your upholstery, so it might be worth while to provide plastic covers for the nearest and most vulnerable parts of the layout.

A separate engine-room is preferable, but sometimes owners and designers get so carried away by the attractions of this that they insist on

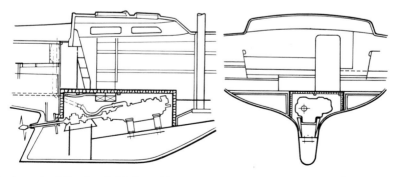

The layout of the ketch Nylanni's *engine installation where particular attention has been given to noise insulation.*

Noise reading being taken over **Nylanni**'s *engine. Even with the insulated top removed, the noise level is lower because the sound is being absorbed in the keel.*

The 53 ft ketch **Nylanni** *which has very sophisticated engine installation.*

having one in a yacht which really is not big enough for it, making the engine almost totally inaccessible. There is no need for an engine-room to have full standing headroom, as much of the work around the motor is done sitting down. The minimum requirement of any engine-room is that there is room to move around in a seaway without actually touching any part of the engine itself. With a heftier centre cockpit yacht, the engine-room is usually under the cockpit itself, and can thus be provided with a hatch and good ventilation.

In smaller craft where the engine is installed in a box, it is a source of constant wonder to me that many owners will tolerate a level of engine noise which they would not abide for one second in their cars, and that despite the fact that the sound insulation of almost any standard cruiser-racer can be greatly improved to bring noise down to a more acceptable level.

Noise
With a very light-displacement boat, a simple diesel engine will cause reverberation no matter what you do, as noise abatement is to a considerable extent related to absorption of the sound in the weight of the boat, but in the average cruiser a strongly anchored engine, using the latest forms of bearers and with sound insulation in the engine box, noise can be at low level. In the 53-ft ketch *Nylanni*, which was completed in 1971 in foam sandwich GRP, the engine noise was reduced to little more than a hum even at high speed with a system designed by Sound Attenuators Ltd. of Essex.

Nylanni was fitted with a 115 h.p. 6-cylinder Perkins horizontal diesel, and the installation of this engine is of interest in many ways as it involved detailed attention to the material of the internal ballast keel, the mounting of the engine on this keel, the vibration isolation of the engine and all auxiliary services, the acoustic enclosure of the engine and the elimination of drag from the propeller when the yacht was under sail.

The engine mountings are connected solely to the internal ballast keel which is made up from lead strips layered in the keel envelope and infilled with a fluid mix of lead shot and resin which sets solid and bonds the lead in place. Thus any residual vibrations not removed by the rubber in the shear vibration isolators under the engine are absorbed in this 8-ton mass, and vibration left is further isolated by lead ingots attached to the engine bearers, thus reducing any chance of vibration in the steel section engine mounting, while further anti-noise precaution is to be found in the twin flexible couplings between the stern tube and the drive flange, and the final touch is the fitting of flexible couplings to all water, fuel and other connections to the engine.

With this all then installed in an acoustic enclosure, the reduction of noise level when the yacht is under power is truly remarkable. Obviously such an installation has to be worked towards from the earliest design stage, and *Nylanni* being an experimental boat, few owners would want to go the level of expense involved in her installation. But when we go to the expense of acquiring yachts in order to find a little peace and quiet, then surely a little extra expenditure on keeping noise levels down is desirable. By contrast the owner of *Moonduster*, when he found that the provisions of the International Offshore Rule made it necessary to have an engine in his new yacht, insisted on fitting it in the noisiest way possible in order to ensure that it would have minimal use.

Propellers
One point touched on in the requirements list of *Nylanni*'s auxiliary installation was the need for elimination of drag from the relatively large propeller when the yacht was under sail. In her case, the problem was solved by having a Hundested 3-bladed variable pitch propeller, and I must say it continually amazes me to see the number of cruising yachts with a performance orientation which are expected to drag huge propellers around with them.

However, with a variable pitch arrangement you introduce expense and complication, anathema to some cruising types, and they insist on staying with a simple three bladed prop, but even this can be modified with benefit, for instance the big steel ketch *Verna* has a sailing clutch fitted which enables the propeller to turn freely, and in so doing provide the power for the ship's Robertson self-steering gear.

However, for most yachts a great deal of attention is necessary to make sure that the propeller selected provides the best of all possible worlds. In my own little Galion 22 we had a $1\frac{1}{2}$ h.p. Watermota Shrimp which worked through a variable pitch prop, and it was interesting to note that if we were sailing along with the blades in the drive position and shifted into the sailing position, that is with the blades running fore-and-aft, the speed would rise from 5 knots to $5\frac{1}{2}$. This indication of the unexpectedly large drag exerted by a fixed propeller is borne out by other cruising men.

One benefit of the International Offshore Rule is that it provides a real encouragement to have an auxiliary of worth-while power, as generous allowances are made both for engine weight and propeller size. In the hothouse of offshore racing, folding propellers have been refined to a remarkable degree, such that there is very little difference in real drag between, say, a folded propeller of 14 in diameter and one of 18 ins diameter. The most skilfully designed fixed 2-bladed propeller, with a pitch to the greatest limit allowed under the rule, has so much extra drag by comparison that it is not worth having.

With a large fixed 3-bladed propeller, at least ensure that a sailing

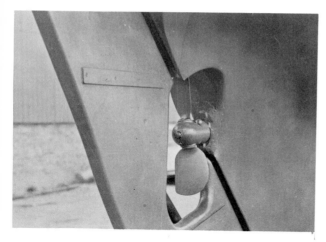

Two-bladed propeller in aperture. In this case a variable pitch prop makes the sailing resistance minimal, but handling under power is poor because the aperture is in the rudder.

clutch is fitted to make some reduction of resistance; better still is a variable pitch prop. If your propeller works through an aperture, a 2-bladed variable pitch propeller has even less resistance when in the sailing position, but there is still an acceptable reduction of drag if a 2-bladed fixed propeller is installed, provided that the shaft is marked

A worthwhile aperture installation with fixed two-bladed propeller. With most of the aperture taken from the deadwood, the almost straight steering under power is good.

inside the boat so that you can be sure the propeller is in the minimum resistance vertical position.

Shafts

An exposed propeller shaft arrangement is one of the least desirable features of fin-and-skeg yachts, as the set-up is extremely vulnerable to any obstruction in the water. Such a prop and shaft can get wound up in a mooring. When it does, there is a risk of bending the shaft and

A very large fixed three-bladed propeller protruding from the quarter of a sailing cruiser. A propeller installation intended to cause the maximum of harm to sailing performance, would be designed something rather like this. . . .

damaging the 'P' bracket, and the only advice that can be given is not to get fouled up in moorings.

There is more protection if the shaft emerges from the aft side of the fin, with the propeller fitted close to the keel, but to do this it is usually necessary to have some special drive unit installed in the keel itself, such as the hydraulic units which have appeared in recent years. It is probable that such units will become popular as time goes by, as they eliminate the skilled task of engine alignment; the drive unit comes complete with enclosed shaft, and relatively unskilled operatives can fit them into the boat, the power from the engine being carried by heavy duty hoses.

Drive

With a propeller thus installed aft of the fin, the yacht is particularly easy to control when going astern, as the prop is working in clear water, but there is a reduction in forward control, as the yacht has to gather way before the rudder begins to work, whereas with a propeller located immediately forward of the rudder, the water pushed out by the prop can be redirected by the rudder itself. This aspect of rudder location is something which is all too often overlooked by designers, because it makes a great deal of difference to control in confined waters if you can push the stern of a yacht around without any significant forward movement. Some yachts have been built where the propeller is mounted on a little skeg above, and sometimes well aft of, the rudder: from the control point of view such an arrangement is very poor. I have often seen yachts with this set-up at low speeds being blown around completely out of control in confined waters.

People with aperture installed propellers often feel that they have the best installation for such slow speed control, but often this is not the case as the aperture may be cut out of the rudder as much as the keel of the yacht; thus when the rudder is turned it does not redirect the thrust from the propeller at all; for slow speed control, the aperture should be entirely in the hull itself, with the leading edge of the rudder a straight line.

The best initial forward control under power comes from a spade rudder. This makes the most positive job of redirecting the propeller thrust, so much so that I remember once seeing someone being thrown off the foredeck of an Excalibur when a sudden course alteration was made under power. There is nothing new under the sun, for nowadays all the latest designs seem to have spade rudders of one sort or another, and a yacht such as the Contention 33 would be expected to control extremely closely even under very reduced power.

Installation

It is the 'outside connections' of an engine which require the most attention. The experimentation with *Nylanni* has shown what can be done with the engine bed, the connection to the hull itself. We have seen too how significant is the selection of the best propeller configuration; but as well, considerable thought and continuing attention have to be given to the other connections – the fuel supply, the cooling water intake, and the exhaust system. I have to confess to a primitive preference for gravity feed with the fuel, but larger cruising yachts will carry diesel fuel in tons rather than gallons, and such weights should be

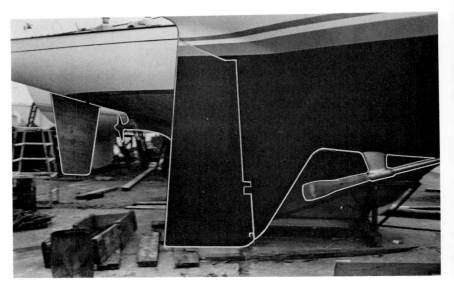

Typical modern cruiser-racer installations. The Frers 39 in the foreground has a folding propeller with an exposed shaft supported by a P-bracket, functioning via direct drive from the engine with the prop immediately forward of the rudder skeg. In the background, the older van der Stadt designed Excalibur has a spade rudder (a configuration once again favoured by the highest performance yachts) and auxiliary power is transmitted through a variable pitch two-bladed prop with the shaft supported by its own special skeg.

as low down as possible. Fuel tanks need baffles to prevent undue surge, accessible inspection hatches, and the lead system itself must be accessible for clearance of blockages, or more usually for bleeding when an air-lock has been caused by letting the tank get too low. Nowadays most engines are fitted with fuel pumps.

It is too often assumed that the cooling water alone is sufficient to keep engine temperature at acceptable levels. In some countries, regulations insist on a required amount of positive engine space ventilation through fans. As such fans are only needed when the engine is running, and thus the power is on hand to run them, their installation seems logical anyway. As for the cooling water, it is usually this dreadful stuff salt water, that we do most of our sailing on, and which will attack anything it can get in contact with, so the water cooling system is something which needs to be checked at regular intervals.

Exhaust systems are the real heroes of the auxiliary cruiser. In a normal day they will have to endure every temperature from the near freezing to the red hot; they have to withstand noxious fumes and doses of this dreadful salt water stuff; and yet many owners give not a thought to their exhaust system, that is until the poor thing collapses when the yacht is heeled, tramping along under sail. Admittedly there is a likelihood that the exhaust will have been closed off with a seacock, so the yacht will not sink immediately, but he will get his own back when the engine is started and he shares with everything aboard the fumes and muck he has had to endure alone until then. Joking apart, there are probably as many people killed by faulty exhaust systems on yachts as are drowned off them, so do ensure that your exhaust system is at least up to the engine maker's requirement. Check it frequently.

Nowadays it is possible to install instruments which will give readings of the more important aspects of an engine's functioning, though such instrumentation should not be used as an excuse for avoiding regular proper check-ups of the engine itself. Some navigators insist that such dials should not be installed as part of the chart-table arrangement, but on smaller cruising yachts it is difficult to see where else they could usefully be placed, and navigators are such intelligent chaps that it is surely not asking too much of them to monitor the engine as well.

In larger yachts you can of course have a crew-member who is an engineering specialist and his set of dials can be installed elsewhere, usually convenient to the engine, thereby ensuring the continued purity of the navigator. Increasingly the more important engine instruments now have secondary dials in the cockpit where the helmsman has his

Good engine access on the Biscay 36, with extensive use of insulation which can be removed by panels.

controls and the engine switch, and while this is a good feature it is wise to have separate instrumentation down below as well.

The location of the engine controls in the cockpit is an important feature which sometimes receives far too little attention. A minimum requirement in smaller yachts is that the engine controls should be reachable by the helmsman at least when he is sitting down at the helm, without any need for undue bending down, or having to move away from the helm itself. In larger yachts with wheel steering the controls are sometimes actually fitted to the wheel pedestal, and provided this does

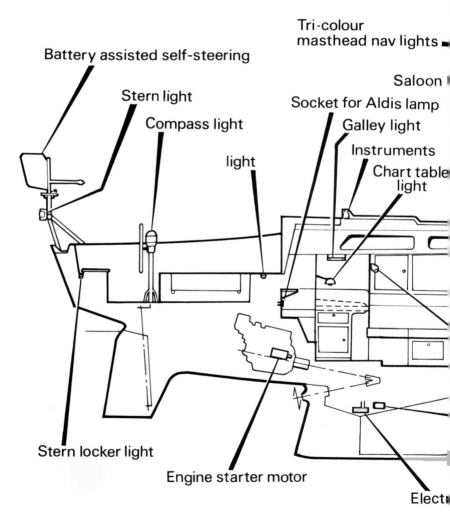

The electrical requirement of the fully-equipped cruising yacht.

not interfere with the compass or the sailing of the yacht, it makes for the most effective control when manœuvring under power in confined conditions. Nowadays an engine is much more than just an auxiliary to push us along through a calm. Like it or lump it, most of us have to keep our yachts in harbours where space is so restricted that an engine is vital to almost all initial manœuvres, and unless we want to be little better than a nuisance to everyone else we have to have a reliable easily controlled engine which is a positive asset for quick and efficient movement in port.

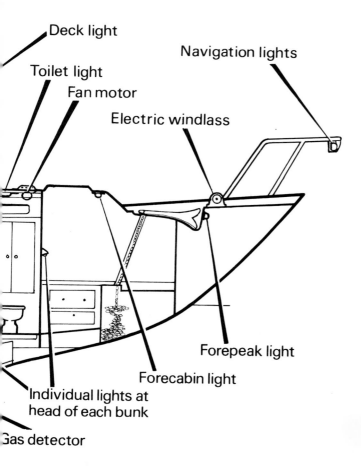

Deck light

Navigation lights

Toilet light

Fan motor

Electric windlass

Forepeak light

Forecabin light

Individual lights at head of each bunk

Gas detector

Electrics

'You can't see it, you can't put your arms round it, you can't kick it, and it doesn't like salt water. . . .' Thus speaks a cruising man of at least average technical competence describing his bafflement in trying to sort out electrical problems with his yacht. But the modern auxiliary cruising yacht is more than ever reliant on an increasingly complex system of electrics, and even if we do not have an advanced technical knowledge of the whys and wherefores of the system, at least we should know enough to have some idea of what is going wrong, and how to put the more elementary things right, as well as knowing what to specify when the yacht is being built.

At the most basic level, the smallest cruiser which may rely on an outboard engine will still have a simple electrical system to power her navigation lights and provide a couple of lights in the accommodation. It is possible if you have a real aversion to electrics in very small boats to have each light with its own separate little battery, but such fittings tend to be somewhat toy-like and I have noticed that even out-and-out sailing enthusiasts who will not have an engine of any kind tend to favour a proper electrical system with one or two batteries. These can either be charged aboard the boat with one of the windmill chargers which have come on the market in recent years, or else you take the batteries ashore to have them charged at your local garage. Carting heavy batteries around seems irksome, but you do not have to do it all the time, with normal use a re-charged battery will supply power for many weekends, and if you plan to spend a couple of nights at sea, or are doing an overnight race where a lot of power will be used up working over the chart-table, then that is the time to top up beforehand.

As the size of the boat increases, so inevitably does the complexity of the electrics, until even a fairly ordinary 35-footer can have the starting motor for the engine, a fridge, all the navigation instruments, the radio-telephone, the navigation lights, the deck lights, the compass light, the cabin lights (which will include a separate light for each bunk, special lights in the navigation area, galley lights, overhead lights in the saloon, lights in the toilet, bunk and overhead lights in the forecabin), lights in cockpit lockers and a power point for an Aldis lamp all relying on the electrical system. Astonishingly enough though many such cruisers do not even have a voltmeter to warn if the battery charge has by some accident or other become low.

Even with a voltmeter, sudden loss of power can leave you in a jam unless there are ways of getting the engine going again. With smaller craft hand-starting of the engine seems an obvious answer, and it is of interest to note that the ocean cruising Tradewind 33 was specifically fitted with a Buhk 15 h.p. diesel as this was the largest size which designer John Rock felt he could comfortably hand-start. In some racing orientated boats, special location of the engine has been carried to such a stage that it has been located immediately aft of the mast with no way whatever of hand-starting the thing – the S & S 34s were a particular case in point. A story to illustrate the problems of restoring power where it has somehow drained away was the big offshore racing ketch *Ondine* at the start of a Sydney–Hobart race. Heading out past Sydney Heads it was discovered with horror that the batteries were all completely drained, and *Ondine* was an all-electric ship – electric cookers, deep freezers, even a sauna. So they removed the big watertight hatch in the cockpit floor above the engine, wrapped a genoa sheet round and round the flywheel, and the strongest men aboard started winding away like blazes on the biggest winch; they just got enough speed in the flywheel for the engine to burst into life, and gradually life returned to normal.

As with almost every item of marine equipment, the sheer growth of the market has seen the steady refinement of seagoing batteries in recent years, one welcome development being a battery fitted with its own power reserve which retains sufficient voltage just to restart the engine even though for all other purposes the battery is flat. A pair of batteries is useful, one solely for the engine and the other for everything else, an alternator increasing the flexibility of the system. As the size of the boat increases, so room becomes available to carry one of the many portable generators which have appeared in recent years. Some owners object to these as a number of them are run on petrol; having gone to the trouble of installing a diesel engine for safety reasons, the precaution is rather defeated by having a petrol driven generator which can fall about. If that is a prime concern then paraffin-driven generators are available. With all portable generators be warned that exhaust fumes can be dangerous, for if allowed into the boat they sink to the bilges and during a cruise can build up to dangerous levels, poisoning people, or causing an explosion risk.

Of course, once you reach the size of yacht which has an engine-room, then the installation of a separate diesel-driven generator is well worth considering; apart from functional and safety problems, a great deal more can be done with it for noise abatement. A portable generator rattling away on the very end of a yacht's counter, or even ashore on the marina pontoon, may be very safe, but it is anti-social.

One of the problems with the high standard of finish being obtained with today's series produced cruising yachts is that much electrical wiring is hidden behind interior furniture which may make for a neat appearance but poses problems in the event of breakage. Get hold of a wiring diagram from the builders, and also check all the vulnerable places in the wiring, such as where it comes through the deck for navigation lights, particularly the electrical wiring going into the mast. One belt and braces merchant in building a new boat decided that for safety he would duplicate his wiring system, with two complete installations, one on each side of the boat. Sounds sensible, but unfortunately it was found that when he tried to take radio bearings his double wiring circuit had created an enclosed electrical field which made the RDF useless until the circuit was all disconnected.

Another cause of radio interference is the use of fluorescent strip lights, which usually have to be switched off if anyone is trying to take radio bearings or get a weather forecast, indeed trying to use the radio at all.

The vital central feature of a worth-while electrical system is a clearly-marked switchboard-cum-fuse-box – in recent years a number of attractive examples have come on the market. Obviously to get the best value from such things, they have to be installed in a place both accessible and easily seen, and once again, in small and medium size yachts at any rate, the chart table area seems the obvious choice.

The external lights we cover in Chaper 9 in the safety section. However, one final thing to remember is that however well you may maintain your electrical system, a couple of really good torches kept securely in *known* positions are an absolute necessity; regrettably it is usually the yachts which never need such things which have them, while yachts with erratic electrics often have equally erratic torches. Knowing, too, of the constant battle to keep electrics functioning in face of the hostility of salt water and damp generally, many cruising men see to it that they still have a couple of the little gimballed oil lamps which may seem more appropriate in an antique shop, but can be a friendly source of light when electricity fails.

8 Instrumentation and equipment

One sure-fire topic for discussion among cruising people is the relative importance and usefulness of the many different instruments which are available to assist in a yacht's sailing, pilotage and navigation. There is general acceptance of the main compass as being first priority. After the compass there are ten or so instruments which you can have, if you can afford them; and if you cannot, then obviously a ranking of comparative usefulness is important if the available money is to be used in the most effective possible way.

My own preference for the coastal-short sea passage and continental sailing which is the main activity of cruising folk everywhere would be:

1. Compass
2. Echo Sounder
3. RDF set with built-in bearing compass and including ordinary radio receiver
4. Barograph or barometer
5. Distance run indicator
6. VHF radiotelephone
7. Radar
8. Apparent wind indicator
9. Wind speed indicator
10. Speedometer
11. Sextant

This is essentially a list for cruising; if you want to do a spot of racing, obviously the extra performance instruments which occur towards the end of the list would move up in rank, and radar would be discarded as it is disallowed under most offshore racing rules, and in any case would cause unacceptable extra windage. Even with these provisos, understandably many people will disagree with this order of things, so perhaps a brief discussion is in order.

The first two will probably be conceded, but ranking the radio and RDF set ahead of the distance run indicator might be disputed. However, it must be remembered that a yacht's good basic RDF set, from something like the little Seafix by Electronic Laboratories at one end of the scale to the Brooks & Gatehouse Homer Heron at the other, fulfils multiple functions. To begin with it provides us with radio bearings, whether direct from nearby stations or over longer distances on the Consol system. But the radio's usefulness does not stop there, we can also use it for weather forecasts. A good knowledge of the general weather pattern which is evolving is invaluable. A further use for the multi-purpose set is that its compass installation can be used as an ordinary hand-bearing compass when something on which a bearing can be taken is visible. Using it thus is something of an economy measure, but some of us find the little pocket compasses less than perfect. Usually this is because of a sight defect, which is compounded by the magnetic variations caused if spectacles are worn, but whatever causes it, we need as big a hand-bearing compass as we can get, and if we cannot afford a proper hand-bearing compass, then the compasses which are part of the RDF set provide the best substitute.

Barometer and barograph

The barometer and barograph are placed fourth in importance because the workings of the weather should be of prime interest to any cruising skipper, not just what it is like at the moment, but what it has been, and what it is likely to become. In smaller yachts, certainly yachts of less than 25 ft, it would be difficult to get a barograph to function satisfactorily, and so a barometer will have to do, though it is of little use unless regular readings are taken as part of the proper keeping of the log. As the size and displacement of the yacht increases, it should be possible to install a really worth-while barograph. They used to be thought of as expensive items, but they now seem reasonably priced when compared to some of today's more expensive equipment. The best chance of successful functioning lies in placing them in the position of least motion, which is roughly a third of the waterline length forward from its aftermost point. However, even in larger yachts an ordinary barometer is preferable every time to a non-functioning barograph, so if you find that the barograph has to be located somewhere unsatisfactory, install a barometer instead, and it usually comes in a useful double set with a ship's clock.

As the old-fashioned log spinning merrily on the taffrail used to be the very symbol of cruising, it may seem peculiar to have our distance run indicator only half way up the list of priorities, but it seems to be the case that the development of other navigational aids has steadily eroded its significance. As it is, it merely gives the distance moved through the water, often with questionable amount of accuracy, and that water may be drifting through wind action, or moving with tidal streams, so the figure on the log is only one component of an often complex equation. As a cruise progresses it is remarkable how accurately the helmsman can gauge the speed being made, and if each watch enters the estimated distance covered in every hour in the logbook, a surprisingly good idea of the distance covered emerges. Be that as it may, although I did much of my early cruising without a log – from time to time we threw wood chips over the bow and timed them to the stern – I do not think I would fancy going to sea these days without a proper distance run indicator.

Radio-telephones

One of the more unexpected developments from the economic recession of the mid-1970s was the growth in popularity of electronic yacht equipment which previously had been thought of as being just luxury gear. This was because people who normally would have traded up into a larger yacht made do with the one they had, and contented themselves instead with adding some extra items of equipment which they might not otherwise have done. The growth in such specialist items was happening in any case, but in that particular period it easily out-stripped everything else in a marine industry which was otherwise in a period of some shrinkage. The most popular item in this growth was in radio-telephones, particularly in the small VHF transceivers specially developed for yachts, the increase in their usage being nothing short of phenomenal.

Not everyone is wholly enthusiastic about this proliferation. That great cruising man Eric Hiscock, discussing various aspects of the world sailing scene after he had reached England in 1975 to conclude his third voyage round the world, weighed into radio-telephones with gusto. We had been discussing his new 8-track stereo system which a friend had installed for him during a stop in the voyage. Like him, my own knowledge of music is limited, but I do know what I like, and feel that in the right circumstances appropriate music can add immeasurably to the pleasure of a sail. Indeed, I even went so far as to remark that given the choice I would always have a stereo system before a radio-telephone, but did not get a chance to add that if at all possible, particularly in certain areas where a radio-telephone is almost essential for civilized cruising, I would very much like to have both.

There was no opportunity to make this point as the doughty skipper of the *Wanderer IV* was holding forth on top of his form. 'In the unlikely event of my being asked to advise on legislation', he said, 'the first thing I would do would be to ban all yachtsmen from having radio-telephones.' It seemed that in various parts of the world where radio-telephones are already popular, particularly on the West Coast of America, with his receiver he had heard several examples of gross abuse of the system. One notable case had been an auxiliary yacht with a broken-down engine which had demanded in light winds that the Coast Guard come out and tow them in. As an advocate of 'cruising without fuss', this had disgusted Hiscock – 'I fully expect next time I'm there to hear them calling up the Coast Guard to come out and clear a blocked toilet. . . .'

Certainly when you hear people making an absolute nuisance of themselves with the RT, you begin to wonder about the value of the system, but it is probable that anyone who makes trouble in this way would probably be a damned nuisance in other ways, were he deprived of radio. Far from being an unwelcome intrusion of the outside world, the radio-telephone can in fact minimize your contact with the workaday world, particularly if your cruising is done in the more crowded waters of the world. This is because the harbours and marinas in such places are now geared to contact through radio. So much of the ship's business which can take up so much time can be done through it beforehand. This is one everyday immediate benefit of radio-telephones, and the more complex the shoreside infrastructure on the coast you are cruising, the greater benefit you will derive from it. Whether or not you use it as well for idle chatter with friends is your own affair, many people get fun out of operating gadgets and good luck to them. In a more serious vein, in the event of the yacht getting into difficulties, a radio-telephone which you can use with the same unconscious effort as the phone at home may make all the difference.

The usefulness of a VHF is in direct ratio to the crowded nature of the waters you are sailing, as it works on line-of-sight reception, though varying somewhat with the weather conditions prevailing.

Radar
It may be because man is essentially a visual animal, but whatever the reason, I have to confess that I find a properly functioning radar set to be something which has an ethereal beauty of its own, apart from its great usefulness in pilotage. This usefulness depends to a considerable extent on where you do most of your cruising; in places like the foggy coast of Maine, or on the west of Scotland where a 'soft' day makes visibility very poor, radar will make a real contribution to peace of mind; but it has complexity – you may come to rely on it too much. If it breaks down, it will take an expert to fix it and meanwhile you have to readjust to doing without.

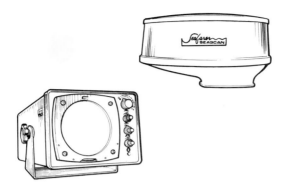

The 'Seascan' small craft radar has 16-mile range and is fitted with an enclosed scanner to minimize possible damage. Dimensions of radome: $34\frac{3}{4}$ in × 20 in; transceiving unit: $13\frac{3}{4}$ in × $7\frac{1}{2}$ in.

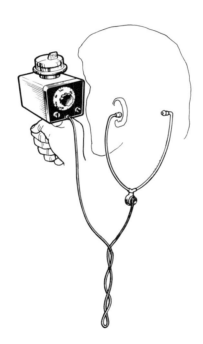

The Seafix hand-held RDF is a useful instrument for smaller cruisers, and is often carried in larger craft as a reserve against the possible failure of the main RDF. The great advantage with it in smaller craft is that the operator has the opportunity to place himself in the best possible position to withstand the inconvenience of the boat's motion.

The majority of sailing cruisers will not carry such an extensive range of instrumentation, but it is worth noting that where instruments are carried they should be located as effectively as possible near the helmsman's line of sight to the stemhead.

Wind instrumentation

It may seem curious that in a sailing cruiser the instruments for the direction and speed of the wind are reckoned of such little importance, but I find that when the wind speed is changing the last thing I look at is the anemometer, if such a thing happens to be fitted.

An electronic wind-direction indicator is probably more useful in the actual sailing of the yacht, as relatively inexperienced helmsmen often find it easier to steer by a dial rather than watching the set of the sails, and it may help to prevent unexpected gybes. It is still necessary to look at the sea ahead and to weather for the wind patterns coming in and other things which instruments cannot tell you about.

Sextant

If you happen to have a log which only tells you the distance run, then a speedometer as such is way down the list of priorities. Traditional sailors may find it lamentable that in the ranking a sextant has such minor significance, but in many boats where one is carried with great reverence, it often never gets out of its box. In coastal and continental cruising, celestial navigation is nowadays seldom used, and indeed a sextant's best use in such circumstances may be to take the vertical angle of some shore features in order to calculate distance off.

Inevitably, many cruising people will regret the preponderance of gadgets on today's yachts, and occasionally you will come across someone who quite deliberately equips his yacht with no more gear than was available at the turn of the century. 'What was good enough for McMullen and Worth, is good enough for me,' he will say. Perhaps, but really such an approach is even more artificial, as both McMullen and Worth set out to achieve a standard comparable and possibly better than that of professional seamen, using the best of equipment then available. Thus Claud Worth sailed at times with two logs streaming, as he wished to compare their performance, and in his day he was something of an inveterate gadgeteer. Were he alive today, I imagine that his yacht would be covered with the best of today's equipment. The difference from him and other cruising men being that he would know just how everything worked.

Even so, a line has to be drawn somewhere. Recently I was sailing with a man whose fine yacht has all sorts of gear, radio-telephones, radar, just about everything, and I asked him if he expected to progress further and install one of the navigation systems, such as Loran or Decca. 'Oh no, I don't think so,' said he, 'after all, that would take the fun out of it.'

Compass location

The location of each instrument and the layout of all the equipment in its most usable form will depend to a large extent on the type of gear selected within each category. Starting with the compass, for instance, the choice will depend on the size of the boat and the kind of steering gear fitted. With wheel steering, a binnacle compass fitted on top of the wheel pedestal makes the best possible use of this method of steering.

The best location for the steering compass is one which requires only a minimum of distraction from the helmsman's prime task of keeping an eye on the sea ahead of the yacht. Thus a compass which is as nearly as possible in the line of sight towards the stemhead seems to be the most nearly ideal, but it is one which in many yachts the layout of instrumentation makes impossible. Even the binnacle compass with wheel steering, though it looks undeniably nautical, will involve the standing helmsman in a sight alteration of about 45°, admittedly less when sitting down, but in either case it is not only uncomfortable, but can be dangerous if you get the kind of helmsman who insists on sailing with his eyes glued to the compass.

Thus the bulkhead mounted compasses which have become popular in recent years offer the advantageous alternative of being sited on the aft bulkhead of the coachroof, and provided that no one is persistently sitting in front of them, can help the helmsman both to keep his course and keeping a weather eye on the sea ahead. Aboard *Barbican* Bernard Hayman has, in a clever arrangement, located a steering compass on each side of the boom gallows, thus the helmsman is not only looking ahead, but is even casting an eye aloft which forces him to take cognizance of the set of the sails.

For straightforward steering purposes, the easiest compass to read is of the grid type, and aboard the Hustler 35 *Setanta* we had a Neco repeater. With this, the main compass was in a lead-lined box down below, clear of anything which might cause deviation, and the steering was done from the repeater dial which fitted neatly in as part of the general instrument console at the forward end of the companionway. For a yacht of this size, this was the best arrangement for the instrumentation, as in theory nobody was allowed to linger in the hatchway at any time, and the instruments were just nicely distant from the helmsman – near enough for him to read comfortably, particularly the compass where all he has to do is keep a line parallel between two others, placed such that he has to keep a lookout ahead, and yet not so close that they are totally distracting. All too often as a yacht gets bigger the helmsman finds himself in his own little area with his own separate instrument panel, cunningly placed, for instance, in a special recess down the side of the cockpit. It sounds good in theory, but all too often

Not only is it essential to have navigational instrumentation which does the job for which it is designed, but as well a carefully planned layout around the chart-table greatly increases its value for the navigator.

it means that he is looking down almost vertically in order to get some information from his instruments.

Just because a compass has been carefully installed, and then the ship has been swung in order to check any deviation, does not allow us to ignore its welfare thereafter. Compasses are liable to suffer to some extent from magnetic objects within their field, and attention has to be maintained at all times to ensure that absent-minded crew-members do not go wrecking your careful navigation with beer cans and suchlike.

Instrumentation to a greater or lesser degree leads a sort of double life, as its information has both to get to the watch on deck and to the navigator in his den. Thus in planning the yacht's instrumentation a compromise has to be made between the needs of the cockpit crew and the navigator. With the more expensive examples of most instruments, this presents little difficulty, as the main unit can be placed at the chart-table while one or more repeater dials can be out on deck.

Echo sounder

The echo sounder can be one of the more complex variety, with a separate cockpit repeater, or it could be a cheaper model where everything is contained in one unit. In the latter case, in smaller yachts the unit can be located on the inboard end of the chart-table semi-bulkhead, and can thus be easily read both by the navigator at his chart-table and the cockpit crew looking through the main hatch. An alternative method is to have the echo sounder mounted on a hinged board immediately inside the cabin, which can swing round either to face into the accommodation or outwards towards the cockpit. Some owners with a particularly tidy frame of mind fit a porthole to the aft bulkhead, so enabling the echo sounder to be read from the cockpit and then swung round for cabin reading.

The installation of the unit and its possible extra dials is only part of fitting the echo sounder. Particular care has to be given to the location of the transducer. With more sophisticated instruments, a transducer is fitted either side of the yacht, at what could be called an 'average' angle of heel from the vertical, thus providing a true reading of the depth when the yacht is sailing along heeled. With just one transducer, the location is vertical, and allowance has to be made for real depth when an artificially high reading is being obtained as a result of heel. Anyone interested in sailing performance will of course go to some trouble to ensure that the transducer mounting causes a minimum of drag, while anyone interested in using the echo sounder not only as an aid to navigation but also as an aid to pilotage with the exploration of shallow creeks and harbours will require to know the exact reading which occurs when the yacht is just on the point of grounding. This may seem such a basic requirement as scarcely to require mentioning, but it is astonishing how often arguments occur at crucial moments about just how much depth there is between the transducer and the bottom of the keel. Such information should be affixed to the echo sounder. Some cruising men are so enthusastic about an echo sounder as a navigational aid that they equip themselves with hydrographic echo sounders to provide them with recorded depth and seabed information; it can be useful, but such equipment usually costs at least five times as much as a straightforward echo sounder.

As the radio direction finder is the basis of navigation (as opposed to pilotage) in many small cruisers, it must be installed in such a way that it is easy to reach and comfortable to use – in other words, the navigator should be able to chock himself into his seat, held in by a harness if need be, when he is using minimal equipment such as the Seafix. More complex installations where adjustments are made to a set fixed on a bulkhead should be easily accessible, and not stuck away in some corner where the operator has to reach over an awkward locker or some other obstruction. With either instrument the navigator has to be able to write down his readings immediately.

Distance run indicators

Distance run indicators are available these days in an almost bewildering variety of types; it is still possible to obtain a trailed log, where the recording unit is mounted on the yacht's taffrail and is driven by a spinner trailed on a line astern. A modern development of this is the popular 'Sumlog', made in Germany, where a propeller-type impeller attached under the hull turns a flexible metal cable in a tube which in turn rotates the mechanism within a dial. The installation instructions for this ask that the cable be kept to as large curves as possible in order to minimize friction; installing one in my Galion 22, I went to enormous trouble to have the cable in just one fair curve, with the dial angled into the side of the cockpit; seemingly I had overdone it, for even with the maximum adjustment our Sumlog always over-read by 12 per cent and since than I have seen other installations where a number of curves in different directions have been accommodated, and yet satisfactory readings are obtained, so presumably the manufacturers allow for considerable friction. But once we had measured the level of over-reading, the instrument was otherwise remarkably accurate, and the Sumlog has a deserved reputation as one of the better cheaper distance run and speed indicators on the market.

Moving into the more expensive equipment, electrics come into use, the best known types being based on impeller units working from a small propeller, while a recent new development has been the use of a little paddle wheel where just one blade at a time protrudes below the hull. Particularly with propeller units, development has been carried to an advanced level, and a high degree of reliability has been obtained. Of course, merely to have the best equipment available is not enough – the installation of the impeller unit requires careful thought, and the best position seems to be immediately forward of the keel, where the impeller is functioning in clear water, and yet is far enough below the waterline to remain under water even when the yacht is heeled. It is possible to go to the extent of having an impeller on each side in somewhat similar style to the more sophisticated echo sounder installations, but that inevitably involves further clutter in the bilges forward. Fortunately nowadays most designers incorporate a 'skin fittings compartment' somewhere immediately forward of the mast, as any impeller, particularly the propeller type, is liable to be fouled by weed and must be easily withdrawn into the hull for clearing, but particularly in small cruisers a line has to be drawn somewhere as to how much paraphernalia can be stuck onto the hull. An enthusiastic cruising friend of mine, determined to get accurate distance run readings, insisted that his 26-footer be fitted with impellers either side immediately forward of the fin keel; the builders fitted one of these immediately aft of the toilet outlet, and as each cruise progressed with the already healthy crew becoming even healthier, it was noted that for considerable periods each day the impeller on the toilet side came to a stop; at such times there was considerable reluctance on everyone's part to withdraw the impeller and find out what was slowing it up.

Such problems may be solved by the introduction of Doppler and magnetic logs, which involve only the most minimal protuberance from the hull. With the Sonar Doppler log, a transducer mounted in the hull skin projects a narrow beam of ultrasonic waves forward, and by measuring the difference in frequency in the amount of sound beam returned to the source, an estimate of speed is obtained. At the time of writing this equipment had only been available for three years, a relatively short time in terms of marine equipment development, and it has been found, for instance, that location of the transducer to within very close limits is particularly critical for accurate readings, so though the Doppler log certainly solves the fouling problem, a number of other factors must be considered in order for it to be of use in relatively non-technical hands.

Perhaps the best solution if you feel a hull unit without moving parts is needed would be one of the small craft developments of the electromagnetic logs which have been used by ships for some years now, where a magnetic field is projected into the water, and the water movement produces a small potential difference which gives a voltage reading between two electrodes. In ships the sensor probe stands out about a foot from the hull, but it has been found that in small craft an almost flush sensor can produce satisfactory results. However, the success of the method depends on consistency of water movement past the sensor, and if this is affected by even a slight growth of slime on the yacht's bottom, the readings begin to become a little peculiar; for the racing brethren, this is yet another inducement to have their boat's bottom sparkling clean, while the minimal resistance of the electromagnetic log is an added attraction in itself, but for cruising folk who may be making long voyages this fouling problem with its increasingly inaccurate readings may militate in favour of the older impeller-type units where even if the unit gets fouled, at least it can be pulled into the hull for clearing.

Radio-telephone siting

The latest VHF sets are compact units and they lend themselves particularly well to installation under the side-deck beside the navigator's seat. It is a great improvement if the radio-telephone is installed where the operator is comfortably seated with a convenient writing surface in front of him, and in the vast majority of yachts only the chart-table fulfils this requirement. It is a great help to everyone involved in radio if, when complex messages are involved, you write down beforehand what you are trying to say, and furthermore are easily able to write down the messages you are receiving.

Radar location

Location of the radar set often poses problems as many of the units tend to be rather bulky, while some are notable for their sharp corners, something almost unforgivable in equipment designed for small craft where people can be thrown about. One possible location is under the deckhead above the chart table, but if it is facing fore-and-aft the navigator has to be able to stand up to see the screen. If it is placed athwartships he has to get out of his seat altogether to read the thing, but with radar the navigator is only one of possibly two or three people who may be operating the equipment, so possibly this is the best solution. Most units have handholes attached to enable one to continue reading in rough weather, but an extra handhold or two attached to the yacht rather than the set might be a good idea.

The biggest problem with radar is the location of the scanner; a height of somewhere between 12 and 15 feet above sea level seems about optimum for yachts of up to about 70 ft. Below that your horizon is greatly reduced, while above it means there is rather a lot of weight and windage flailing around, while any unnecessary lengthening of the cables between the scanner and the screen should be avoided. Just where to put it is often the problem, and if you are keen on radar it may be worth having a ketch rig just for this purpose alone; handy old things, mizzen masts, even if the mizzen is not much use as a sail. Theoretically in

While wheel steering may save cockpit space, in the first instance the cockpit layout should be designed to accommodate as large a wheel as possible. Here a 47-footer is roaring along on a close reach, bound past Land's End and on for France.

single-masted yachts it should be possible to mount the scanner on the foreside of the mast, protecting it from the assault of genoas and lines with a protective cage, but understandably owners are reluctant to do this, and resort to having the scanner on top of the coachroof. Apart from greatly reducing the effective range, this may be dangerous for crew-members, as it is believed the pulse emitted by the scanner is harmful, so in desperation owners of single stickers have been known to build oil-rig-like structures on their after decks to carry the scanner. So if you want radar, perhaps you should have a ketch.

Steering gear

Tiller steering used to be not uncommon in cruisers as large as 40 ft LOA or even more, and of course back in the Golden Nineties such famous giants as the mighty cutter *Satanita* were steered with a tiller (admittedly some 17 ft long) but the trend has always been towards having wheel steering in ever-smaller craft, and these days the dividing line is probably around the 35 ft mark, with many cases of wheel steering in yachts even smaller.

While tiller steering has a certain attractive simplicity, there is no doubt that in anything over 35 ft it can make for brutally hard work for the helmsman, and wheel steering has the further advantage of taking up much less room in the cockpit, while also making the cockpit a somewhat less dangerous place for its occupants. As well, there is a much greater choice of helmsman's position if a wheel is fitted – assuming that the wheel is fitted on the aft side of a pedestal, you can sit or stand behind it, you can also at least sit on either side and if there is room stand on either side, and if need be you can even steer while standing in front of the pedestal, whereas with a tiller you are necessarily restricted to sitting or standing on either side, facing athwartships if both hands happen to be needed, and any other position involves some gymnastics.

Any advantage allowed for wheel steering, however, is made on the assumption that some thought has been given to the wheel position and the ergonomic requirements of the helmsman operating it. Within the limits of the space available, the wheel should be as large as possible (if there happens to be room I do not think it is possible to have it too large) and the wheel should be smooth rimmed, without any projecting spokes. Fancy nautical-looking wheels with projecting spokes belong on the walls of pseudo-maritime bars.

Generally wheels without projecting spokes have a plain rim of varnished wood, or else they are in plastic-covered alloy, but it can be a pleasant indulgence to cover the rim in pigskin or some such exotic material to give extra grip. Having fitted as big a wheel as possible, then make sure that the helmsman has a choice of comfortable positions; a surprisingly large number of boats have the main helmsman's seat too near the wheel, which makes it impossible to stand at the helm in any comfort. It is also a good idea to have fore-and-aft wooden footgrips to hold him in place when standing with the boat heeling, perhaps the best solution of all is to have a deeply-dished cockpit sole in the helmsman's area.

People who have been brought up with tiller steering are usually pleasantly surprised by the ease with which one can steer a large yacht if a really worth-while big-wheel steering gear has been fitted. Going off on a wheel steering craft, the first thing we usually do is to check out the emergency tiller arrangements, and another beneficial offshoot of the International Offshore Rule is that such equipment is mandatory on offshore racers and as a result has become virtually standard on most sailing cruisers. Also with rudders and helmsmen being moved as far aft as possible these days, wheel steering has been greatly improved by being based on more direct gearing, doing away with the troublesome cables of times past which were inevitable when the wheel position was a long way from the rudder head.

One of the real design improvements of modern boats is the tendency for rudder posts to be more nearly vertical, and this has improved tiller steering as well. I remember once doing some sailing on a venerable gaff cutter which had a tiller at least 6 ft long, and yet she hung on her helm like a ton of bricks despite the theoretical leverage which this mighty stick provided. The reason was clear when we dried her out one day – her rudder post was very raked, it must have been at least at an angle of 45°, and so our effective tiller length was really only about a couple of feet, while the steeply angled rudder was not much use either. Nowadays the length of tiller you see in a yacht with vertical rudder stock is the *real* length, and consequently it is often possible to make do with a considerably shorter tiller than would have been the case with similarly-sized boats of older type. As with the wheel, the longer the tiller the more comfortable the steering, and one should always have as long a stick as is consistent with keeping the cockpit habitable by other occupants.

Self-steering
Talk of self-steering immediately brings to mind the plethora of vane-steering gears which has appeared in recent years; vane-operated self-steering started with model yachts light years ago, it had its first seagoing test with Marin Marie's single-handed motor-cruiser crossing of the Atlantic in 1936 with *Arielle*, and then there was a further burst of new development in the 1950s – Ian Major's *Buttercup* crossed the Atlantic in 1955 to the West Indies using vane self-steering. In the same year the innovative yachtsman and designer Mike Henderson raced and cruised successfully offshore with his little JOG sloop *Mick the Miller* steered by an attractively simple vane system known as Harriet.

The single-handed transatlantic race gave extra impetus to the development of gears which could steer a yacht at a constant angle to the apparent wind. Development has been such that equipment which will steer the yacht is now available from a number of manufacturers. Particularly to windward it is better than most helmsmen, and is an invaluable aid when cruising as it is the equivalent of having at least one and possibly two extra people aboard. One objection to the use of this gear is the safety factor, critics arguing that no lookout is kept when there is no one on the helm, but in fact on ships large and small experience indicates that a helmsman is a remarkably poor lookout and in a fully crewed ship he is not expected to be one. In a yacht, he will be so busy with the mechanics of steering, with keeping an eye on instruments, on watching the set of the sails, with looking out for awkward seas coming from the windward side, and as often as not with just keeping as comfortable as possible, that very little effort is given to keeping an all round lookout. Thus, where the yacht is being well steered by a vane gear a normally well-sheltered and lightly worked crew-member standing a watch will actually keep a far better lookout than if he were clinging to the helm.

Just which type you select is dependent on the size of your yacht and her steering arrangements – with a transom-hung rudder, trim-tab equipment can be fitted, such as the Hasler with the tab fitted to the aft

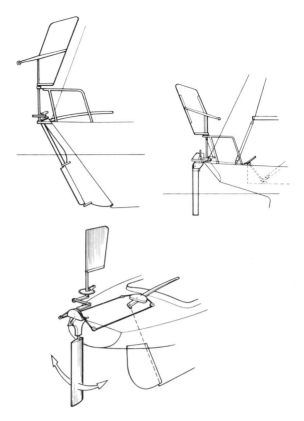

Vane-operated self-steering gears. Although somewhat unsightly, they nevertheless represent a real boon for cruising convenience.

end of the rudder blade itself, or the Quartermaster with the tab hung separately.

Where the rudder is inboard, the usual solution is a pendulum-servo gear where the alteration of the apparent-wind angle on the vane turns the horizontally-hinged servo blade in the water, thus generating the power to alter the main rudder angle by means of lines to a quadrant on the main tiller. It sounds complex but is very simple in practice, and all commercially manufactured vane steering gears have now been developed to the stage that they can be put in use or – perhaps more important – taken out of use for the manual helming to start within seconds.

Of course, it should not be expected that a newly-installed vane steering gear will work perfectly first time round. It is true that the better a boat sails and balances in the first place, the more ready is she to lend herself to vane steering, but all yachts are individuals and it is reasonable to expect a certain amount of initial experimentation, even if we have now got to the stage that in most cases it will not be necessary.

Vane steering really comes into its own with windward work, as it will make the best possible job of getting to windward, though in such circumstances it is up to the navigator to be on his toes to calculate just where such efficient helming has got the boat to. Once sheets are eased, the vane steering continues to steer a course at a pre-determined angle to the apparent wind, and here naturally the human helmsman with his eyes glued to the steering compass will make a better job of holding to the navigator's desired course, because even at sea, away from the influence of the land, a wind constant in direction is more usual, and an alteration of even as little as ten degrees will soon result in a marked deviation from the proper course.

With larger yachts where there is a regular throughput of a large amount of electrical power in working much of the equipment, auto-pilots can be a realistic proposition, and the latest ones use relatively little power, but for the purely sailing man such equipment has the disadvantage of merely steering a course, instead of sailing in relation to the wind. In this case a compromise solution has been arrived at with electrically powered vane gears; only a tiny vane is needed to show the apparent wind direction, the electrics provide the power to alter the helm, and the unsightly clutter of the wind-operated vane gear is avoided on the afterdeck.

Dinghies and all that

One of the hallmarks of a real seagoing cruising yacht is that when she does happen to reach land, her crew have means of getting ashore without having to come alongside a quay or go into a marina berth. Just as convenient and worth-while ground tackle gives you an independence of choice in selecting anchorages, so you have further encouragement to visit desirable and out-of-the-way places if you know that when you get there you can go ashore independently of shore facilities and services.

There has now been almost universal acceptance of the use of inflatables as yachts' tenders. Admittedly the safey factor of an inflatable is much greater than the traditional dinghy's, for even if filled with water, provided it is not punctured, it will still keep people afloat, a useful factor when it is remembered that in the old days it was reckoned the most dangerous bit of water that you crossed on a cruise was the half mile in the dinghy between the yacht and the shore. Despite these advantages in extreme situations, the inflatable loses out in just plain all-round usefulness, as generally it does not row well and even when powered with an outboard as so many are, it tends to be wet and uncomfortable.

In theory the small space in which a deflated inflatable tender can be stowed will make it a real asset aboard a sailing cruiser, but in practice during port-hopping crews find daily pumping and deflating irksome, and the dinghy tends to be stowed, often somewhat untidily, on deck.

The disadvantage of an outboardless inflatable was forcefully illustrated for some friends of mine cruising the west coast of Scotland during breezy weather; having anchored in a sheltered loch off an inviting village, the gusts sweeping down from the hills were such that there was no way they were going to be able to row ashore direct to the fleshpots. Nothing daunted, they got into the tender and were blown ashore on the lee side of the loch; they then set off to walk round to the village, marching along the foreshore carrying their dinghy with them, and finally came to the the pub; after some time spent absorbing the local culture, they then continued their dinghy-carrying march on round the shore until they were directly to weather of the yacht, upon which they all got into the dinghy and were blown back on board their cruiser. . . .

Of course, if you do go to the trouble of having a rigid rowable dinghy of sound hull shape, it must also have sufficient buoyancy to support the complement if swamped. But it has to be admitted that for the majority of yachts, certainly any under 30 ft and many under 40 ft, such a dinghy just takes up too much room on deck, and in this case an inflatable stowed away is preferable every time to towing a dinghy astern, even if some inflatables are so much trouble to pack or unpack, and inflate or deflate, that they lie undisturbed in hidden lockers from one season to the next, defeating their purpose entirely.

For larger yachts, the newer type of inflatable with rigid bottom section provides a handy, fast and safe runabout, but from the stowage

Outboard powered inflatable in davits. For port-hopping in sheltered water this is an ideal arrangement, but in heavy weather there is a risk of damage.

point of view generally seems to have little advantage over the orthodox rigid boat. In recent years stern davits have increased in popularity as a means of coping with the stowage problems of such types, and for short hops in sheltered water these davits are a great convenience if the yacht has a stern configuration suited to them, but it must be remembered that they are essentially a smooth water facility. Undoubtedly you could make long passages with a dinghy stowed in them, many people have, but in really heavy weather a dinghy stowed in this manner is positively dangerous for the safety of the yacht as a whole, and so if open sea passages are contemplated alternative means of securely fastening the dinghy inboard on the yacht's deck must be devised.

A cruising man's attitude to his tender reveals more than almost anything else the kind of cruising he prefers. For almost all the most interesting places one can cruise to, a useful yacht's tender is essential. Admittedly when cruising with small children aboard, lying in a marina berth can be a great convenience, and even with a tough and fully experienced crew it makes a pleasant change to come in alongside a quay in the heart of some fascinating port. But the real essence of cruising often is to be found in visiting remote anchorages where there may not be another soul around, let alone a quay to come alongside or a boatman to take you ashore. In such places a reliable and convenient tender adds immense pleasure.

9 Safety and emergencies

One of the most interesting things about a yacht is that virtually everything about her can contribute to her safety. There are features such as a sound hull with efficient skin fittings, based on a properly engineered construction topped out with a deck and cockpit structure which can withstand the strains of heavy weather sailing. But there are less obvious things: if properly designed, the attractive interior furniture should further contribute to the hull's strength, and perhaps most important of all, a comfortable layout makes for livability and workability down below which keeps vital crew morale at a high level. Some would-be rugged cruising types may scorn the luxurious toilet and wash-rooms which are a feature of the best of today's standard cruising yacht. If making a difficult landfall in poor visibility after a long and hard passage, I find by contrast there is nothing more refreshing, more conducive to thinking things out just that little bit more clearly, than having a wash in as much comfort as a hard-sailing yacht can provide. Indeed my daily progress through the yacht heading 'wash-roomwards' with a kettle of hot water in almost all weathers has been a matter of mirth for many crews.

Safety is not a matter of just taking the right course of action in an emergency, it is a matter of continuous attention to virtually every aspect of the yacht, and all the hazards which she has to withstand vary from the continuous to the merely occasional. Yet the merely occasional hazards, because they tend to be dramatic, get all the attention.

The most continuous problem is just keeping the boat afloat even when she is not in use. Even if your yacht is built in one piece of GRP, with encapsulated keel, she is full of holes, cluttered with skin fittings for inlets, outlets and instruments. Once when I built a yacht it was found that we put no less than thirteen holes in the hull for such things, and one of the wags on the job suggested that any future yacht be built with pegboard, and we would just fill in the holes we did not need. Keep an eye on those skin fittings, and if you are building a new yacht, see if you can get the number of them cut down a little. Seacocks should be the cone type, forming a seaworthy unit right on the hull skin, but very rarely are these fitted, and the usual types some inches in from the hull are prone to all sorts of damage.

It may well be that an old fitting can manage for years, but one brisk sail and the whole lot could disintegrate, as the engine exhaust did on one old boat I was sailing. It is not funny, starting to sink through the engine exhaust in the small hours. Nowadays too, all sorts of fancy and hard-wearing hosepipe is available for lines and tubes. It is surprisingly tough, but do check that the connections are up to the job – a friend of mine sailing along in his newly-acquired 50 ft ketch suddenly discovered her sinking quietly under him – a bagged sail thrown into a cockpit locker had knocked a cockpit drain hosepipe off its skin fitting, resulting in an impressive inrush of water.

Bilge pumps

Strictly speaking, bilge pumps are mainly in the emergency equipment category, but before we have actually reached the stage of a dire emergency, ordinary bilge water control is a safety factor. A seagoing yacht requires a minimum of two bilge pumps, and in recent years this need has been institutionalized racing regulations. One of these pumps must be operable from the cockpit without the need to open a cockpit locker hatch and with the main companionway closed off, and as a result the manufacturers have devised a number of neat flush fittings which do the job. Often such pumps are not complete and require a handle to be plugged in; in an emergency it is essential that the handle is readily available in the cockpit, set in clips beside the pump so that there is no need to open lockers. There is a risk of the pump handle being lost: someone could easily kick it out of its sockets, so many cruising men prefer to have a complete pump with handle permanently installed.

The main bilge pumps will be operated from within the accommodations, usually in the galley/navigation/engine area. All too often such pumps seem to be installed as an afterthought, with little attention given to the physical needs of the person operating them, and so preferably at the design stage, and certainly at the installation stage, close attention must be given to ensuring that the pump is easily worked and readily accessible for clearing; all inlet and outlet pipes must also be easily reached. So another safety factor which should be standard is the need for the cabin floorboards to be easily lifted.

One main bilge pump worked down below is only a minimum requirement; for smaller yachts it is sufficient, but for anything over 30 ft it is not unreasonable to think of an extra pump located forward, and for comfort if not for emergencies a small portable hand-pump can be a great convenience. In yachts large enough to carry an extensive range of equipment, electrical or auxiliary-powered bilge pumps are carried as a matter of course, but it must be remembered that means have to be provided for manual pumping of the yacht in the event of power breakdown. Smaller electrical pumps are now often fitted as well to the more racing-orientated contemporary designs where the shallowness of the bilge means that even a cupful of water finding its way below will wander all over the place creating more havoc than you would think possible. Owners of such yachts when sailing in brisk conditions know that the only way to preserve some modicum of comfort is to switch on the pumps every time they tack – a skilful operator can catch most of the loose water as it swills across the top of the keel!

Fire

Having ensured that the yacht will not sink at her moorings or start to sink the moment she goes to sea, we can look at two of the more dramatic causes of unexpected immersion, fire and explosion. Because it seems such an unlikely thing when you are surrounded by all that water, the notion of a fire afloat has a special horror, a horror which it thoroughly deserves, because a fire can spread through a yacht with alarming speed, and whereas with a house fire you can stand back to fight the thing, with a boat fire you are in the middle of it with the only escape being into the sea, so in terms of safety provision, fire prevention ranks high in the priorities.

The most destructive fires usually result from explosions. These are invariably related to the cooking or heating systems, or the engine fuel, and often to a combination of them, although with today's increasingly complex products new and unexpected causes can be provided. A cruising skipper of my acquaintance had a fortunately small hole blown in the side of his yacht when an aerosol spray can which had fallen off a shelf during a brisk sail became overheated through contact with the engine exhaust while motoring through the subsequent calm, and exploded. Aerosols themselves, particularly those which are used to inspire life in recalcitrant diesels, constitute potential hazards, and engines have been known to blow up with fatal results when there has been an over-heavy hand with the spray can to help with starting.

Prevention of explosions is a matter of constant vigilance in proper maintenance of everything to do with volatile fuels, but there are wide diversions of opinion as to just what does constitute the safest installation; general agreement supports diesel as the least dangerous fuel for auxiliaries, and anyone who uses a petrol engine does so because he feels the smooth running advantages outweigh the fuel hazards, but in cooking and heating there are a number of viewpoints, each with voluble adherents.

In theory a paraffin or alcohol cooker is the safest, but careless users often get potentially dangerous flare-ups when lighting, and the sheer convenience of gas means that in the majority of cruisers it is the favoured cooking fuel, although in larger and more complex craft electric cooking is finding increasing favour. Gas can serve perfectly well if the hazards are known; and of course most maritime nations and national boatbuilding authorities now have stringent regulations to ensure that there is safety consciousness at every level, though in some cases, as for instance Sweden, this has led to the banning of gas altogether and a proliferation of alcohol-fuelled stoves as a result.

This may be adequate if you are content with a camping kind of cruising, but for a yacht where the crew really live aboard, and where an elaborate meal at least occasionally is regarded as an integral part of an enjoyable cruise, more versatile fuel is required in order to provide an oven, and where this is done gas has a real advantage. But having accepted the need for it, the problem is whether to have long pipes with the gas bottle installed outside the accommodation in a separate well which vents directly off the ship, or else to have pipes of minimal length with the bottle beside the cooker where the cook is responsible for turning off the gas after use. My own preference is for this latter arrangement, as long pipes introduce new hazards, and from an administrative point of view it seems better to have everything to do with the gas worked directly from the galley, instead of getting the cockpit crew involved as well. If you do prefer to have the gas bottle well away from the cooker, a gas bottle well draining outboard or into the open cockpit is required, and if this cannot be provided, then it is better to keep the bottle in the open in the self-draining cockpit. Never must gas fumes from such a cooker be able to reach the bilge.

Another fire hazard is to be found in electrics; this is at its greatest when the engine is running and power output is high, but with more complex systems breakdown can occur when the yacht is not in use, and so unless there is some requirement for the power to be left on when the yacht is unoccupied, a convenient means of disconnection of power at the battery is desirable.

Apart from all the precautions taken to ensure that fire-creating circumstances do not arise, warning devices are of course available to give an alarm if a dangerous level of combustible material has accumulated in the yacht, usually in the bilge. A mixture of gas and petrol used to be the most common thing, now it would tend to be gas alone, and even this hazard may in future be reduced by new types of cooking and heating gas which is lighter than air and will eventually find its way out of the yacht. But even in this case the process takes time, and a potentially explosive situation can arise, so obviously an alarm is an aid, but do remember that it is just that – an *aid*; it does not prevent an explosion, it merely gives warning that one could happen.

Consideration of the more dramatic causes of explosion and fire tends to obscure the fact that a significant number of fires on yachts are caused not by equipment failures but rather by crew carelessness; if we include the explosions caused by inept handling of cooking equipment or the engine, then the majority of such happenings have an immediate human element, but as well there are the even more idiotic fires caused by good old smoking; after a hard day's sail with the relief of reaching a comfortable and secure anchorage, even the toughest matelot can find himself nodding off after supper; in his bunk having the final cigarette or pipe of the day, this can be really dangerous. Obviously the golden rule would be no smoking in the bunk, but having sailed in some of the 'smokingest' ships afloat, I know that in some cases this is just too much to expect, and so proper ashtrays conveniently placed for the bunk-bound smoker represent a regrettable but inevitable compromise with the awful weed.

Fire extinguishers

Despite all your precautions, fire may nevertheless break out from all these possible causes or even something else, and then the priority is both to get it under control and ensure that anyone below is not trapped by the flames or overcome by fumes. The strategic location of fire-extinguishers is all important. Some experienced cooks I know, well used to the hazards of their particular job, often come aboard complete with their own little safety kit of a handy first aid box and a small fire-extinguisher to deal with any minor outbreaks in the galley with a minimum of fuss. A thoughtful owner will of course have already provided a fire-extinguisher specifically for the galley; there should be one as well which can be reached from the cockpit without having to go down the companionway, and in smaller yachts this one will also be accessible to the navigator. On larger craft an extinguisher should be provided for the navigator's own use, because it should be remembered that in the constant movement of personnel in the accommodation of a cruising yacht, the navigator on his perch is one of the few constant objects, and so provision can be made for him to be the quickest man into action fighting a fire.

The number of extra extinguishers provided will depend on the size of the yacht, with special extinguishers for engine installations, but there should also be at least one extra one located forward, and in average-

While proper life-lines are a worthwhile safety feature, they can be a hazard in that they can induce a feeling of false security, as it is remarkably easy not only to fall over the top, but also to slither between the lines. Somebody has taken this latter hazard seriously aboard this Nicholson 32 with 'child-proof' netting fitted all round.

sized cruisers of standard layout the toilet is often a handy place to keep it, but as this may involve the opening of a door at a time when every second counts, it may well be preferable to have the forward extinguisher more accessibly located. In considering fire dangers and coping with them from forward, the problem of opening the forehatch inevitably arises. From a security point of view many owners prefer to lock their forehatch when the yacht is left unmanned in her berth, though realists will tend to point out that any villain worth his salt can break into a closed yacht in seconds, so from the damage point of view it may be better not even to try to keep him out – a gloomy thought. However, when the yacht is occupied the hatch must never be left locked; it *must* be possible to open the main forward hatch from outside. Fortunately today's mass-produced hatches usually have this provision.

Falling overboard

The ever present safety element in everything to do with cruising must be evident from the fact that we have already covered so many topics which can arise without even having to take the yacht to sea, but even in sailing itself the safety problems tend in the majority to be of the undramatic sort – yachts foundering in heavy weather tend to attract the

news, but at all other times there is the danger of someone falling overboard without being noticed, while a constant hazard of sailing in busy
waters is that of collision.

Preventing people from falling overboard comes under four main
headings – the provision of useful working deck space with a really non-
slip surface, the installation of adequate handholds, the erection of
stanchions and life-lines, and the supply of personal safety harnesses
with workable means of attachment.

Good deck space comes in at the design stage, and if your yacht does
not have it, there is not really a lot you can do about it, though many
older yachts often would benefit from the removal of some superfluous
deck fittings which make rapid progress forward something of an
obstacle race. Non-slip surface is of course essential, but be warned that
what is sometimes claimed to be non-slip really is no such thing. For
instance, in production GRP yachts an alleged 'non-slip' surface is
claimed to have been moulded in, but although there have been
improvements in this in recent years, all too often the theoretically non-
slip pattern just holds water and a foot placed thereon does a spot of
aqua-planing with painful and possible dangerous results. A teak-laid
deck is still the best surface – there is no denying its attraction, but it is
expensive, and heavy. However, the 'She-deck' simulated teak in GRP
with non-slip inlay in the 'seams' has become popular and makes an
attractive and workable sustitute.

However, for straightforward provision of a non-slip surface, any of
the non-slip deck paints which are on the market do very nicely indeed.
If you happen to have bought a GRP cruiser with one of those
moulded-in patterns, just paint over the patterned area and crew
adhesion will be greatly improved. On new yachts where the decks
have been left clear for the provision of non-slip surface, the attractive
Treadmaster material really does give a fantastic grip. It has a
disadvantage shared with any abrasive surface that it wears holes in
trousers or even in your knees!

Handholds running fore-and-aft along the top of each side of the
coachroof are a feature common to most cruising yachts, but it is seldom
enough that you will see handholds in other places where they could
usefully be deployed, such as around the companionway and on the
foredeck, particularly around the forehatch, the message being that
handholds are most useful where people tend to be moving a lot to and
fro. It may seem so obvious as scarcely to require comment that such
handholds should be securely attached (by through bolting), but this is
not necessarily always the case, and should be checked in getting to
know a new boat. The attachment of the stanchion supports for the life-
lines is also something that often leaves a great deal to be desired.

It is worth giving some thought to making the life-lines snag-free, ensuring that the fitting at the top is as flush as possible and so will not foul ropes and sails, and having a convenient means of keeping the rails taut, for slack life-lines not only look sloppy, but are very dangerous. Offshore racers tend to make up a cat's cradle of lines on the life-lines in the foredeck area to stop sails being washed or blown off the deck under the lower rail. There is not the same degree of sail changing going on aboard a cruiser, but when it is being done there is if anything a greater risk of sails going overboard, and so this notion is desirable. It is a great help too if you sail with young children aboard.

Teak deck surface on the Biscay 36. This is a surface with positive non-slip qualities. The coachroof here appears slippery.

Harnesses

Merely to have a harness attached to anything which seems convenient is not enough: there should be special attachment points in strategic locations, and attachment wires running forward along the deck on either side. It must be remembered that they must be massively strong in themselves and well anchored, for when the pull comes on them, it will be at an angle, inducing savage strains.

In far too many cruisers, the use of safety harnesses has not been sufficiently well thought out. All too often the harnesses are kept in a jumble in the oilskin locker, and when bad weather comes on there is inevitable confusion. It is the duty of the skipper to give each crew member a harness, to make sure it is adjusted to fit him or her, and then to allocate each harness its own stowage location. Over the years I have become so disenchanted with the neglect by different skippers of these simple procedures that I always bring along my own harness and rather than put it on one of the hooks provided, stow it instead in my personal clothes locker, all utterly selfish I know, but at dead of night with the yacht crashing around it makes all the difference to the convenience of getting kitted out to go on deck. The same thing applies to lifejackets; when things are calm before leaving port, the skipper should allocate lifejackets, but all too often a soggy mess has to be sorted out when the going is rough. If you are a skipper it is up to you to see that such things do not happen, but if you are sailing on someone else's boat, rather than count on it, instead bring along your own lifejacket with your own safety harness, stow it in your own locker and do not hesitate to beat hell out of anyone who tries to borrow this vital gear.

Having hopefully got our yacht to the stage that she will not absent-mindedly sink under us, blow up, go on fire, or carelessly chuck her crew overboard, the next problem is to add further equipment to prevent her being run down by someone else.

Radar reflectors

Little yachts being biffed by big ships always reminds me of the old Turkish proverb about the stone and the egg, viz: A stone falls on an egg, the egg breaks; egg falls on stone, egg breaks. In other words, whatever the rights or wrongs of any collision situation, if it comes to a bump you will come off worse. Forget about the romance of the sea, and all the old palaver of steam giving way to sail, today's huge ships just cannot manœuvre that way, and even the smaller ones which can do not keep such a great lookout, so do not expect them to avoid you (though many of them do, because seamen are still seamen) and give them every chance to know that you are there.

Which means being picked up on their radar screens. At night good lights may be a help, but at any time the old radar is there, working away, and as big a radar reflector as you can reasonably carry is more use than all kinds of fancy lights. Once they get you on their screen, then they will look out to see you or your lights depending on whether it is day or night, but the harsh reality is that unless they see you on radar first, then they will hardly spot you otherwise, and even if you have a big radar reflector, do not be complacent in the vicinity of shipping; one cynical skipper of my acquaintance told me that he always preferred to go round busy headlands in poor visibility – at least then he knew there was a reasonable chance that somebody on the many ships flashing by was keeping an eye on the radar!

One sensible development in recent years has been the way some realistic cruising men have been affixing their radar reflectors to the masthead; up there it has more chance of showing above the clutter which comes on radar screens when a sea is running, and it is well clear from causing chafe to sails and ropes. Considerable trouble should be taken to ensure that the attachment is strong, and it should be checked for corrosion every year, for if it came adrift it could cause a nasty injury falling on anyone on deck. But for masthead-rigged cruising yachts, this is quite the best place for the reflector; with a three-quarter rig, it can be made a little less unsightly by having it on the for'ard side of the mast above the head of the forestay, and inevitably for racing yachts where the windage would be unacceptable other ways of attachment, usually low down on the backstay, have to be found.

Lights
Revised lighting requirements have been in force from 1977. One of the best new features is the tricolour light, as it means that instead of having three relatively weak lights, more power can be put through just one bulb to give three powerful sectors, well clear of any chance of being obscured. The electric cable running the entire length of the mast must inevitably run greater risk of breakdown than anything shorter, and while navigation lights located on the pulpit may not have the same range as those at the masthead, at least if anything goes wrong they can be much more easily reached for repair.

Just because of the dominance of radar use, navigation lights should not of course be dismissed as an irrelevance. Every reasonable precaution should be taken to ensure that you are seen, and with so many people cruising these days, two unlit yachts run a real risk of being in collision with each other. Your light power will also be increased by having white flares located convenient to the cockpit, and if the yacht's electrical system is adequate, an Aldis lamp or something similar can be a reassuring thing to have around. If this cannot be provided, a powerful torch should be readily available for the cockpit crew, always kept in one place which is sacred.

Foghorns
In fog conditions the last resort is to sound. Foghorns may be an awful

nuisance when some clown is sounding them off in a crowded anchorage just for the laugh, in the awful chill of nil visibility a foghorn properly operated by yachtsmen can be a great aid to professional seamen for whom coping with fog is just another part of the day's work. Today's aerosol foghorns do very well for most craft, but remember the dangers already mentioned of aerosol cans, and have a spare.

Heavy weather

Having covered the principal hazards which face a yacht and her crew in everyday use, whether in port or at sea, perhaps we can now turn our attention to that aspect which most people tend to think of first when thinking of safety at sea, coping with heavy weather. In producing a standard cruiser or cruiser-racer, the designer and builder are immediately faced with the problem of creating a yacht which looks good, provides comfortable accommodation, performs reasonably well for family use when making a coastal cruise, and can look after herself well enough if caught out in bad weather.

It is a difficult matter, because favouring one requirement almost invariably leads to a lowering of standards elsewhere, and this is particularly the case in making a yacht hefty enough to withstand really heavy weather offshore, because a yacht which could confidently face absolutely any conditions in open water becomes well nigh useless for anything else.

To understand what this means, it is necessary to be aware that by heavy weather I do not mean just Force 8 or even 9 for a brief period, but rather winds of Force 9, 10 and more for a prolonged time, during which a yacht may be kicked around by the sea like an ineptly handled football. Even in these conditions it is possible by skilful helmsmanship to avoid the worst of the breaking water, but particularly at night the risk of a knock-down is ever present, when the yacht may be hit by a large breaking crest, or even caught up within it, and receive a dreadful battering.

In such conditions provided they have searoom the craft most likely to stay afloat would be something like a giant ping-pong ball, but such a 'yacht' would have no directional control, and even a proper sailing hull with upper-works and rig made strong enough to withstand any kind of weather at all will end up with a ballast ratio so poor, with consequent inadequate windward performance, that anywhere near land she runs a real risk of being embayed on a lee shore. So at all times a compromise is needed between the needs of offshore sailing and coastal performance, and somewhere at the top of the scale in these categories comes a modern cruiser-racer like the Swan 44.

But few people would see in the Swan 44 an ideal family cruiser, as her deck is not designed for lolling around, and anyone down below is effectively cut off from the outside world. She is strictly a sailing machine, and for family cruising one would turn more to something like a Salar 40 which provides a more comfortable and sheltered cockpit – very important – but while that shelter is a real boon in a gale, in a storm there is a real risk of it being damaged, possibly with further more dangerous damage to the coachroof to which it is attached.

However, for 99·5 per cent of the time there will be no risk of this, and a vigilant skipper making normal coastal passages can ensure that for that potentially hazardous 0·5 per cent of the time, he is safely in port. This is the situation with the average production sailing cruiser; she is designed for a wide spectrum of the market and a great variety of uses, and with good sense she can cope with extremes of weather while cruising. But it is absolutely essential that any skipper is aware of his yacht's limitations, and plans accordingly.

If your cruising is going to involve a great deal of open sea work, then obviously you will tend to have a really sound self-draining cockpit (draining through the transom if possible), hatchways with steps above deck level, and minimal and very strong houses on deck. A large doghouse with big windows may be a real asset for family cruising in sheltered waters, but it is a menace in open water, leading one to the somewhat extreme conclusion that glass-houses belong in gardens, they have no place on the deck of a seagoing yacht.

Which is all very well in an ideal world, but most of us have standard cruisers with a coachroof of some sort on top, and when from time to time we want to make a longer passage across open water, clearly we are going to want to do it with our own boat without getting involved in the absurdity of fitting her with a flush deck. In such circumstances the sensible thing to do is to have a real think about the structure of the yacht, particularly areas of weakness such as the windows and portlights, the hatchways and cockpit, and see what can be done to provide an extra margin of safety.

In 1973 I met Miles Frankel who wanted to sail from Europe via Iceland to Newfoundland where he worked as a doctor with the Grenfell Association. His yacht *Conche* was a Nicholson 38, a hefty centre-cockpit motor-sailer with an especially good performance under sail for her type, and as I had once sailed to Iceland aboard a Vertue he wanted to know of anything extra I could think of for the yacht to make her more suitable for the voyage ahead. The thing I remembered particularly about the sail up had been prolonged periods of strong winds from the north-east; though this had given us a reach, it had been uncomfortable sailing, as the North Atlantic Drift sets eastward at a speed of at least half a knot, and so we were sailing in seemingly endless 'wind over tide' circumstances, with the result that every so often a really hefty breaking crest would crash over the little boat with an almighty bang, making us

Cockpit protection fitted to the Nicholson 38 Conche *for a transatlantic passage.*

fear for the coachroof, which fortunately had very small portlights. I suggested that some protection for *Conche*'s portlights, for all that they were smaller than the 32's, was essential.

My own thoughts on the matter had been towards the provision of something for use in the event of window breakage, such as a sheet of stout ply held in place by an internal batten tightened up by a large butterfly nut over a heavy bolt, simplicity of application being the keynote. On the same lines, if your coachroof happens to be of wood you can just nail the boards in place in the event of breakage, the important point being to have them readily available in the first place; as for the nail holes, in the event of you coming through the bad weather, they would make for entertaining conversation pieces afterward.

However, aboard *Conche* things were done much more stylishly, Miles Frankel reckoning quite rightly that prevention is better than cure, so he had deadlights made in marine ply of more than $\frac{1}{2}$ in thickness fitting neatly around the windows and held in by bolts screwed into female sockets which in turn were bolted into the coachroof. The bolts themselves were specially machined with large knurled heads so that they could be screwed in by hand; it might be possible to make them in such a way that they are permanently installed on the storm boards, thereby minimizing the chance of loss, or confusion during installation, but as it is they were kept in their own special box in the bo'sun's store, during the voyage they were easily fitted when bad weather threatened, and the transoceanic passage was successfully completed.

Further developments with 'The Storm-Proofing of *Conche*' came in 1974, when owing to pressure on time she was brought back across the Atlantic by Peter Haward, the deservedly renowned delivery skipper who probably knows more about all sorts of different yachts in varying weather than anyone. As the passage from Newfoundland to Ireland was to be made at the end of August, when the chances of severe weather were substantially higher than mid-summer, he made further preparations for really heavy weather in open water. I have to confess that at the time of my meeting with *Conche*'s owner in the previous year, it had never actually occurred to me that she would not have a self-draining cockpit, as at that time I had not been aboard a Nich 38. This was a silly assumption for a central cockpit configuration is sometimes hard to make self-draining. The Nich 38 is no exception in this respect, so Peter Haward spent some time strengthening the somewhat light doors of both companionways with $\frac{3}{4}$ in plywood washboards, and then he put together a wooden cockpit cover which reduced the effective cockpit working area by two-thirds, but meant that most of any heavy sea breaking aboard would be deflected. In the event, *Conche* had a fast and relatively uneventful passage from St. Anthony to Kinsale, with no winds of more than Force 8, but just two days after she got in, the storm of September 1974 swept across the coasts of Western Europe, which would have given her every chance of demonstrating the undoubted usefulness of her skipper's preparations.

Most of us hope that our cruising is a relatively relaxed business in which we do not stick too rigidly to a prepared plan, because experience shows that the weather can easily alter it, or unexpected events such as finding that some port on the itinerary is even more attractive than was hoped can cause delays. However, such relatively carefree waterborne wanderings can only be undertaken with confidence if all preparations have been made beforehand, not only in making a proper job of victualling the yacht and ensuring that all pilotage and navigation gear is aboard, but also in making her as safe as possible in relation to the type of waters on which the cruise is being undertaken. Hopefully this section has shown that every yacht has certain hazards even when she is serenely afloat in her marina berth or at her mooring; even when sailing on the gentlest of days further dangers are possible, and when out in open water among shipping or in heavy weather such risks are compounded by the addition of other hazards.

Emergencies
Despite all the safety preparations possible, it would be unseamanlike to assume that emergencies may not occur. In the long run the best

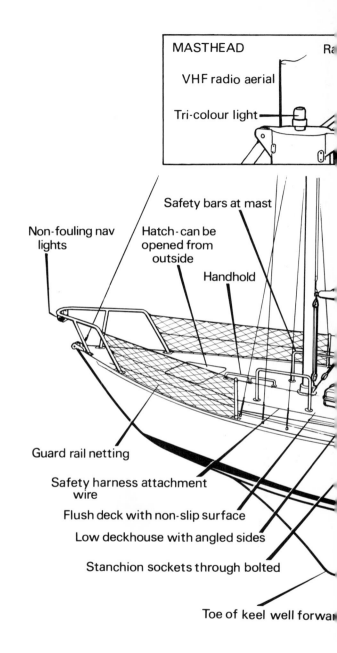

The safety points on a cruising yacht.

READILY ACCESSIBLE INSIDE:
Fire extinguishers, Flares, Emergency radio,
First aid kit, Safety harnesses, Lifejackets,
Main bilge pump, Tool kit.

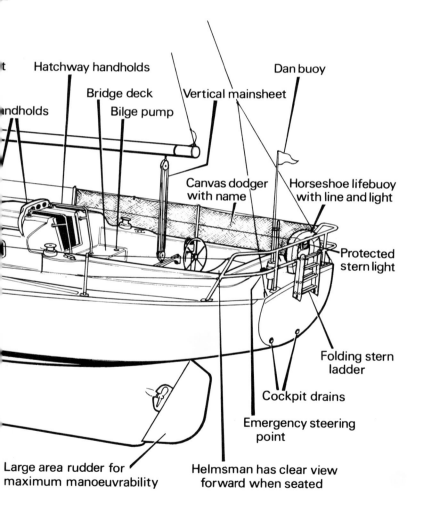

Hatchway handholds

Dan buoy

Bridge deck

Vertical mainsheet

ndholds

Bilge pump

Canvas dodger
with name

Horseshoe lifebuoy
with line and light

Protected
stern light

Folding stern
ladder

Cockpit drains

Emergency steering
point

Large area rudder for
maximum manoeuvrability

Helmsman has clear view
forward when seated

equipped yacht in the world is no better than her crew's ability to handle her and her equipment, so at all times human fallibility can bring about emergencies.

Inevitably one tends to think first of the more spectacular emergencies such as fire or foundering, but a host of more minor happenings are liable to happen, happenings which in effect are emergencies because they can create circumstances which rapidly worsen; a breakdown of the steering system, for instance, may be only an annoyance in open sea well clear of other craft, but in crowded waters or in rough weather in a narrow channel, unless it is possible to rig emergency steering in a matter of seconds, disaster can quickly result. As well, the loss of motive power, whether through dismasting or engine breakdown, can be a setback which can quickly escalate into a serious situation unless solutions can be found, whether in clearing away wreckage, getting the engine re-started, or getting an anchor rapidly over the side to prevent the yacht being driven ashore.

Before giving consideration to the many emergencies which can arise in relation to the yacht and her gear, the first priority should be to the personnel aboard. Everything possible has been done under the safety heading to minimize the risk to crew-members, but it is still possible nevertheless for someone aboard to injure himself, or fall ill or overboard. For the first two possibilities, a minimum of medical equipment is essential on any cruising yacht, and any skipper with a proper concern for the welfare of his crew will acquaint himself with a basic grounding of medical knowledge – *Reed's Almanac*, for instance,

Fishermen and cruising enthusiasts get together for a safety and emergency equipment demonstration at the author's home port. Knowledge of emergency gear obtained this way may make all the difference when it is needed in earnest.

gives an outline of this, even down to instructions for childbirth – and will ensure that this first aid kit is adequately supplied and, most important of all, maintained in good order, for all too often you hear of something being needed and then it is found that it was used up earlier in the season. Standard equipment on any yacht should include a small basic first aid kit in the galley/companionway area, with a more complete selection of medical gear stowed further forward, a first aid locker in the toilet/wash-room is the usual arrangement. In the event of serious injury or illness, a radio-telephone really comes into its own, and many yachts carry R/T mainly with this eventuality in mind. If any member of your regular crew suffers in any way from something which could become serious at any time, clearly this militates in favour of a radio-telephone if there is any debate about the matter.

'Man overboard'

One of the benefits of the special regulations for offshore racing has been that they have institutionalized provision for this emergency, resulting in the proliferation of equipment on the market. There are Dan buoys with flags on long poles for daylight marking, flashing lights which are invaluable at night, lifebuoys with whistles which have proved particularly useful on a number of well-documented occasions in recent years, and a variety of heaving lines which make actual contact once the man is found much easier.

Further problems arise once he is found, as someone in the water can be surprisingly heavy to get on deck; there are all sorts of old salt's tricks to deal with this – for instance, you can make a genoa sheet fast to the stemhead and then lead it over the side of the yacht aft to the winch in the cockpit; get the person in the water to stand on the rope and as it is winched home he gets that vital lift from below to get him on deck. Another ploy is to lift with the mainsail – take it out of its luff groove or track, heave it into the water, and just wind away on the main halyard. There are other more direct methods of winding aboard with halyards, or craning in using the topping lift, but all such methods can involve risk of injury through hitting against the yacht as she rolls, and so it is a welcome feature to find some yachts which include a boarding ladder over the stern or let into the topsides as standard equipment. In such cases, it is essential to ensure that at least two and preferably three of the steps of the ladder are well under water, because the first couple of steps upwards are the most difficult.

Broken steering gear

A breakdown of the steering system may be caused by a number of factors, but it is essential to ensure that an alternative method of steering is readily available and known to all crew-members. Basically this will consist of an emergency tiller in both tiller and wheel steered yachts. A benefit from racing is the requirement that such a tiller is available and easily installed. Even so in most yachts a spanner will be required for this changeover, and this points to the fact that one of the most important items on any list of general emergency equipment is a first class tool kit, properly maintained moreover, for even in the 'driest' yachts tools can very rapidly deteriorate.

Most steering breakdowns can be coped with by the emergency tiller, always remembering that in large yachts with wheel steering a tackle of some sort will be required on the tiller in order to have even a minimum of control. However, if the fault is caused by the rudder head becoming detached from the stock, or the stock coming adrift from the rudder, then alternative means of turning the rudder must be devised, and with this in mind it is a worth-while precaution to have a hole in the trailing edge of the rudder to provide the means of attaching control lines which come over the sides of the yacht. This sounds easy enough in theory, but in practice, particularly when water temperature is low, it can be surprisingly difficult and potentially very dangerous for someone working under the counter, so in such a case you should be prepared to devise an emergency steering oar using something like the spinnaker pole and the top of the saloon table.

This implies a minimum of tools and equipment, and in fact any yacht's tool kit worthy of the name should include a selection of bolts, screws and large nails for such situations. Some friends of mine bringing the 35 ft sloop *Taharra* westward across the Atlantic had their rudder come adrift in mid-ocean; they made up a steering oar as shown in the sketch using a spinnaker pole and the table, and did it so neatly that on the successful completion of the voyage the table reverted to its proper function. Note from the sketch that the controlling of the oar was done by means of a line led from the end of the oar to the lee side, done so because otherwise the oar tended to float upwards once *Taharra* was making any sort of speed.

Dismasting
The thought of dismasting rightly produces the shivers in every sailing man as it is a three-pronged attack! Crew-members can be injured by the stick coming down, the yacht can be holed by crashing against the mast lying in the water, and if you manage to cope with these little setbacks you then have no means of getting anywhere except by engine, a most unpleasant state of affairs, as a mastless sailing yacht will roll her guts out when motoring in any sort of sea. With the jagged edges inevitable with a broken alloy mast, most people's reaction is to cut everything clear, and almost invariably the mast goes straight to the bottom. In some circumstances this is the only possible course, but if at

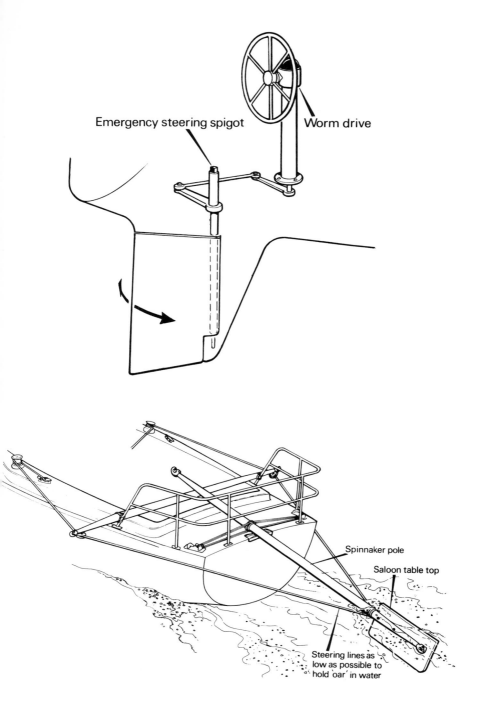

Emergency methods in the event of loss of wheel steering and of whole rudder.

all possible save the stick as it may make all the difference later on. Whatever course is adopted, almost invariably some item of rigging will have to be undone, and at such times you will bless yourself for keeping cotter pins in good order, and having at least two pairs of well-maintained pliers. In the event of wire having to be cut, most yachts nowadays carry hefty bolt-croppers to do the job, but people who have actually had to deal with the problem of cutting wire in a seaway, particularly stainless steel or rod, assure me that a handy little hacksaw is easier to operate in difficult conditions and can do the job surprisingly quickly.

The bo'sun's store should include bulldog clamps, or similar, in order to shorten up rigging where necessary. Although an alloy mast is less easily altered than a wooden one, do not abandon hope altogether – when my friend Bill McKean and his crew were dismasted in the Excalibur *Siolta* while sailing to Norway from Scotland in heavy weather in 1972, admittedly they had to get a tow from a trawler to get there, but once in Norway they got hold of a pine tree and as they had saved the bits of the mast they were able to push the tree into the two parts and under what looked to a casual observer to be standard Excalibur rig, *Siolta* sailed back to Scotland.

Engine breakdown

Unless dismasted, an engine breakdown should only be of serious consequence in confined waters where wind or tide can drive the yacht ashore or on to some obstructions, the one exception to this state of affairs being a sailboat becalmed in a shipping lane where a short burst of the engine may well be vital to get out of the way of a ship which either has not seen you or can do nothing about avoiding you. Obviously avoidance of such breakdowns is as a result of proper engine maintenance with special regard to engine accoutrements such as the fuel lines, but despite such regular attention it is as well to remember that breakdowns are a possibility, however remote, and that a breakdown in confined waters can very quickly become an emergency. In such a situation, the yacht with anchor and cable readily available is at a real advantage, and as has been already pointed out, unless your yacht is trimmed for racing down to the 'nth' degree, there is really no excuse for a proper sailing cruiser not to have an anchor ready on deck for instant use.

Fouled propeller

Nowadays with harbours ever more crowded, a fouled propeller is a not uncommon cause of breakdown, particularly with today's fin-and-skeg configuration where an exposed propeller on a bracket-supported shaft is much more vulnerable to obstruction than the relatively enclosed aperture propeller of traditional design. When this situation arises, you may be lucky and get clear with a quick reversal of the propeller, but it is a very slim chance, so instead of trying any further turns (the engine will probably be brought to a halt almost instantly) accept the fact that you are fouled and get it properly cleared. In some cases this can be done by getting a crowd on the foredeck sufficient to lift the propeller almost out of the water, and work from the dinghy. Thirdly, try turning the shaft with the starting handle to unwind it. Finally go swimming, and for thoroughness you should find a local sub-aqua enthusiast or diver. Count yourself lucky if you have not bent the shaft or bracket, or damaged the propeller itself, and put it down to experience. A friend of mine, Jack Toogood, who cruises to all sorts of obscure little harbours with his cutter *Tarka*, modified his shaft in order to be able to cope quickly with such foulings. There is good clearance between the propeller and the leading edge of the rudder, so if he picks up warp he just detaches the shaft from the engine drive (it is easily accessible) and can slide the shaft and propeller 5 inches aft. Usually fouled warps will go into a jammed ball between the propeller and the deadwood, and this move exposes the knot enough for him to be able to see it (*Tarka* is transom-sterned) and cut everything away with a saw-edged breadknife on a special pole; Jack goes into all sorts of creeks and canals and inevitably picks up rope and fouling from time to time, but so far he has always been able to clear it himself.

Foundering

The ultimate emergency is a yacht's foundering, which can be brought about by a multiplicity of causes. More than ever the seas are full of rubbish, the wreckage and timber of times past now being added to by things as lethal as cargo containers which have been washed off the decks of freighters. Like icebergs, they float in a semi-submerged condition, and with their sharp corners can be disastrous not only for small craft, but even for ships; this latter state of affairs is fortunate for the cruising man in that it results in naval vessels making efforts to sink drifting containers by gunfire. However, if you happen to get a calm day in open water, it is quite astonishing how much junk of one sort or another is seen to be floating around.

Sinking by whales seems to have become almost a vogue, but the increased incidence is probably due to more yachts cruising the oceans with life-rafts to which survivors take and thus can subsequently tell the tale. If anything, the number of whales has probably decreased, but in any case it is scarcely a hazard of coastal cruising. Much more likely in such cases is the yacht beginning to sink as a result of a breakdown in a skin fitting or the pipe running from it – earlier we referred to the case of a 50 ft ketch which started to go down while out on an afternoon sail because a hosepipe with a loose connection had been knocked off a skin fitting. Another dramatic case was the huge ketch *Great Britain II* which successfully completed two round-the-world races, and then in the summer of 1976 put out a PAN alarm call because she was taking in water on the first stage from Plymouth to Tenerife of the Sail Training Association's transatlantic series. Eventually the substantial leak was traced to a skin fitting hidden under the cockpit.

The first rule in a sinking situation is that abandoning ship is only the very last resort. Just lately I have heard of people who are working on ways of making inflatable life-rafts 'to sail', however limited their performance, but nevertheless it must be remembered that a jury rigged yacht kept afloat only by the efforts of her crew at the pumps is a better proposition for getting somewhere than a life-raft. Moreover she will provide better protection from exposure, and is more easily seen by rescuers. Rather than trying to make a life-raft 'sailable', why not a big inflatable rubber dinghy fitted with a drift-sail for downwind courses?

So if you feel there is a danger of the yacht sinking, make a damned good battle against it before giving up. In such a situation you will bless the extra pump fitted in what seemed a moment of extreme caution and extravagance. You will bless the tool kit and spare timber put aboard for just such emergencies. It is possible to buy an umbrella-like item of equipment which can be thrust through a hole and then opens out to be held in place with water pressure, but do not count on being able to use such a thing, the interior of most yachts is a complex honeycomb structure which makes easy access to any hole in the skin difficult, and the good old method of hauling a sail over the hole can still make all the difference to staunching a flow of water.

With a situation worsening, communication with the outside world is vital, and here again the radio can come into its own, but for straightforward emergency calls special distress radios are available which you can take with you if you do have to finally take to the life-raft. As well as flares, carry the emergency flags of the international code of signals. Communication in an emergency is everything, and a highly experienced cruising man I know of made a point of carrying a blackboard and chalk aboard his remarkably well-equipped yacht, knowing full well that in emergencies noise is often overpowering (a black felt pen for writing on the back of a chart has the same effect), and not everyone has a radio or can read Morse or flag signals. His system came into its own one time when he rescued a yacht that had been dismasted — not a word was spoken, he calmed down the somewhat panic-stricken crew of the dismasted yacht by showing them written instructions, and soon had them in tow and brought them safely to a port twenty miles away.

If it finally comes to an abandonment, the location and installation of the life-raft will become all-important. Royal Ocean Racing Club rules insist on a life-raft being stowed in such a way that one man can get it to the life-lines within ten seconds, and so dangerously located life-rafts hidden away in cockpit lockers under other gear should be a thing of the past. In cruising yachts where the distribution of weight is not so vitally important, life-rafts may be stowed in special containers mounted on supports on deck; wherever the raft is placed, it has to be done with attention to ease of launching and ease of access when afloat, for all too often it has been shown that the most dangerous part of the whole business is getting the raft afloat, and getting the crew into it.

Just when this should be done is a matter of endless debate. My good friend Don Street in his book *The Ocean Sailing Yacht* quotes a large number of cases where crews have taken too readily to the life-raft, and their supposedly foundering yacht has been found weeks, even months later, still afloat. Against that I remember once riding out a 65-knot blow off Land's End; being a rather fierce headland, the sea was pretty rough, and though we did not know it at the time, somewhere in the same area a 34 ft yacht was foundering; she went very quickly, and only one of her crew of two was able to make it away safely in the life-raft. Street suggests that if you feel the yacht is going to sink, inflate the life-raft on deck and get into it, but do not cut her adrift until the yacht actually goes down physically under you. I am sure he had his tongue somewhat in his cheek when making this suggestion, but even so he has a point; however, if you follow his advice, do make sure you do not get caught up in the yacht's rigging, or you will defeat the purpose of the exercise. Whatever way you go about it, remember it really is the last ditch stand. I remember once seeing a French yacht with properly installed life-raft in the cockpit, and the release line conspicuously displayed. Beside its attachment point some wag had written with a felt pen: 'Tirez ici, et bonne chance, mes amis!!' You can say that again.

Doom and gloom
This chapter has been to an extent a trail of doom and gloom, exploring as it does most of the disasters which can befall you when you try to get away from it all for a little bit of gentle cruising. Sometimes I think we all may be becoming almost too cautious – after all, back in the early days of cruising they did not have life-rafts, radio, life-lines, safety harnesses and all the other paraphernalia – they were totally self-reliant, they had to be, and many of them lived to a ripe old age. Possibly if you have been cruising for many years, you see too many potential disasters, and if you are cursed with a morbid imagination these soon become actuality during sleepless nights. In such cases it is possible to cover your boat with so much safety gear that in theory you are ready for anything, but still a nagging doubt remains, and you become like a man who wears

belt and braces but will not go out for fear that his trousers might fall down.

So perhaps with safety equipment as with everything else to do with the sailing cruiser, there is a sensible level of compromise. Where there should be no compromise is in the skipper's knowledge, and hopefully that of his crew as well, about the safety and emergency equipment aboard and its uses and functioning. It cannot be said too often that the time to get acquainted with emergency gear is when the going is good, when things are gentle and you can investigate at your leisure, because lack of such knowledge can only lead to panic and disaster in a crisis. Thus at the start of every season the storm sails should be fitted, and all safety gear demonstrated. Indeed any yacht club which is on the ball makes a point of arranging such demonstrations, it provides an opportunity to let off out-of-date flares, and there is a bit of excitement with a life-raft demonstration. There is much more to using a life-raft than just heaving into the water and jumping aboard – as it inflates, for instance, there will be a whistling noise of a pressure adjustment valve: in emergencies, crew-members are unnecessarily worried by thinking that this indicates a leak. The raft may inflate upside-down – it is easily righted when you know how; once it is properly upright, it is essential to get the drogue out, to control motion and movement; and when your crew is safely aboard the raft, if they are properly positioned round the edges it makes a world of difference to stability and safety.

But yet again let it be said that taking to the life-raft is only the very last resort. Safety precautions on a cruising yacht should be a prime consideration from the word go; having decided the kind of cruising you want to do, then in selecting your yacht you work from a list of priorities which will ensure that she is safe in virtually all of the foreseeable circumstances in which you are likely to place her. You then make further provisions for the safety of the personnel aboard, and the safe functioning of all equipment liable to provide hazards. Having done all this, you still acknowledge that emergencies can arise, and further provision is made for carrying special emergency equipment. And having done that, and acquainted your crew with the workings of all such equipment, you can get on with enjoying cruising, secure in the knowledge that any untoward happenings can be coped with, and with a minimum of fuss.

10 Maintenance, repair and modification

Wandering round a yacht harbour in the spring of 1976 I saw what looked like a new Halcyon 27 about to be launched, but on yarning with the owner I discovered with some surprise that she was actually seven years old. Then it all came out; it seemed he had bought the yacht only three weeks previously, and she had been showing her age. But he happened to own a large garage and since buying the yacht he had put his three best car refurbishers to work on her flat-out, restoring everything. With techniques evolved and developed by the 'carriage trade', they had done a remarkable restoration job, and she really seemed as good as new. An owner doing the work on his own would easily have used a whole winter, and as he would have been learning from scratch as he went along, it is possible that many mistakes would have been made. I am not suggesting that expert car workers could know anything about the condition of the yacht's gear and fittings, but for the massive specialist tasks of restoring GRP surfaces and woodwork trim their highly developed technique and access to special equipment was clearly an advantage, so much so that many yacht-building factories now offer a refurbishment service to owners.

However, this was a special case of a yacht which had been allowed to deteriorate much more than she would have had her previous owner kept up a reasonable level of year-to-year maintenance from the very beginning. As with everything to do with cruising yachts a reasonable level of compromise seems to produce the best overall results. While an immaculately-maintained yacht with highly-polished hull and woodwork kept like a work of art is something which we all admire, the reality is that we prefer a sailing cruiser to have a slightly lived-in and sailed-in look about her, because after all cruisers are for sailing aboard and living in, their *raison d'être* is not the ornamentation of some anchorage or marina.

Thus, an experienced owner will know the level of maintenance which best suits his kind of cruising. Where anything with moving parts is involved there is a constant battle against the invasion by bits of dirt and salt water trying endlessly to make vital equipment seize up. Indeed, much of the maintenance of a yacht in seagoing condition seems to be a matter of dealing with things which should move but do not, such as jammed winches, and things which should not move, but do, such as the mast step. Around the mast is the most constant area of strain on a yacht's construction, and here the alert owner will know how to look for possible danger points, but in such a situation he will also know that if there is any doubt a surveyor's opinion should be asked, yet another example of the need to call in specialist knowledge once a certain stage is reached.

You see this as well with the maintenance, repair and replacement of standing and running rigging; every year at least, and more often if the yacht is used frequently, an owner will make a complete check of rigging; eventually a stage is reached where there is some doubt about some item's continuing fitness for its job, and an expert should be asked. When the rigging is being replaced, it *could* be possible to do it yourself, going through the arduous task of hand-splicing, but almost every time you will do much better to leave it to the experts who have equipment for fitting machined eyes, and if you are rigging a new yacht where stay lengths are not known precisely, as already mentioned, the use of special swageless terminals is much the least painful way of doing things.

If you find that you get more fun out of pottering around a yacht in an almost endless programme of maintenance and modification, then by all means go right ahead and do so, but for most of us a sailing cruiser really is for sailing, not for working at, and so we devise a programme of maintenance which strikes a balance between the needs of economy – after all, there are some jobs which anyone will admit it is money wasted to pay a yard to do – and the need to keep sailing. We acknowledge that we live in the time of the specialist, that in every aspect of maintenance we each have our own level where the involvement of the expert begins to make sense, and so the fitting out of the yacht is planned in such a way that it can manage to be something of a pleasure rather than unrelieved drudgery which makes the subsequent sailing – if you ever do get sailing – rather less fun because every aspect of the yacht is a mute reminder of too much hard work.

Naturally, many owners will insist that they have to do each and every task of maintenance simply because they cannot afford to pay specialists even when their help might be really useful. Allowing oneself to get into

Taking some trouble when laid up afloat can pay dividends when spring comes round – this Tintella 29 is well supplied with fenders, but as well has warps to hold her off the pontoon in addition to the usual springs and lines. Note how the vulnerable moving parts such as the halyard winches on the mast and the windlass have been protected from the weather.

such a situation is surely an example of bad yacht management, because in working out how big a yacht you can afford, the last thing you should do is to spend every last penny you can possibly raise just in buying the dreamship. The age and type of the yacht will be of paramount importance in calculating just how much she will cost to run and maintain from year to year, but for the average cruiser an overall annual figure of 20 per cent of the buying price is not excessive when factors like insurance are included, and if you have to berth in an expensive marina a percentage considerably higher could be expected.

If you can control your natural enthusiasm when making the selection of a new yacht to allow a reasonable margin within available funds for all further recurrent costs, then you will begin to deal with the maintenance problems with everything more fully under control from the word go, and the psychological advantage imparted by knowing that if need be expert help can be afforded will make fitting out a pleasure rather than the burden it can become when people saddle themselves with a yacht which is beyond them both in their technical ability to cope with maintenance problems and their financial capacity to pay for badly needed help.

Most yacht manufacturers provide transport cradles for their standard yachts, and one of these can be modified by the addition of adjustable struts (if they are not already supplied) in order to get support just right and facilitate working at the surface hidden under the support. Most important of all in the cutaway profile is a strut under the bow, and as already pointed out even many long-keel yachts are prone to overbalance forward, so if need be the cradle should be adjusted to include this bow support as an integral component, otherwise it tends to be forgotten. If for some reason a cradle cannot be provided, do ensure that there are two principal supports made fast to the chainplates.

Getting on and off the yacht ashore is something else fraught with potential hazard; at least spend some money on a really good ladder, but be prepared to have your name inscribed on it, and chain it to the boat as well – around yacht yards, ladders tend to be looked on as common property, and do a great deal of 'walking' around the place unless ownership is clearly marked. At best, however, a ladder can be a difficult thing to get up and down, especially if you are carrying anything, and owners who have their fitting out really well organized tend to prefer a staircase such as you get at boat-shows. With such a staircase, there is no benumbed winter reluctance to get aboard and get on with the job, and while you are at it thinking of things to induce the right intitial attitude, buy yourself a proper working boiler-suit to wear when working at the boat. This may seem an almost laughable triviality,

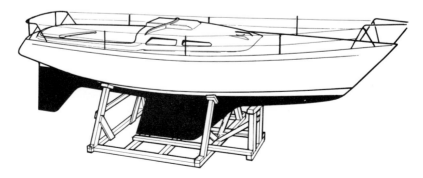

When the yacht is laid up ashore, the use of an effective cradle not only increases safety, but also facilitates maintenance work.

If no shed is available but a sheltered corner can be found, a temporary polythene-covered structure is almost as good, and has the advantage of being very well-lighted.

but I have always noticed that all the owners who make a worth-while job either of doing all their own fitting out, or even doing a basic amount and supervising a yard in doing the rest, seem to make a point of hauling on a boiler-suit beforehand and then they are quite happy to take on any job, however messy. Meanwhile people who turn up looking sloppy in old gardening clothes or such-like seem to manage to specialize in sloppy work.

Fitting out

With perseverance, it is surprising how good a fitting out job can be done in the open, but if there is a choice it is preferable to be indoors, because when the time arrives that a boat-shed becomes uncomfortably hot, you should be out sailing anyway. In a shed it is possible to work all the time and there is not the irritation of having to haul a cover off and on at the beginning and end of the day's work, all of which is conducive to getting the job finished with the minimum of pain. Naturally, it is not always possible to get into such a shed, perhaps economy dictates that you should do so only every three years or even every five years, but in any case forward planning of refitting projects should be undertaken in such a way as to take full advantage of winters spent properly under cover in a shed, and where a shed is just not available at any time, enterprising owners avail of the possibilities of today's heavy duty polythene sheet (awful stuff if you happen to get it round your propeller at sea) and either build a 'tent-shed' over the deck, or if a corner especially well sheltered from the wind can be found, throw up a complete shed in a secluded shelter in the hope that a winter's furious activity will be completed on their boat before the rumblings of the local planning authority become positive action to remove the structure.

Clearly the amount of work involved even in an annual tidy up will involve planning, with lists of priorities; when you get to the stage of having lists of lists, you can be fairly sure that work is proceeding at a proper pace. I have always found that the contemplation of the re-fit in its entirety is best done at home away from the boat, admittedly a very small distance if the pride-and-joy is taking shape just outside in the garden, but if you start contemplating everything that has to be done while on the boat, it is very easy to get bogged down in awed horror of the enormity of it all and fail to get anything done at all. In other words, approach the boat with one or two specific tasks in mind and get on with them with single-minded determination, and perhaps at the end of the day's work you can allow your mind to wander over the myriad of other tasks still waiting to be done.

Laying up
There is a time and a season to it all. When laying up in the autumn, all muck and weed should be cleaned off the bottom; most owners do this as a matter of course, but those who do not find that by the spring what had been easily removable softish stuff has fossilized into something mysterious which almost needs a chisel for removal. Get sails and running rigging removed off the boat, the sails in particular as the autumn is a great time to do business with sailmakers, while they will profess not to know you in the hectic spring. Clean out the bilges – this is the very essence of the lay-up jobs, and a boat which spends the winter with wet and messy bilges just is not laid up at all. 'Winterizing' of the engine is also top priority, and indeed its major servicing should be done at this time in order to have a breathing space before next season if any replacement parts have to be acquired.

With alloy masts and stainless teel rigging there is a temptation not to lift the mast out at all if the yacht is outside; personally I reckon because it has spent a busy seven months up in the air getting precious little attention, it deserves a rest and close inspection, but if you want to leave it in, be sure to get an experienced hand aloft if you are too old and heavy yourself in order to make a detailed inspection *before* the yacht comes out of the water – you will find that experienced yards are reluctant to send riggers up masts with the yacht on the hard, it seems only sensible for amateurs to follow this sound professional practise. If the mast is left up, all halyards should be inspected from end to end by means of a messenger line attached in turn to the end going to the head of the mast, and ideally the halyards should be removed altogether each winter if the mast is left in.

Down below in the accommodation, all the more immediately removable items, such as bunk cushions, should be taken out and put into store, and after the toilet has been cleared for the winter a complete washing of the yacht inside from end to end with fresh water and cleaning material, probably done in conjunction with or perhaps after the bilges, will be the preliminary of leaving the yacht to air for a week or so. Meanwhile, there are all the other vital pieces of equipment we discussed in the safety chapter, from bilge pumps to life-rafts, which need servicing to a greater or lesser extent, either by yourself or through a return to the agents, and while you are mulling over the safety factors, the cooking and heating arrangements, particularly if they are gas, require the most rigorous checks.

For two or three weekends after the yacht has been hauled out of the water you could be working very hard just cleaning and greasing, and checking over gear, without the slightest thought being given to painting or varnishing, but it is a fact that if you get a bit of settled weather in October or even early November it is ideal for getting one or two coats of varnish on, and perhaps a coat of undercoat on the topsides if you have a wooden yacht. This greatly reduces the amount of work to be done in the spring, when winter's wear and tear may mean that three coats of varnish will be needed where the autumnal two would have done, but the whole business of painting, varnishing and polishing a yacht can be made easier by the use of a certain amount of cunning.

Damage repairs

The repairing of cruising yachts falls into two main categories. There are running repairs done as quickly as possible in order to keep a cruise going despite damage to the yacht or her equipment, and major repairs undertaken once she gets to port, or even during the off season as the running repair has proved sufficient to see the summer out. Just how much can be done in the way of running repairs depends on the facilities aboard and the expertise of the crew. From time to time you will come across somewhat hardcase skippers who regard the seas as wholly for sailing and postpone any repairs until the winter. I remember going aboard one such boat, to find that only one winch was working out of four in the cockpit, and great was the ingenuity employed by the skipper and his crew to ensure that they still sailed – and sailed fairly competently – using just this one winch. Perhaps it would be forgivable had the repairs been effected during the winter, but I seem to remember meeting this crowd again the following spring, and not being wholly surprised to find that they were still making do with just one winch. They used more effort and ingenuity in one day's sailing than would have fixed all the seized ones, as well as several other items of gear that were also in no great shape.

At the other extreme I know a hyper-efficient skipper who bristles with annoyance if there is the slightest malfunction in even the smallest item of equipment aboard. Having a large yacht, he has a little workshop

Before and after stages in the resurrection of a timber yacht. Rapid fitting out afloat begins on the Vertue cutter Ice Bird, *which was good enough for one season's cruising, but when the sailing was over the author took her under cover for a complete resurrection. . . .*

. . . and she is seen the following season with her varnishwork restored, GRP sheathing on deck, nylon sheathing to the waterline, and even a replacement suit of sails, acquired second-hand.

aboard where such things can be put right. On the rare occasions when something goes wrong, they are indeed put right very quickly.

These are examples of extremes, but the well maintained tool kit and spares for the engine (particularly a pump impeller and fan belt) are the basis of repairs at sea.

GRP

It is in the maintenance and protection of the large areas of a yacht's skin, whether the hull or on deck, that the real advantage of GRP construction should be evident. Even the most expensively constructed wooden yacht needed some painting on all exposed surfaces every year, whereas a GRP yacht if properly looked after can confidently expect to do without any major treatment for the topsides, etc., for a decade at least. Note that this does not assert that GRP is maintenance-free; it needs *less* maintenance from year to year, but it most emphatically needs care. Regular cleaning removes the soot and grit and other pollutions of the atmosphere which will soon dull a clean surface, while polishing will provide a useful measure of protection while improving the appearance. Special products are available in any well-stocked yacht chandlery to carry out this work, be sure that if you are using a polish it is not of the silicone type as this will have to be chemically removed when the stage of painting is finally reached.

Wooden yachts

Less luxuriously finished wooden yachts with just a single skin planked deck were usually finished with canvas, replaced from time to time and not too bad at keeping out the water, the trouble being that when a leak appeared it could be coming through the canvas at a spot several feet away from the place it was finally getting through to drip on someone's head with a nautical refinement of the Chinese water torture. With a view to curing such leaks, I have twice sheathed the decks of yachts with a three-mat layer of glass fibre; in both cases the result was very satisfactory, strengthening the deck, curing leaks, and tidying up the appearance. When doing this the vital thing is to make a sound job of sealing the edges of the glass fibre, which depends on the particular layout of deck edge. One potential trouble area is around the chain-plates. In both cases we were dealing with internally mounted chain-plates coming through the deck just inside the rail, and we just slapped extra glass around them and hoped for the best. It would have been more thorough to have removed the chainplates and add little deck plates to fit on the deck with permanently flexible sealing compound underneath, but such a removal and reinstallation would probably have taken more time than the rest of the job put together, and we wanted to go cruising that season.

Further attitudes

Creaming along on a sunny day, perhaps it is natural to pretend that everything is perfect in a perfect world, but even in the best run cruising yachts there is almost invariably something which would be much better for a little attention when the going is smooth, for who knows, it could be needed urgently when conditions for making a running repair are not so favourable. One cruising skipper of my acquaintance once found that after a prolonged visit to north-west Spain while heading home across the Bay of Biscay various niggling little things were wrong – being a wooden yacht, there were deck leaks in a couple of places where the intense sun had been shrinking the woodwork, and some equipment needed overhaul. So he hove-to for a morning, and it was make do and mend for all hands, sealing the deck, overhauling gear, and cleaning the ship from end to end of the dirt inevitably brought aboard during three weeks of idyllic cruising from beach to fishing port. With yachts and crew cleaned and refreshed, they got under way again in the afternoon with a very satisfying feeling of having done absolutely the right thing. The morning's work was a lesson for the 'rush-on' school of cruising which all too often confuses movement with action.

Minor changes can be carried out without reference to a designer or surveyor. It must be remembered that a modern yacht is designed as a whole, that the interior layout is often part of an internal structure. Care must be taken to ensure that if modifications are being made, they do not in any way weaken this. Where major changes in layout or rig are contemplated, it is better to consult some expert, at least a surveyor, and perhaps even whoever designed the yacht in the first place.

Yacht designers are generally interesting people, and they are often the most pleasant folk in the marine industry, so doing business with them is generally painless for you, even if your own idiosyncrasies lead the designer to wish, as one leading member of the profession said to me, that they could design the owners as well as the boats in order to produce the perfect seagoing package. But if your suggested modifications are reasonable, I do not think you need worry unduly about being rebuffed by the designer. You will find that even by the time your yacht was launched his ideas had progressed beyond the stage of development she represents, and he may well be glad to have a second bite at the cherry.

Owners of older yachts sometimes take up the modern enthusiasm for open-plan layout, and remove bulkheads with an excess of zeal. It must be remembered that bulkheads are more than just mere partitions, they too, like the modules in a modern GRP yacht, are part of the overall structure of the yacht, and any thought of their removal must be treated with extreme caution. But in this, as in modification of the rig, or in the installation of a new engine, a little bit of expert advice can save a great deal of trouble. Do remember when seeking such advice that, as mentioned, designers generally are very pleasant people who live somewhat in a world of their own. When a course of action is decided on, was it really what the designer thought was possible within the limits of the yacht's basic design, or was it just a tidied-up version of your own obsessive notion imposed on the designer's amiability?

For many cruising men, the most interesting objects are other yachts. Watch a crew coming into a strange harbour and you will see that they give at least as much attention to the other boats in the anchorage as they do to their surroundings, however exotic they may be. Thus it is easy to slip into a way of thinking, where the sailing cruiser and everything to do with her in the way of maintenance, repair and modification is the be all and end all of the sport. To a certain extent such an attitude is most desirable – it ensures that the yacht and her equipment are in the best of order. In the same theme, the good old-fashioned notion of pride of ownership can be carried to such an extent that, coupled with an enthusiasm for do-it-yourself work about the boat, you will find some yachtsmen who scarcely need to sail at all in order to find ownership a rewarding experience. For real fulfilment, the sailing cruiser should be sailed and cruised as much as possible. When used properly, she is the magic carpet to a world unknown to most people: whether your cruising is a modest venture of short hops along a well-loved coastline, or blue water sailing to somewhere beyond the horizon, it is a way of life which never loses its own special sense of excitement.

When it all becomes worthwhile. . . . The 20-ton sloop Querida *outward bound at the start of her annual summer cruise.*

Index